Ripley's Believe It or Not!®

This volume reprints Ripley's Believe It Or Not! ® issues 1 & 2 published by Zenescope Entertainment.
First Edition, January 2019 • ISBN: 978-1942275862

WWW.ZENESCOPE.COM

Joe Brusha • President & Chief Creative Officer
Ralph Tedesco • VP Film & Television
Christopher Cote • Art Director
Dave Franchini • Editor
Christina Barbieri • Assistant Editor
Ashley Vanacore • Graphic Designer

Lauren Klasik • Director of Sales & Marketing
Jennifer Bermel • Business Development & Licensing Manager
Jason Condeelis • Direct Sales Manager
Laura Levandowski • International Project Coordinator
Rebecca Pons • Marketing & VIP Coordinator
Stu Kropnick • Operations Manager

Ripley's Believe It Or Not! ® Trade Paperback, January, 2019. First Printing. Published by Zenescope Entertainment Inc., 433 Caredean Drive, Ste. C, Horsham,
Pennsylvania 19044. Zenescope and its logos are ® and © 2019 Zenescope Entertainment Inc. all rights reserved. Printed in Canada.

'RAMING SEQUENCES
'AGES 5,6, 52, 55, 101, & 102
Vriter Ben Meares
Artwork by Deivis Goetten
Colors by Ceci de la Cruz

'ACT PAGES
AGES 15, 24, 33, 42, 51, 64, 73, 82, 91, 100
Vritten by Ben Meares
rtwork by Renzo Rodriguez
Colors by Robby Bevard

A TALE AS OLD AS..."
AGE 7
Vritten by Howard Mackie
rtwork by Hakan Aydin
olors by Fran Gamboa w/ J.C. Ruiz

'VE BEEN WORKING ON THE RAILROAD"
AGE 16
Vritten by Fox Kavanagh
rtwork by Daniel Mainé
olors by Marco Lesko

'HE RIDE OF HIS LIFE"
GE 25
ritten by Dale Mettam
twork by Allan Otero
olors by Jorge Cortes

1OTHER NATURE"
GE 34
itten by Victoria Rau
twork by Pat Broderick
lors by Robert H. Epps

9 LIVES"
GE 43
itten by Ben Meares
work by Marcelo Basile

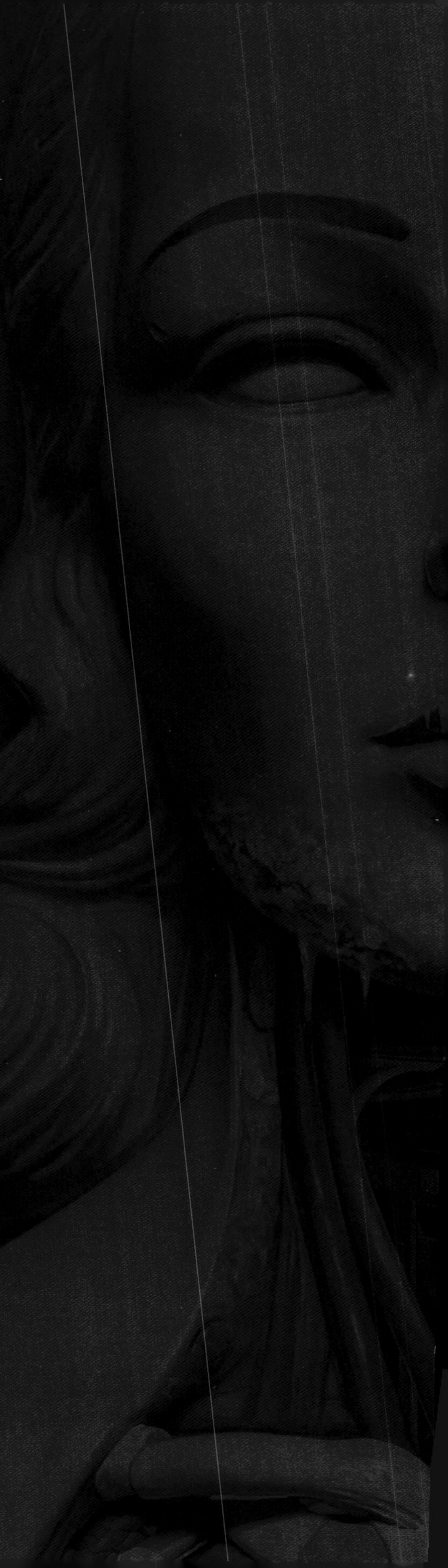

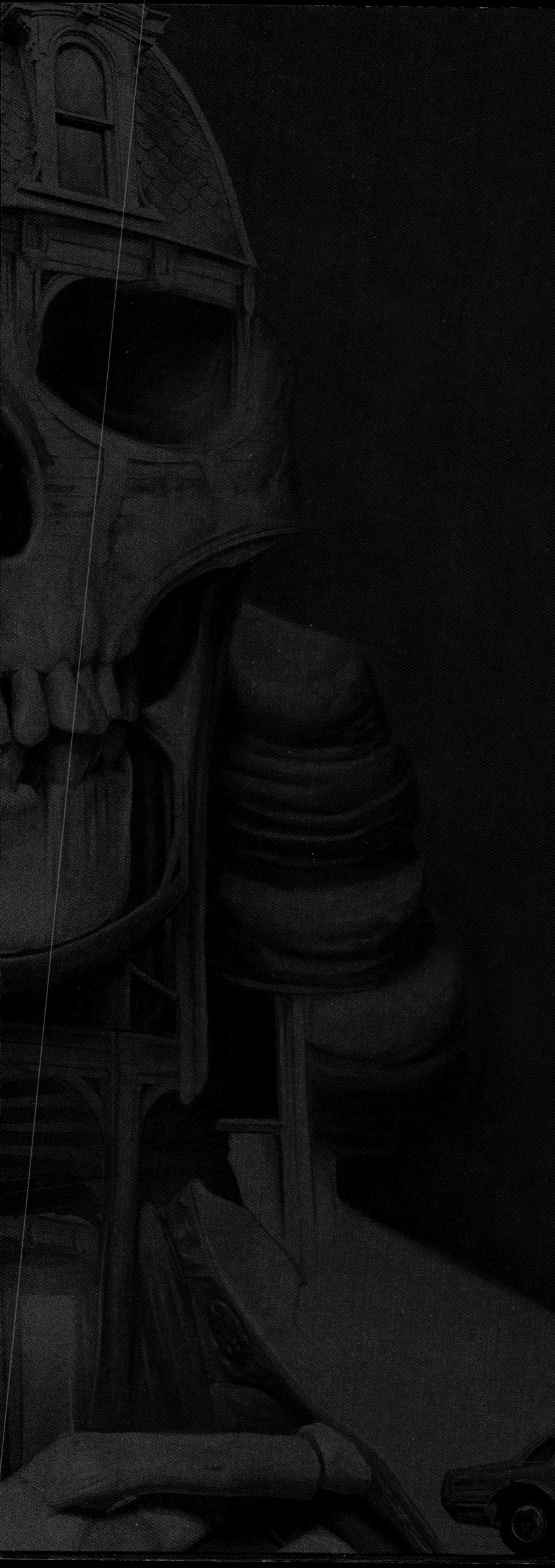

Letters by Charles Pritchett
Edited by Terry Kavanagh
Cover Artwork by David Seidman
Production by Christopher Cote

Special thanks to our friends
(From ©Ripley Entertainment Inc.)
Amanda Joiner
Carrie Bolin
John Graziano
Jessica Firpi
Jordie Orlando
Sabrina Sieck

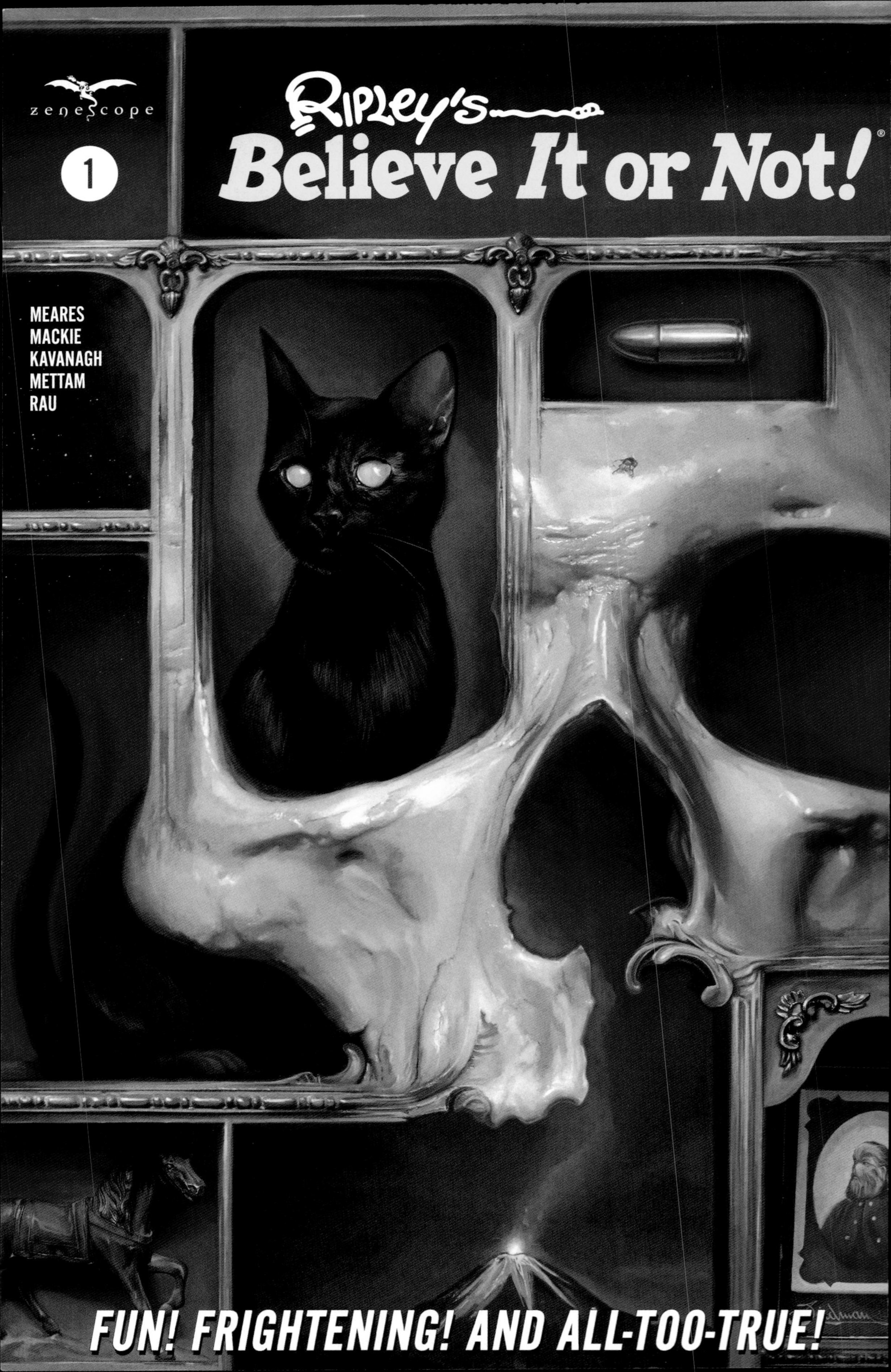
zenescope
1
Ripley's
Believe It or Not!
MEARES
MACKIE
KAVANAGH
METTAM
RAU
FUN! FRIGHTENING! AND ALL-TOO-TRUE!

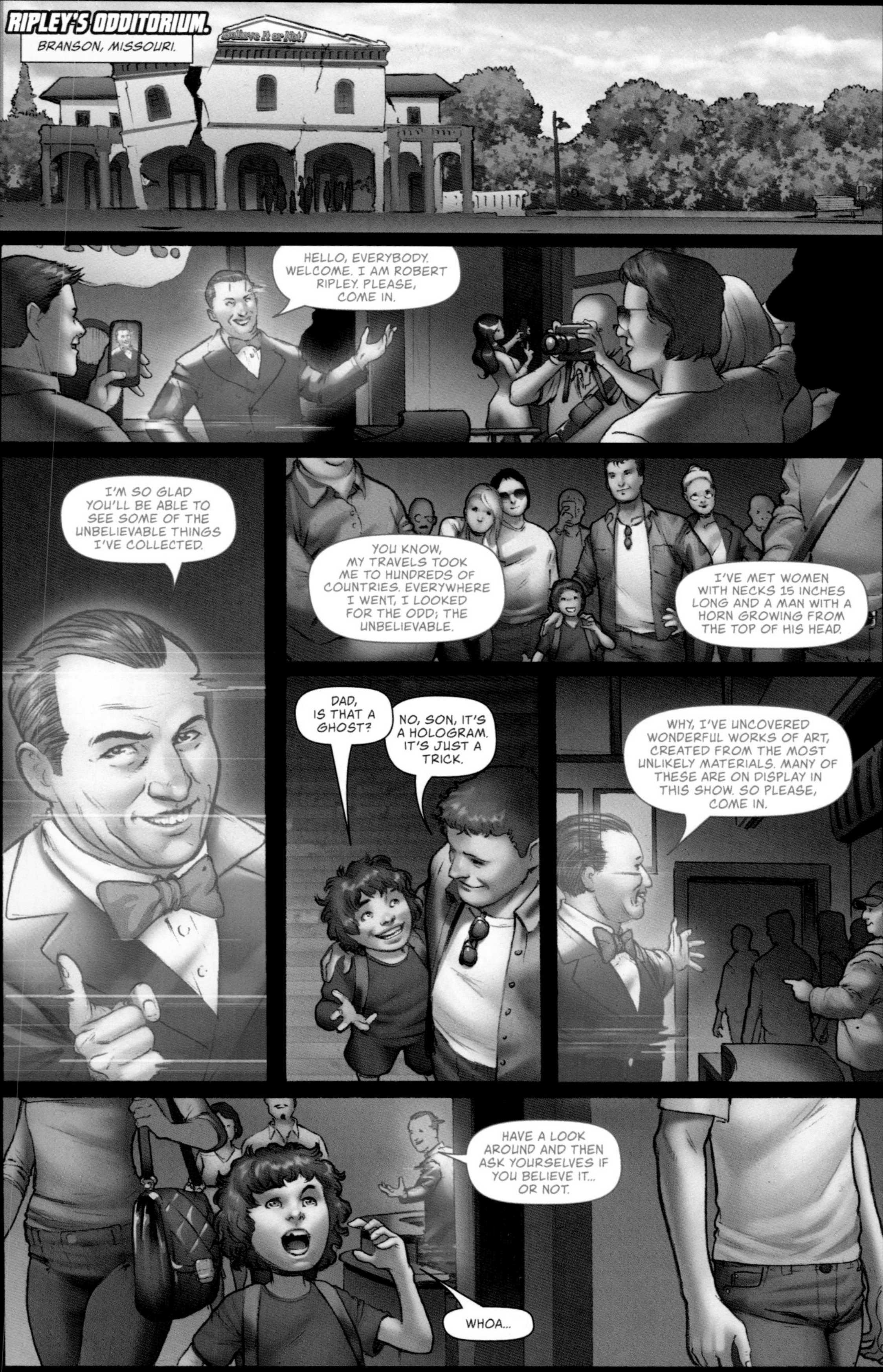
RIPLEY'S ODDITORIUM.
BRANSON, MISSOURI.
Believe It or Not!
HELLO, EVERYBODY. WELCOME. I AM ROBERT RIPLEY. PLEASE, COME IN.
I'M SO GLAD YOU'LL BE ABLE TO SEE SOME OF THE UNBELIEVABLE THINGS I'VE COLLECTED.
YOU KNOW, MY TRAVELS TOOK ME TO HUNDREDS OF COUNTRIES. EVERYWHERE I WENT, I LOOKED FOR THE ODD; THE UNBELIEVABLE.
I'VE MET WOMEN WITH NECKS 15 INCHES LONG AND A MAN WITH A HORN GROWING FROM THE TOP OF HIS HEAD.
DAD, IS THAT A GHOST?
NO, SON, IT'S A HOLOGRAM. IT'S JUST A TRICK.
WHY, I'VE UNCOVERED WONDERFUL WORKS OF ART, CREATED FROM THE MOST UNLIKELY MATERIALS. MANY OF THESE ARE ON DISPLAY IN THIS SHOW. SO PLEASE, COME IN.
HAVE A LOOK AROUND AND THEN ASK YOURSELVES IF YOU BELIEVE IT... OR NOT.
WHOA...

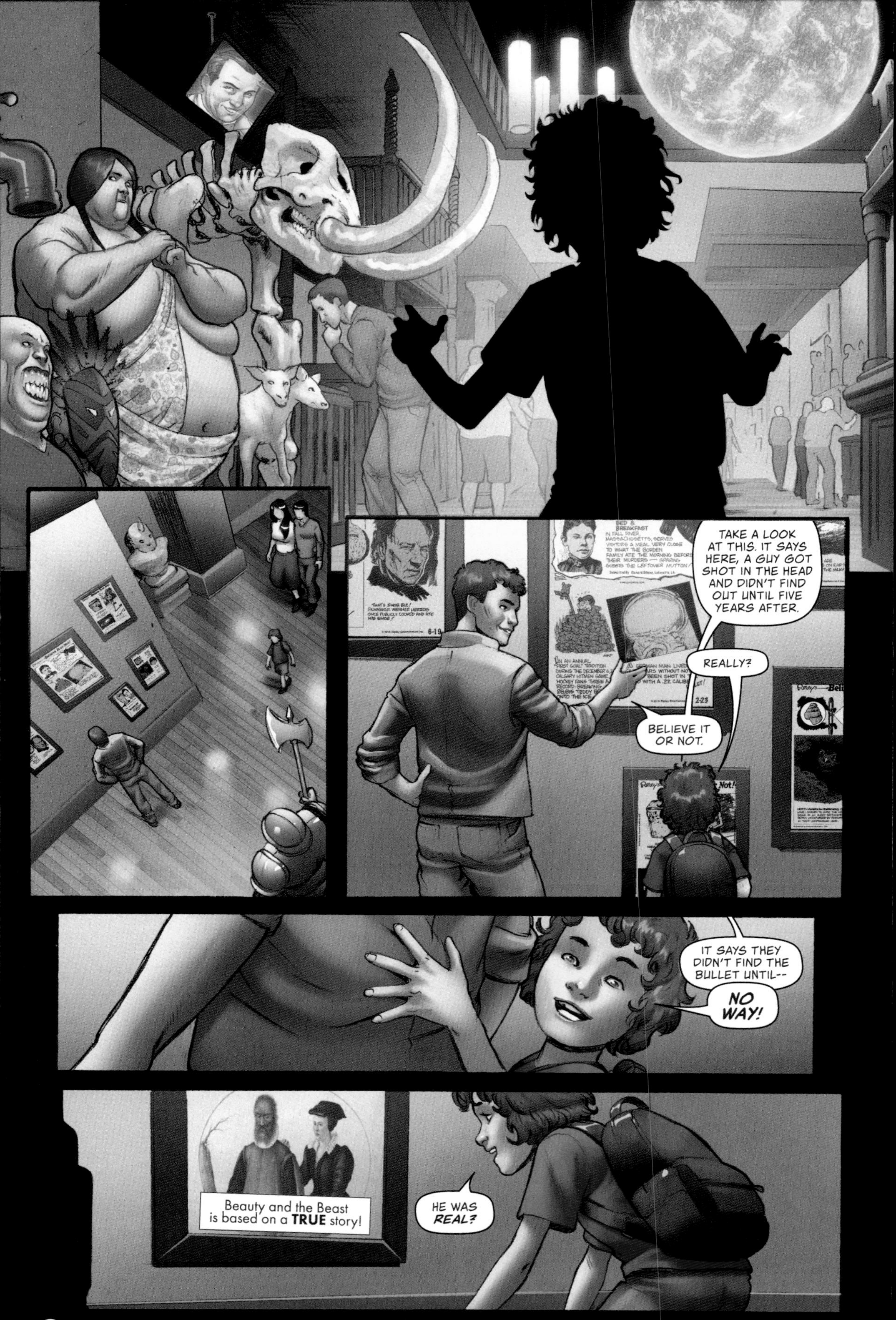

TAKE A LOOK AT THIS. IT SAYS HERE, A GUY GOT SHOT IN THE HEAD AND DIDN'T FIND OUT UNTIL FIVE YEARS AFTER.
REALLY?
BELIEVE IT OR NOT.
IT SAYS THEY DIDN'T FIND THE BULLET UNTIL--
NO WAY!
Beauty and the Beast is based on a **TRUE** story!
HE WAS *REAL?*

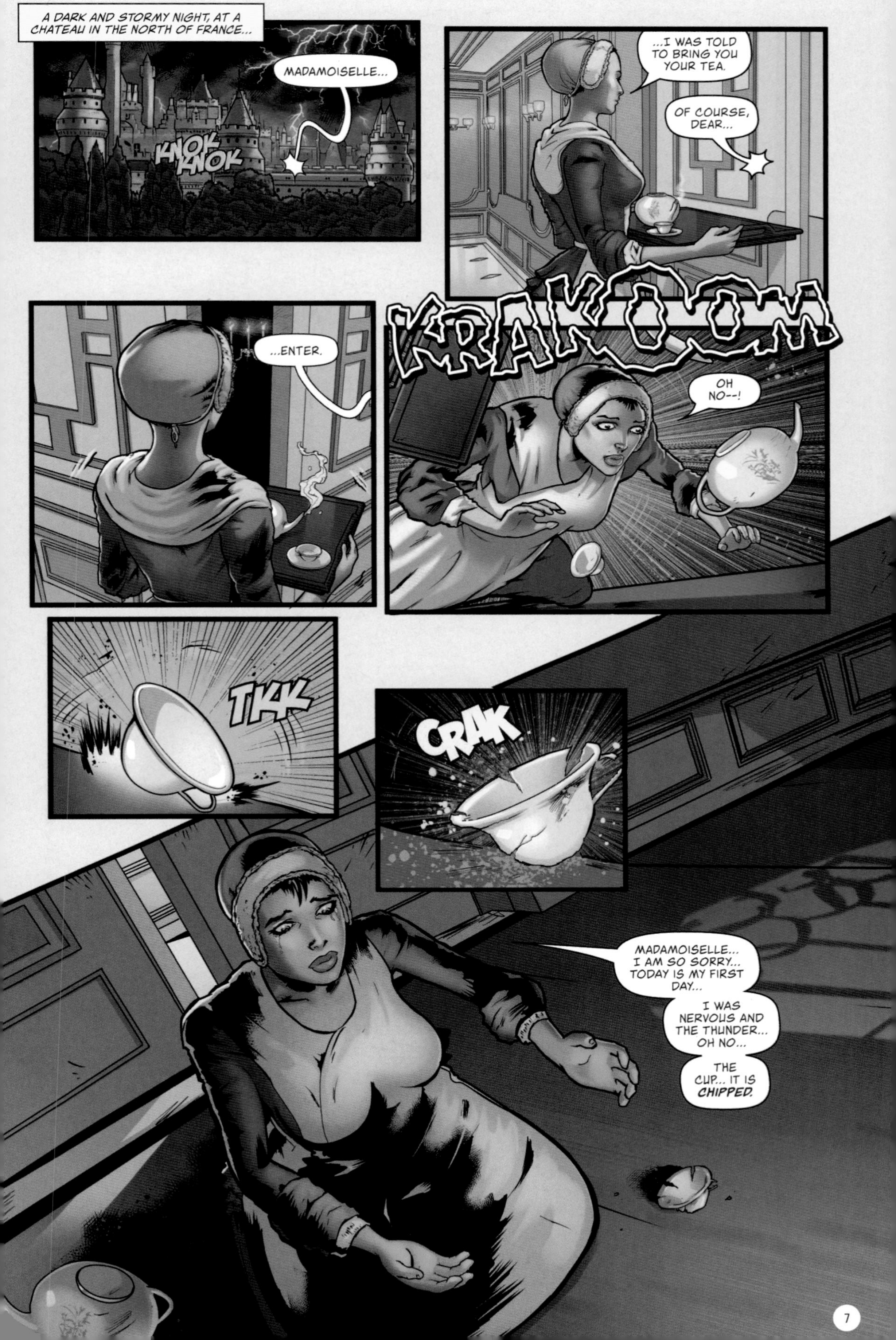
A DARK AND STORMY NIGHT, AT A CHATEAU IN THE NORTH OF FRANCE...
KNOK KNOK
MADAMOISELLE...
...I WAS TOLD TO BRING YOU YOUR TEA.
OF COURSE, DEAR...
...ENTER.
KRAKOOOM
OH NO--!
TKK
CRAK
MADAMOISELLE... I AM SO SORRY... TODAY IS MY FIRST DAY...
I WAS NERVOUS AND THE THUNDER... OH NO...
THE CUP... IT IS CHIPPED.

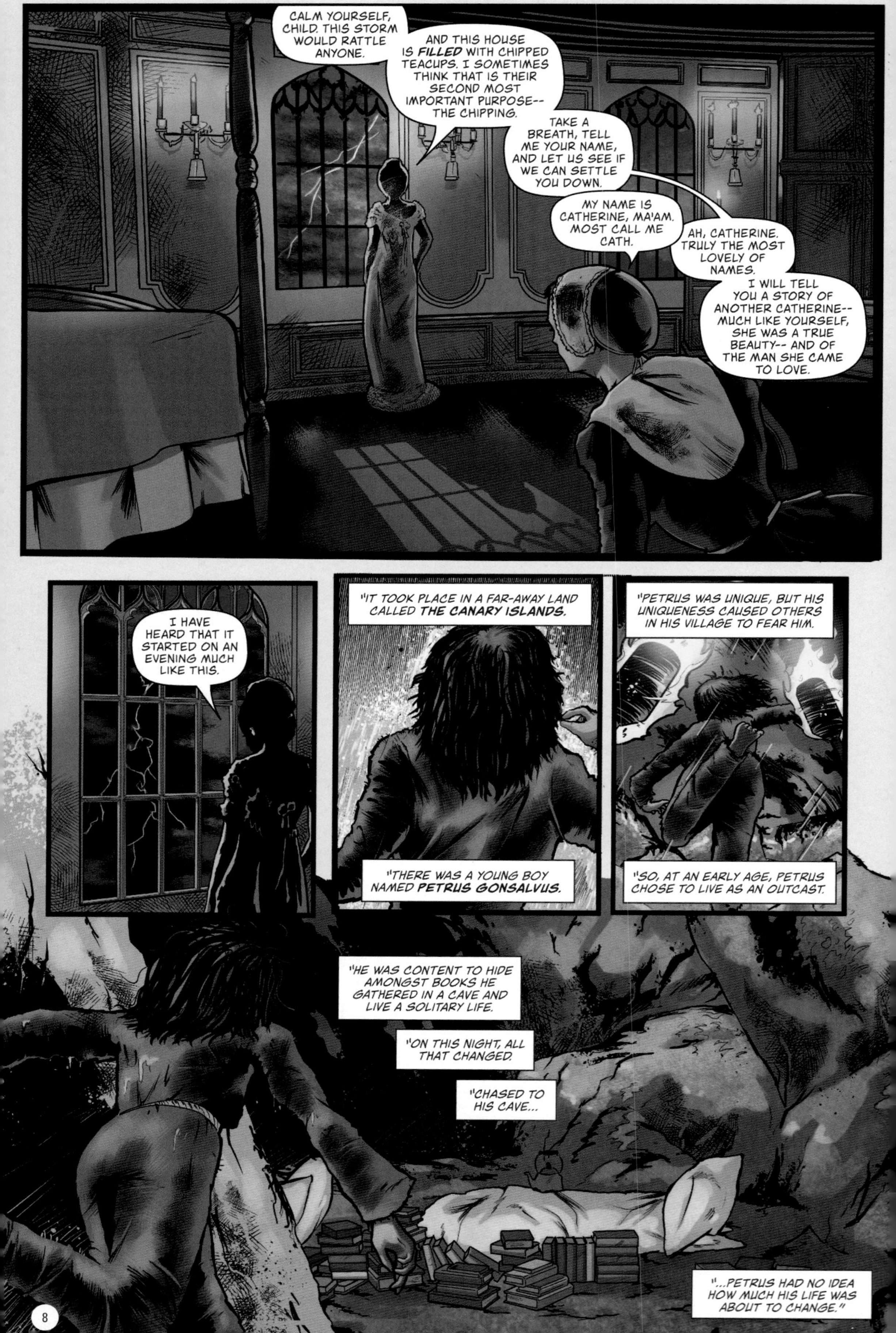
CALM YOURSELF, CHILD. THIS STORM WOULD RATTLE ANYONE.
AND THIS HOUSE IS **FILLED** WITH CHIPPED TEACUPS. I SOMETIMES THINK THAT IS THEIR SECOND MOST IMPORTANT PURPOSE-- THE CHIPPING.
TAKE A BREATH, TELL ME YOUR NAME, AND LET US SEE IF WE CAN SETTLE YOU DOWN.
MY NAME IS CATHERINE, MA'AM. MOST CALL ME CATH.
AH, CATHERINE. TRULY THE MOST LOVELY OF NAMES.
I WILL TELL YOU A STORY OF ANOTHER CATHERINE-- MUCH LIKE YOURSELF, SHE WAS A TRUE BEAUTY-- AND OF THE MAN SHE CAME TO LOVE.
I HAVE HEARD THAT IT STARTED ON AN EVENING MUCH LIKE THIS.
"IT TOOK PLACE IN A FAR-AWAY LAND CALLED **THE CANARY ISLANDS.**
"THERE WAS A YOUNG BOY NAMED **PETRUS GONSALVUS.**
"PETRUS WAS UNIQUE, BUT HIS UNIQUENESS CAUSED OTHERS IN HIS VILLAGE TO FEAR HIM.
"SO, AT AN EARLY AGE, PETRUS CHOSE TO LIVE AS AN OUTCAST.
"HE WAS CONTENT TO HIDE AMONGST BOOKS HE GATHERED IN A CAVE AND LIVE A SOLITARY LIFE.
"ON THIS NIGHT, ALL THAT CHANGED.
"CHASED TO HIS CAVE...
"...PETRUS HAD NO IDEA HOW MUCH HIS LIFE WAS ABOUT TO CHANGE."

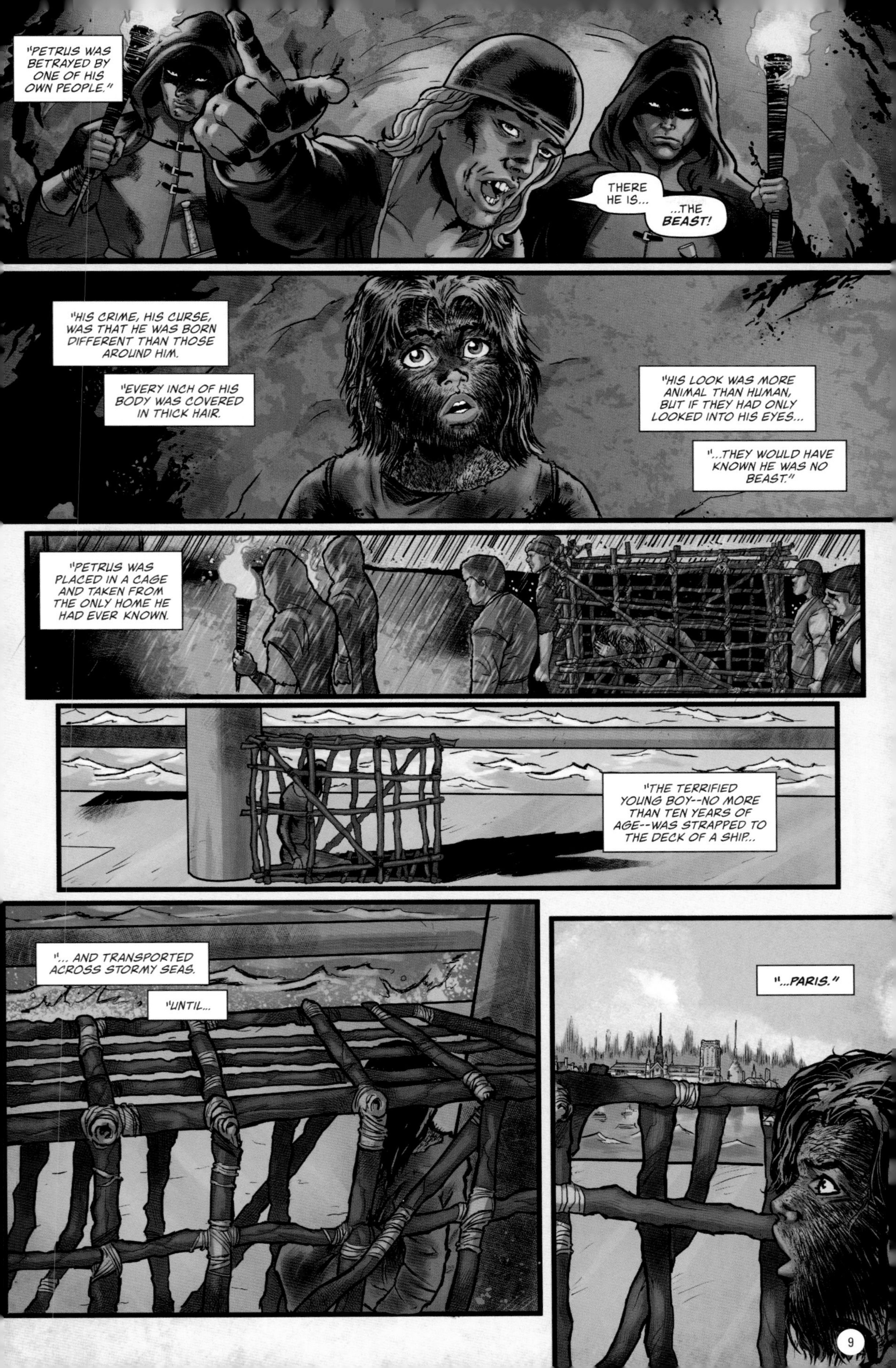
"PETRUS WAS BETRAYED BY ONE OF HIS OWN PEOPLE."
THERE HE IS...
...THE BEAST!
"HIS CRIME, HIS CURSE, WAS THAT HE WAS BORN DIFFERENT THAN THOSE AROUND HIM.
"EVERY INCH OF HIS BODY WAS COVERED IN THICK HAIR.
"HIS LOOK WAS MORE ANIMAL THAN HUMAN, BUT IF THEY HAD ONLY LOOKED INTO HIS EYES...
"...THEY WOULD HAVE KNOWN HE WAS NO BEAST."
"PETRUS WAS PLACED IN A CAGE AND TAKEN FROM THE ONLY HOME HE HAD EVER KNOWN.
"THE TERRIFIED YOUNG BOY--NO MORE THAN TEN YEARS OF AGE--WAS STRAPPED TO THE DECK OF A SHIP...
"... AND TRANSPORTED ACROSS STORMY SEAS.
"UNTIL...
"...PARIS."

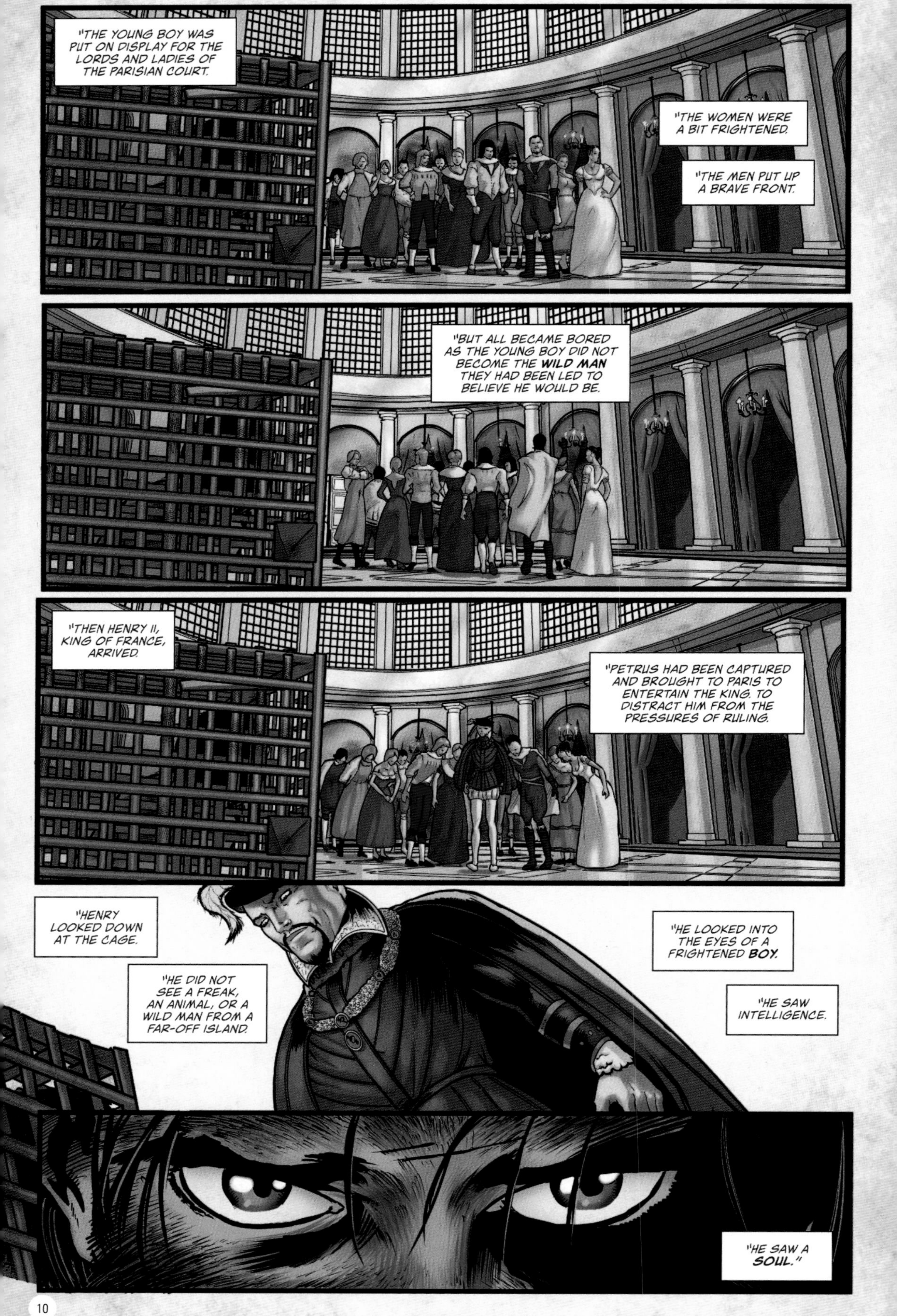
"THE YOUNG BOY WAS PUT ON DISPLAY FOR THE LORDS AND LADIES OF THE PARISIAN COURT.
"THE WOMEN WERE A BIT FRIGHTENED.
"THE MEN PUT UP A BRAVE FRONT.
"BUT ALL BECAME BORED AS THE YOUNG BOY DID NOT BECOME THE WILD MAN THEY HAD BEEN LED TO BELIEVE HE WOULD BE.
"THEN HENRY II, KING OF FRANCE, ARRIVED.
"PETRUS HAD BEEN CAPTURED AND BROUGHT TO PARIS TO ENTERTAIN THE KING. TO DISTRACT HIM FROM THE PRESSURES OF RULING.
"HENRY LOOKED DOWN AT THE CAGE.
"HE DID NOT SEE A FREAK, AN ANIMAL, OR A WILD MAN FROM A FAR-OFF ISLAND.
"HE LOOKED INTO THE EYES OF A FRIGHTENED BOY.
"HE SAW INTELLIGENCE.
"HE SAW A SOUL."

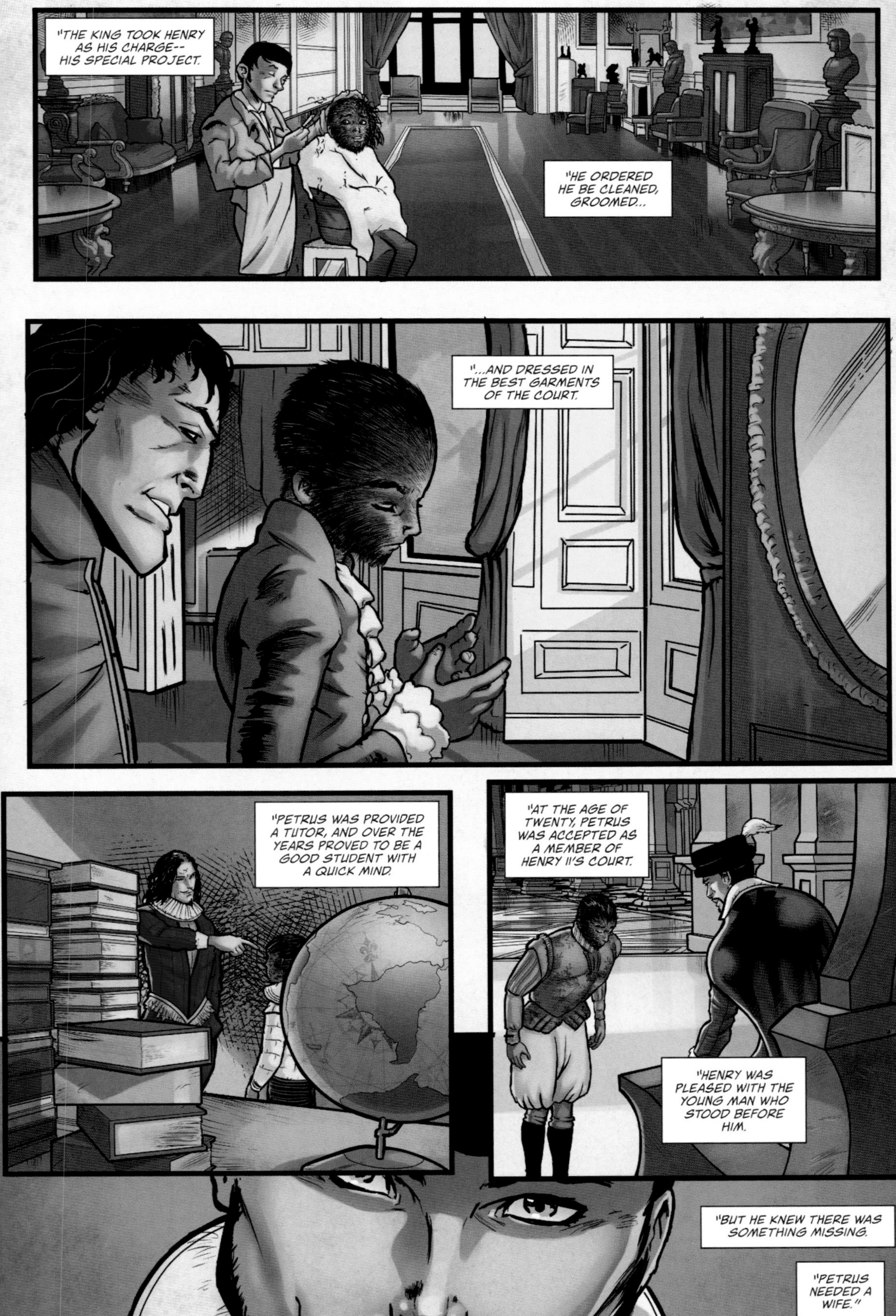
"THE KING TOOK HENRY AS HIS CHARGE-- HIS SPECIAL PROJECT.
"HE ORDERED HE BE CLEANED, GROOMED...
"...AND DRESSED IN THE BEST GARMENTS OF THE COURT.
"PETRUS WAS PROVIDED A TUTOR, AND OVER THE YEARS PROVED TO BE A GOOD STUDENT WITH A QUICK MIND.
"AT THE AGE OF TWENTY, PETRUS WAS ACCEPTED AS A MEMBER OF HENRY II'S COURT.
"HENRY WAS PLEASED WITH THE YOUNG MAN WHO STOOD BEFORE HIM.
"BUT HE KNEW THERE WAS SOMETHING MISSING.
"PETRUS NEEDED A WIFE."

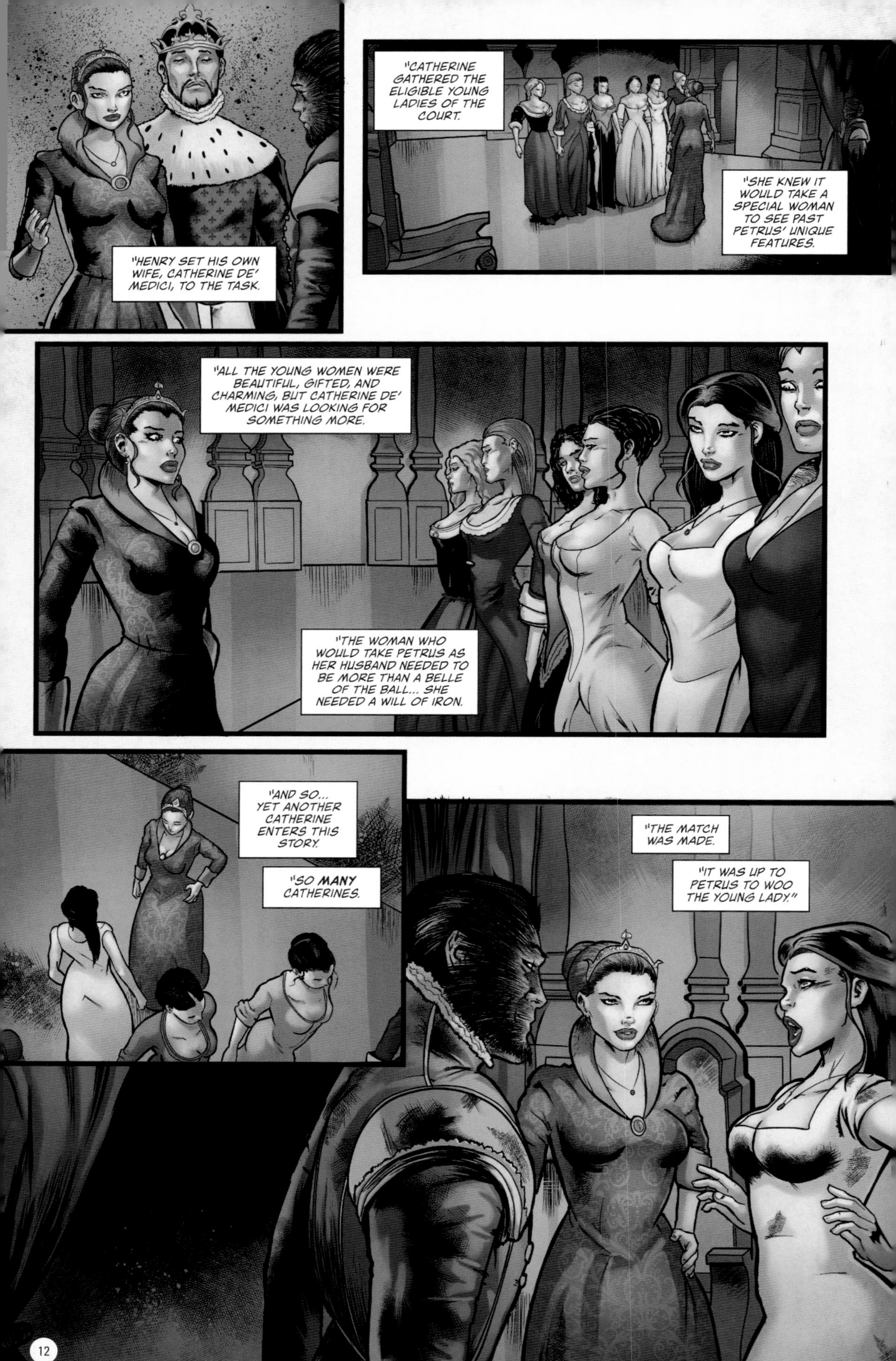
"HENRY SET HIS OWN WIFE, CATHERINE DE' MEDICI, TO THE TASK.
"CATHERINE GATHERED THE ELIGIBLE YOUNG LADIES OF THE COURT.
"SHE KNEW IT WOULD TAKE A SPECIAL WOMAN TO SEE PAST PETRUS' UNIQUE FEATURES.
"ALL THE YOUNG WOMEN WERE BEAUTIFUL, GIFTED, AND CHARMING, BUT CATHERINE DE' MEDICI WAS LOOKING FOR SOMETHING MORE.
"THE WOMAN WHO WOULD TAKE PETRUS AS HER HUSBAND NEEDED TO BE MORE THAN A BELLE OF THE BALL... SHE NEEDED A WILL OF IRON.
"AND SO... YET ANOTHER CATHERINE ENTERS THIS STORY.
"SO **MANY** CATHERINES.
"THE MATCH WAS MADE.
"IT WAS UP TO PETRUS TO WOO THE YOUNG LADY."

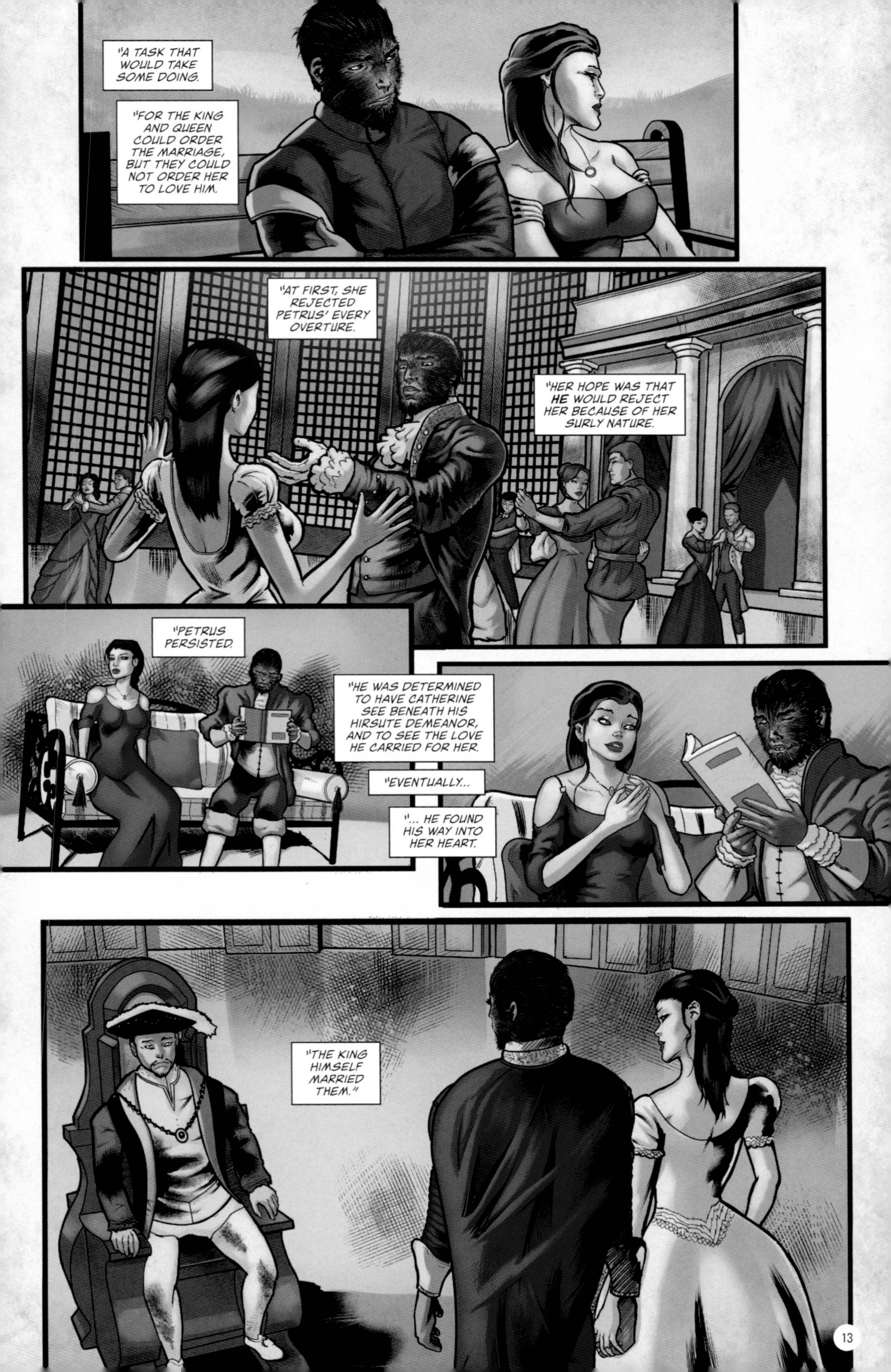
"A TASK THAT WOULD TAKE SOME DOING.
"FOR THE KING AND QUEEN COULD ORDER THE MARRIAGE, BUT THEY COULD NOT ORDER HER TO LOVE HIM.
"AT FIRST, SHE REJECTED PETRUS' EVERY OVERTURE.
"HER HOPE WAS THAT **HE** WOULD REJECT HER BECAUSE OF HER SURLY NATURE.
"PETRUS PERSISTED.
"HE WAS DETERMINED TO HAVE CATHERINE SEE BENEATH HIS HIRSUTE DEMEANOR, AND TO SEE THE LOVE HE CARRIED FOR HER.
"EVENTUALLY...
"... HE FOUND HIS WAY INTO HER HEART.
"THE KING HIMSELF MARRIED THEM."

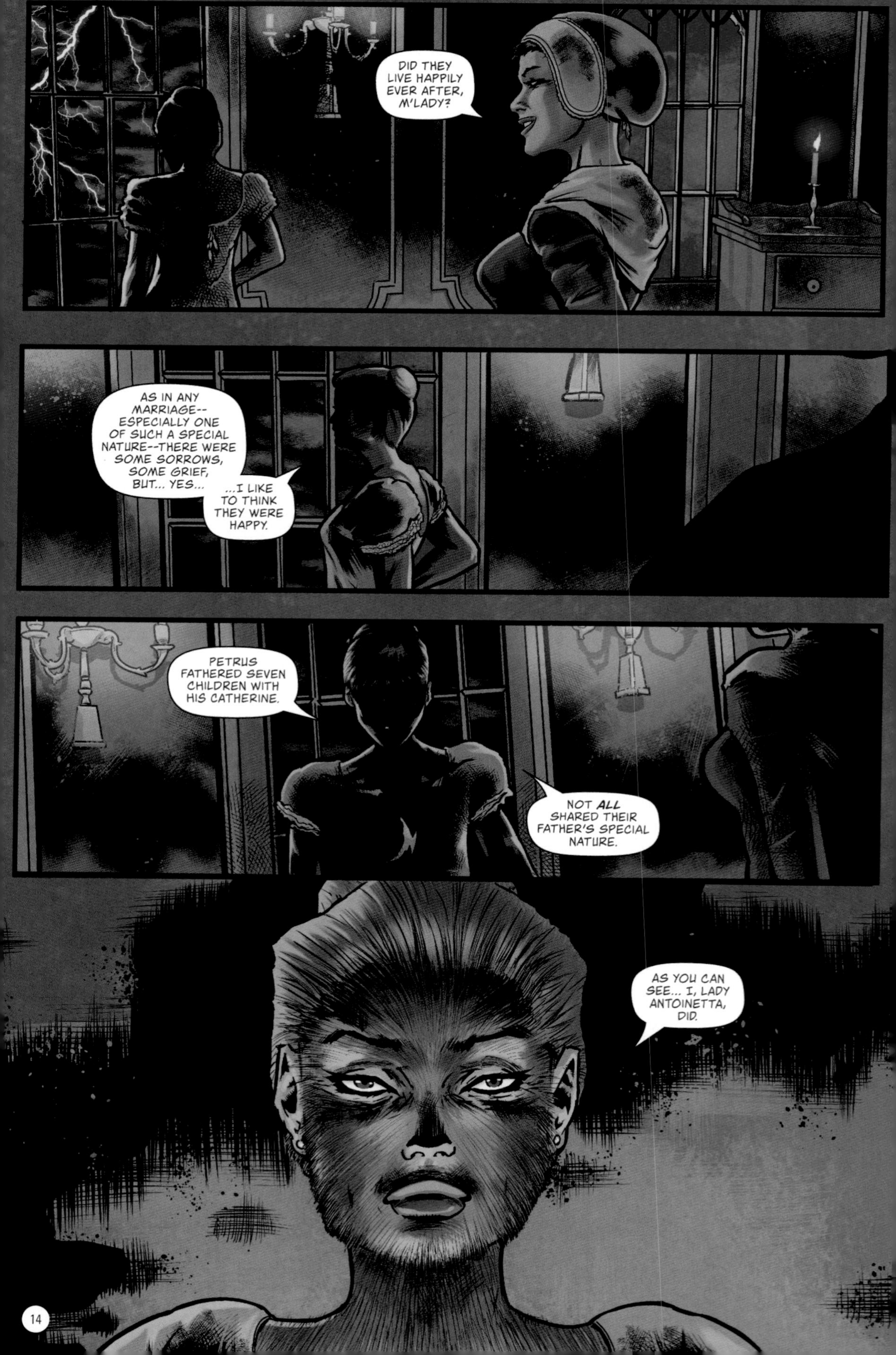
DID THEY LIVE HAPPILY EVER AFTER, M'LADY?
AS IN ANY MARRIAGE-- ESPECIALLY ONE OF SUCH A SPECIAL NATURE--THERE WERE SOME SORROWS, SOME GRIEF, BUT... YES...
...I LIKE TO THINK THEY WERE HAPPY.
PETRUS FATHERED SEVEN CHILDREN WITH HIS CATHERINE.
NOT ***ALL*** SHARED THEIR FATHER'S SPECIAL NATURE.
AS YOU CAN SEE... I, LADY ANTOINETTA, DID.

Ripley's Believe It or Not!®

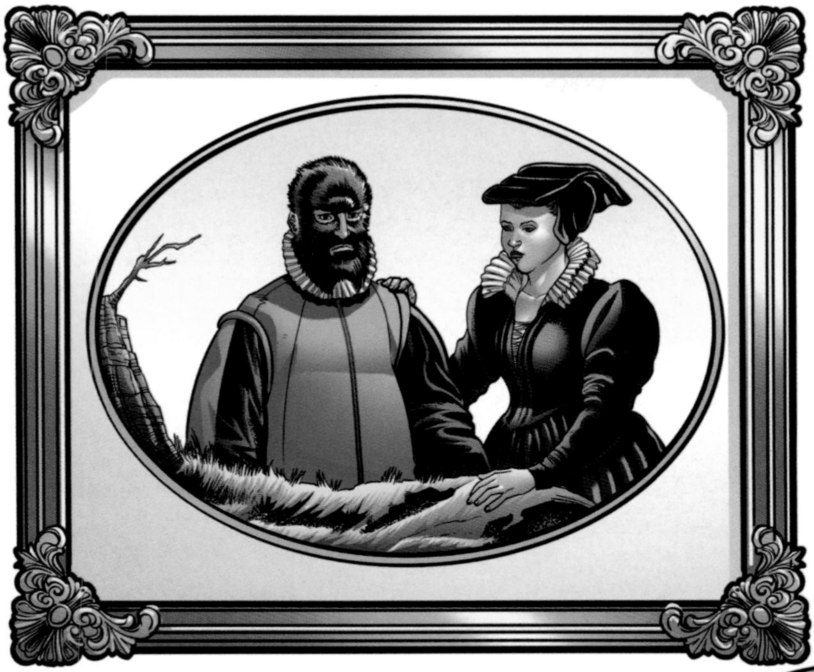

BEAUTY AND THE BEAST

IS BASED ON A TRUE STORY!

PEDRO GONZALES–ALSO KNOWN AS PETRUS GONSALVUS–SUFFERED FROM A CONDITION CALLED ***HYPERTRICHOSIS***, AN EXCEEDINGLY RARE CONDITION MARKED BY RAMPANT HAIR GROWTH ALL OVER THE BODY.

HE IS THOUGHT TO BE THE FIRST EVER RECORDED CASE OF THE CONDITION, AND SINCE HIS LIFE IN THE 1500S, ONLY ABOUT **50** OTHER CASES HAVE EVER BEEN OBSERVED!

ANTOINETTA WASN'T THE ONLY CHILD BORN TO PEDRO AND CATHERINE WHO INHERITED HER FATHER'S CONDITION.

AT LEAST THREE OF THEIR SEVEN CHILDREN WERE BORN WITH HYPERTRICHOSIS!

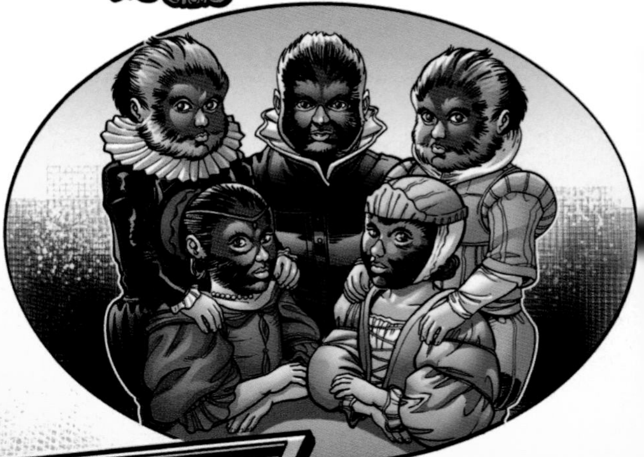

THE FIRST "BELIEVE IT OR NOT!" CARTOON WASN'T TITLED "BELIEVE IT OR NOT!"

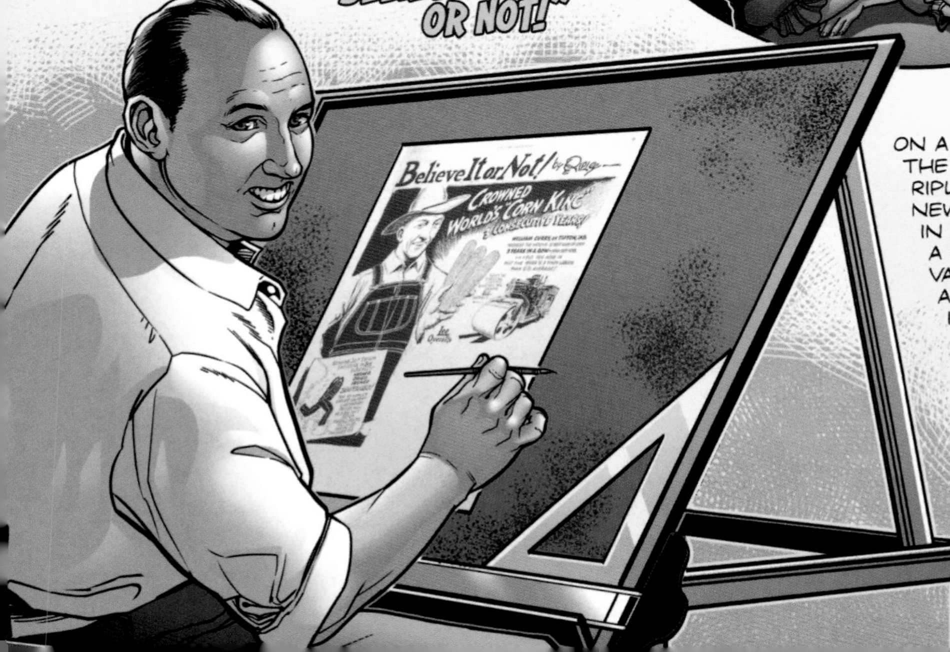
Believe It or Not! by Ripley
CROWNED WORLD'S "CORN KING"

ON A SLOW DAY IN THE OFFICE, ROBERT RIPLEY, WORKING AS A NEWSPAPER CARTOONIST IN NEW YORK, PRODUCED A PANEL FEATURING VARIOUS ODD ACHIEVEMENTS IN SPORTS.

THE FIRST CARTOON TITLED, ***"BELIEVE IT OR NOT!"*** WAS PUBLISHED TEN MONTHS LATER!

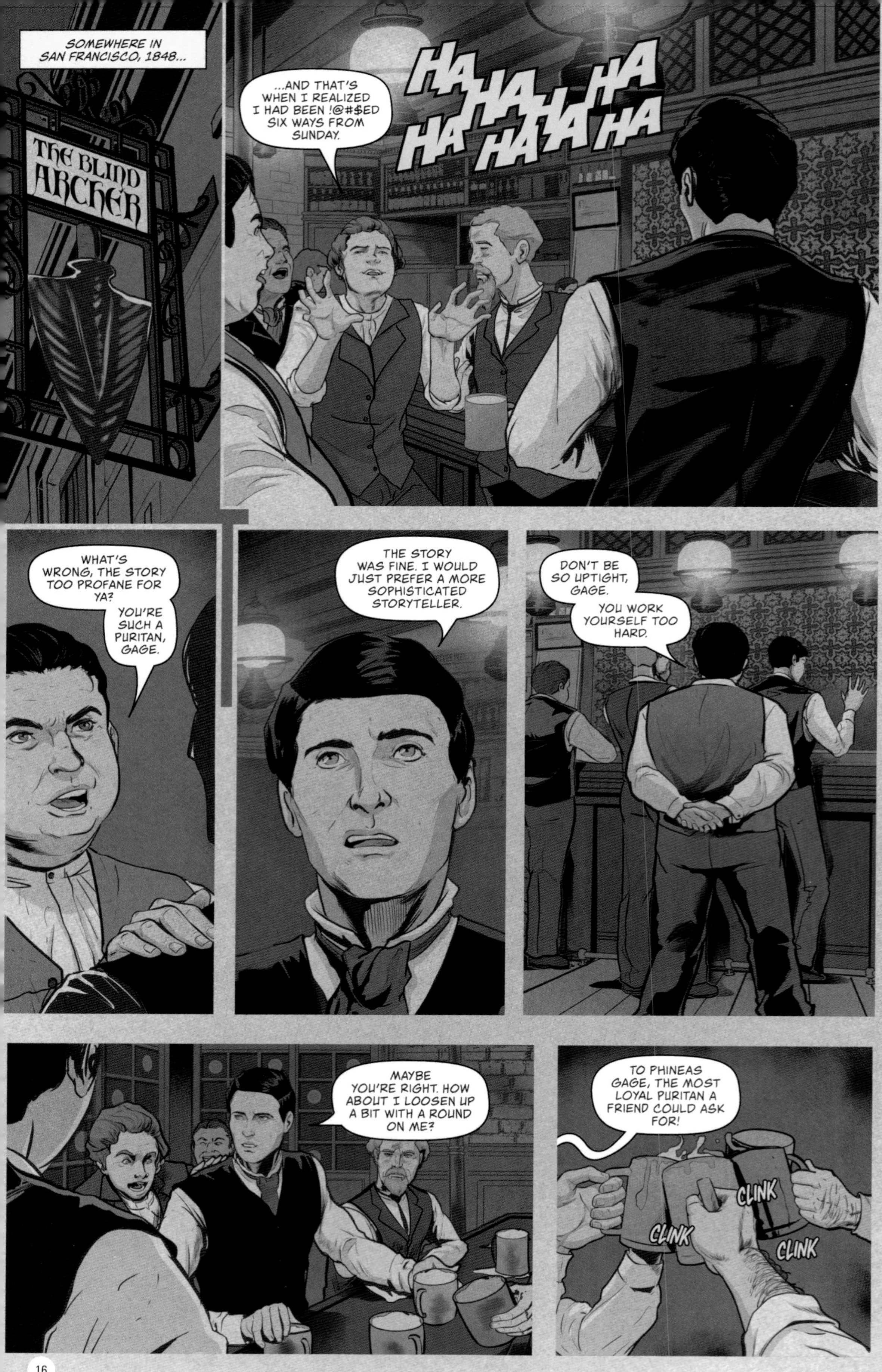
SOMEWHERE IN SAN FRANCISCO, 1848...
THE BLIND ARCHER
...AND THAT'S WHEN I REALIZED I HAD BEEN !@#$ED SIX WAYS FROM SUNDAY.
HA HA HA HA HA HA HA HA
WHAT'S WRONG, THE STORY TOO PROFANE FOR YA?
YOU'RE SUCH A PURITAN, GAGE.
THE STORY WAS FINE. I WOULD JUST PREFER A MORE SOPHISTICATED STORYTELLER.
DON'T BE SO UPTIGHT, GAGE.
YOU WORK YOURSELF TOO HARD.
MAYBE YOU'RE RIGHT. HOW ABOUT I LOOSEN UP A BIT WITH A ROUND ON ME?
TO PHINEAS GAGE, THE MOST LOYAL PURITAN A FRIEND COULD ASK FOR!
CLINK
CLINK
CLINK

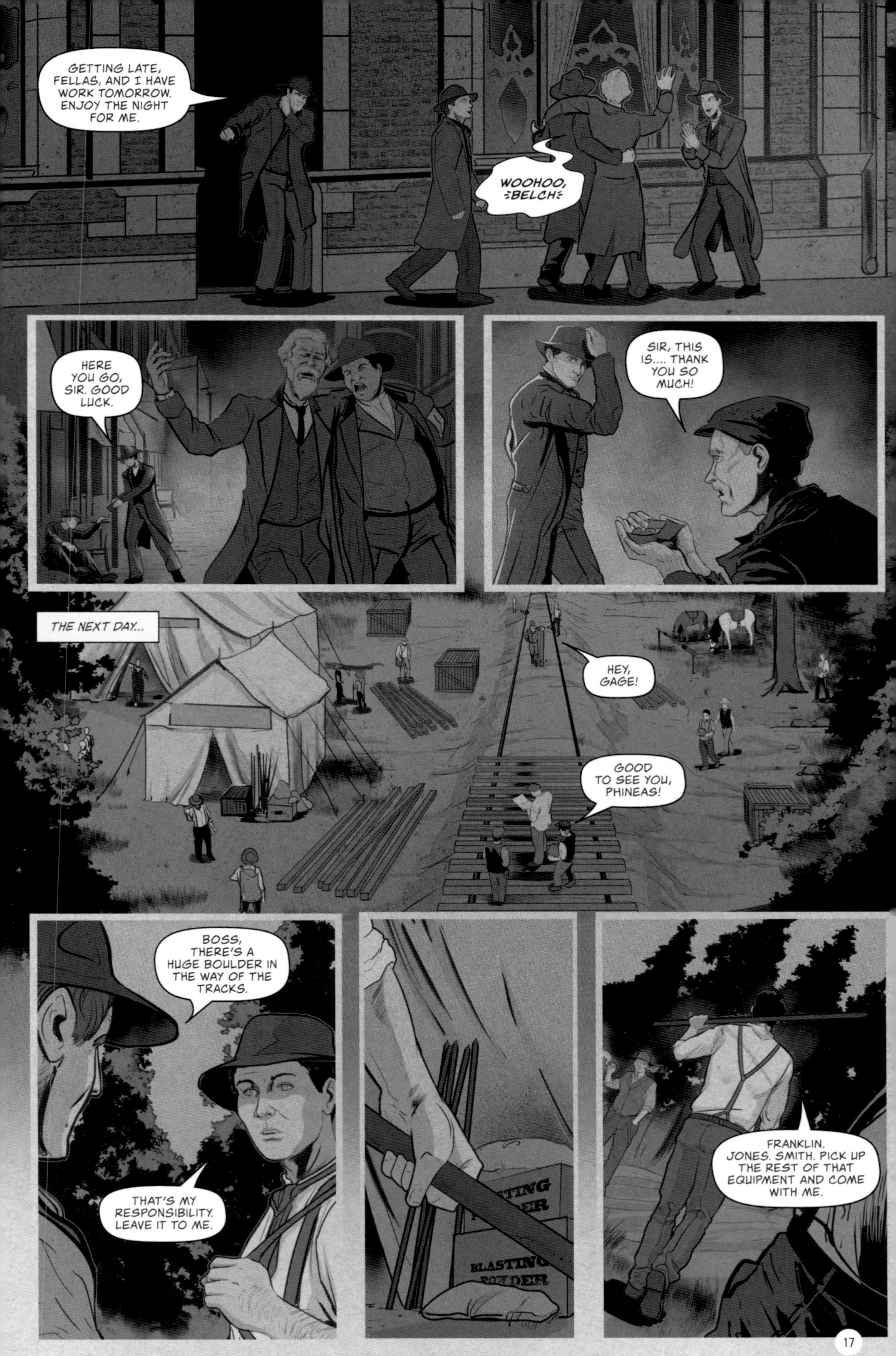
GETTING LATE, FELLAS, AND I HAVE WORK TOMORROW. ENJOY THE NIGHT FOR ME.
WOOHOO, BELCH
HERE YOU GO, SIR. GOOD LUCK.
SIR, THIS IS.... THANK YOU SO MUCH!
THE NEXT DAY...
HEY, GAGE!
GOOD TO SEE YOU, PHINEAS!
BOSS, THERE'S A HUGE BOULDER IN THE WAY OF THE TRACKS.
THAT'S MY RESPONSIBILITY. LEAVE IT TO ME.
BLASTING POWDER
BLASTING POWDER
FRANKLIN. JONES. SMITH. PICK UP THE REST OF THAT EQUIPMENT AND COME WITH ME.

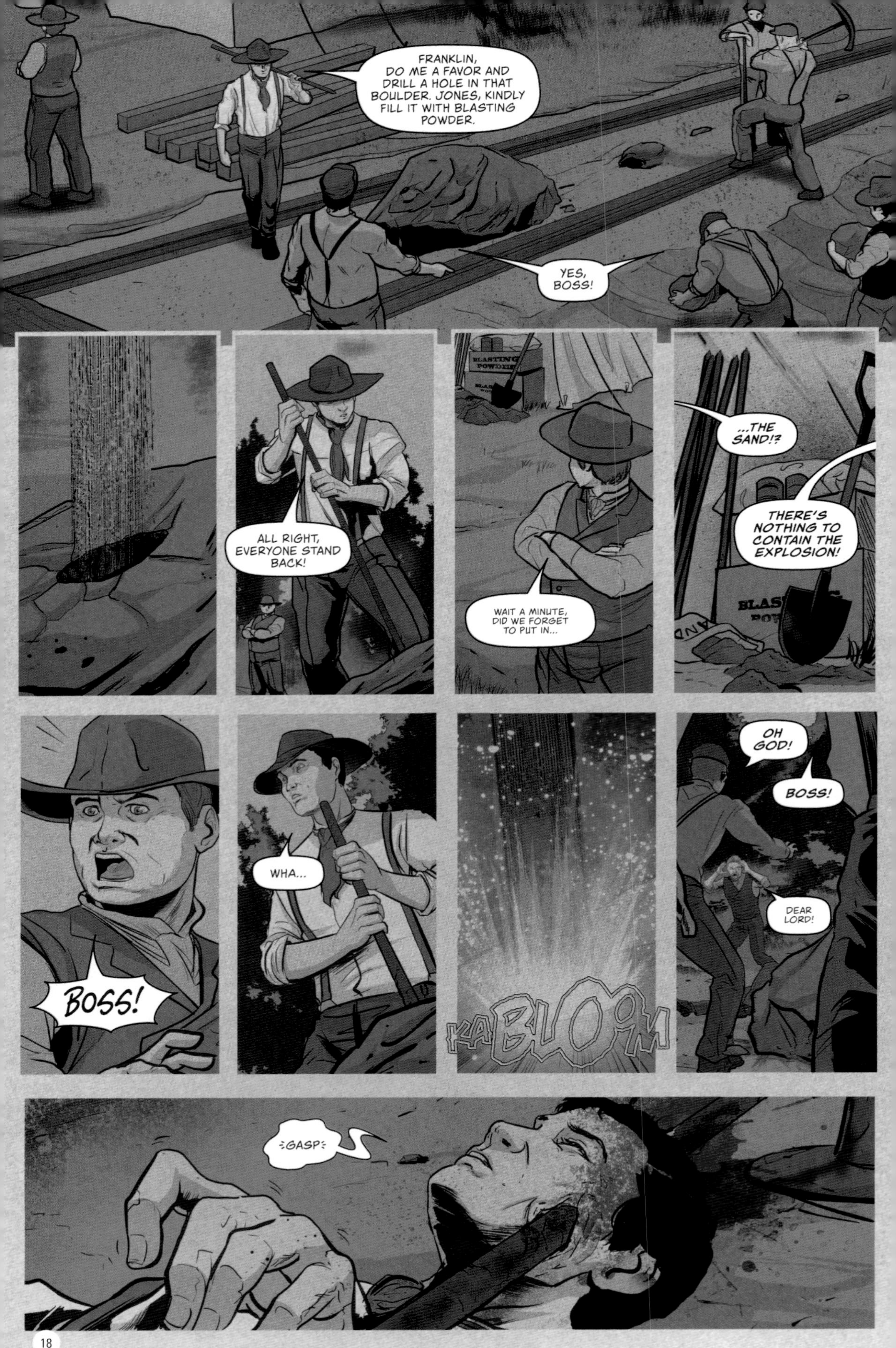
FRANKLIN, DO ME A FAVOR AND DRILL A HOLE IN THAT BOULDER. JONES, KINDLY FILL IT WITH BLASTING POWDER.
YES, BOSS!
ALL RIGHT, EVERYONE STAND BACK!
BLASTING POWDER
WAIT A MINUTE, DID WE FORGET TO PUT IN...
...THE SAND!?
THERE'S NOTHING TO CONTAIN THE EXPLOSION!
BOSS!
WHA...
KABLOOM
OH GOD!
BOSS!
DEAR LORD!
GASP

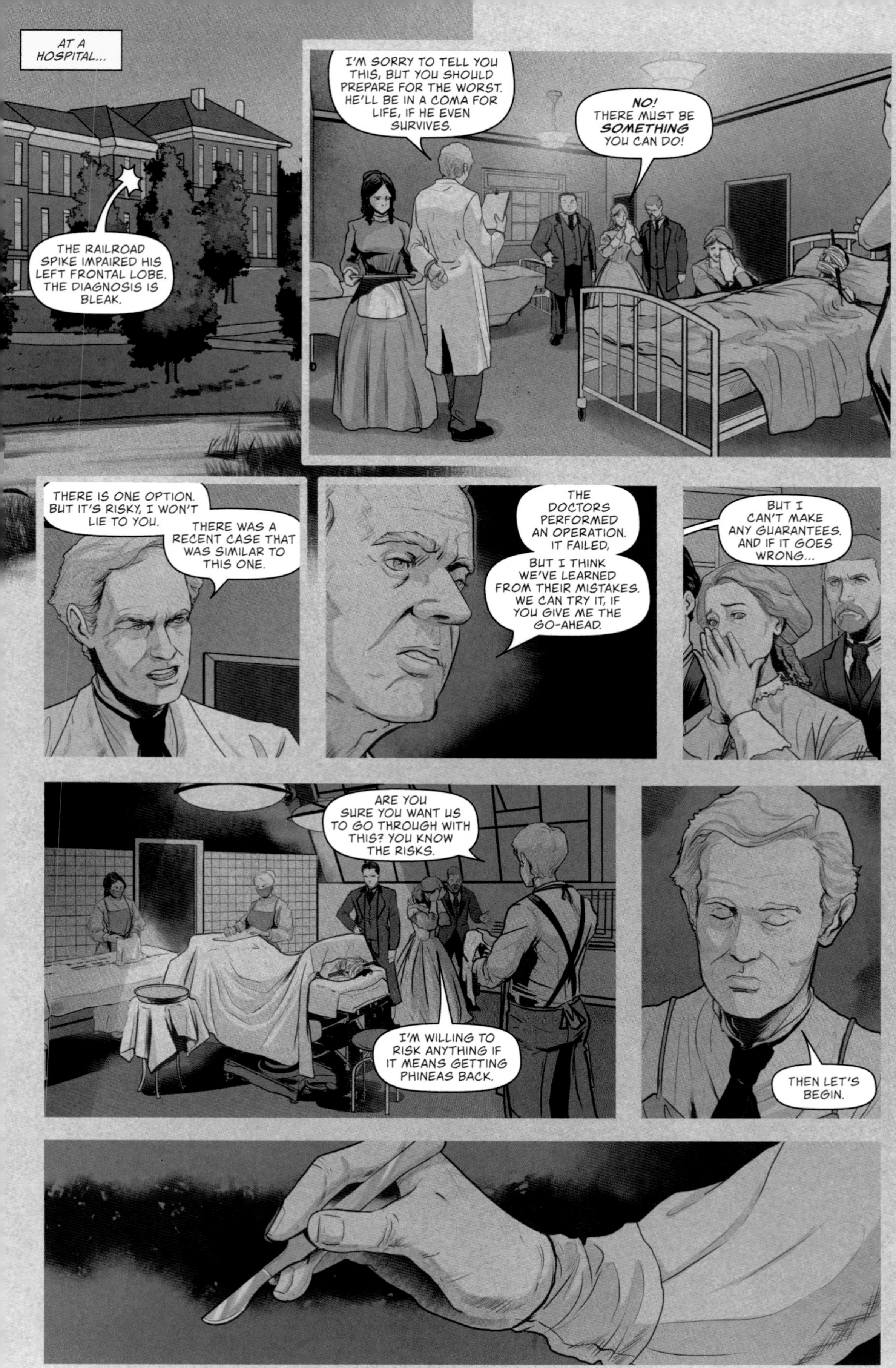
AT A HOSPITAL...
THE RAILROAD SPIKE IMPAIRED HIS LEFT FRONTAL LOBE. THE DIAGNOSIS IS BLEAK.
I'M SORRY TO TELL YOU THIS, BUT YOU SHOULD PREPARE FOR THE WORST. HE'LL BE IN A COMA FOR LIFE, IF HE EVEN SURVIVES.
NO! THERE MUST BE SOMETHING YOU CAN DO!
THERE IS ONE OPTION. BUT IT'S RISKY, I WON'T LIE TO YOU.
THERE WAS A RECENT CASE THAT WAS SIMILAR TO THIS ONE.
THE DOCTORS PERFORMED AN OPERATION. IT FAILED,
BUT I THINK WE'VE LEARNED FROM THEIR MISTAKES. WE CAN TRY IT, IF YOU GIVE ME THE GO-AHEAD.
BUT I CAN'T MAKE ANY GUARANTEES. AND IF IT GOES WRONG...
ARE YOU SURE YOU WANT US TO GO THROUGH WITH THIS? YOU KNOW THE RISKS.
I'M WILLING TO RISK ANYTHING IF IT MEANS GETTING PHINEAS BACK.
THEN LET'S BEGIN.

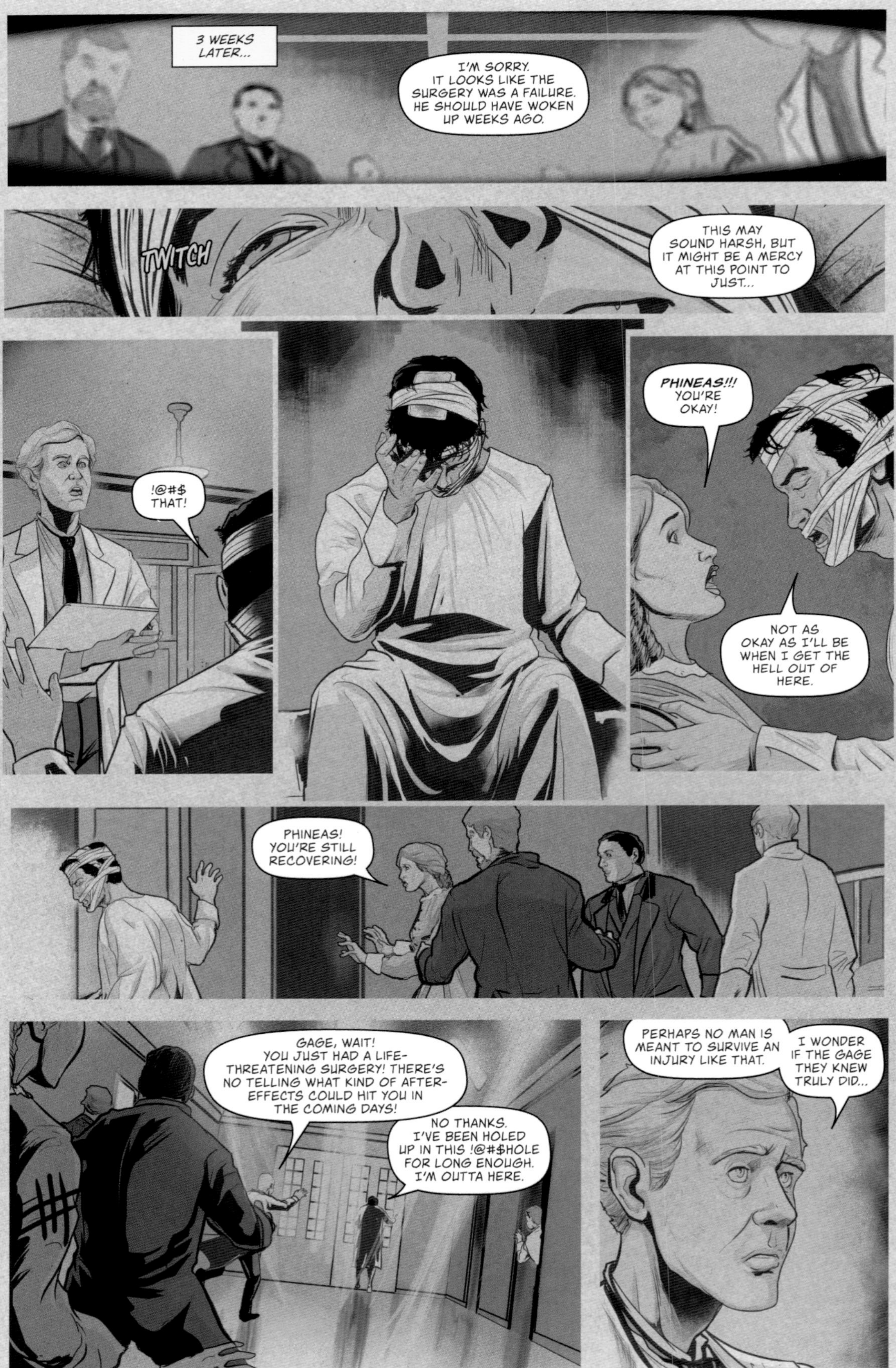
3 WEEKS LATER...
I'M SORRY. IT LOOKS LIKE THE SURGERY WAS A FAILURE. HE SHOULD HAVE WOKEN UP WEEKS AGO.
TWITCH
THIS MAY SOUND HARSH, BUT IT MIGHT BE A MERCY AT THIS POINT TO JUST...
!@#$ THAT!
PHINEAS!!! YOU'RE OKAY!
NOT AS OKAY AS I'LL BE WHEN I GET THE HELL OUT OF HERE.
PHINEAS! YOU'RE STILL RECOVERING!
GAGE, WAIT! YOU JUST HAD A LIFE-THREATENING SURGERY! THERE'S NO TELLING WHAT KIND OF AFTER-EFFECTS COULD HIT YOU IN THE COMING DAYS!
NO THANKS. I'VE BEEN HOLED UP IN THIS !@#$HOLE FOR LONG ENOUGH. I'M OUTTA HERE.
PERHAPS NO MAN IS MEANT TO SURVIVE AN INJURY LIKE THAT.
I WONDER IF THE GAGE THEY KNEW TRULY DID...

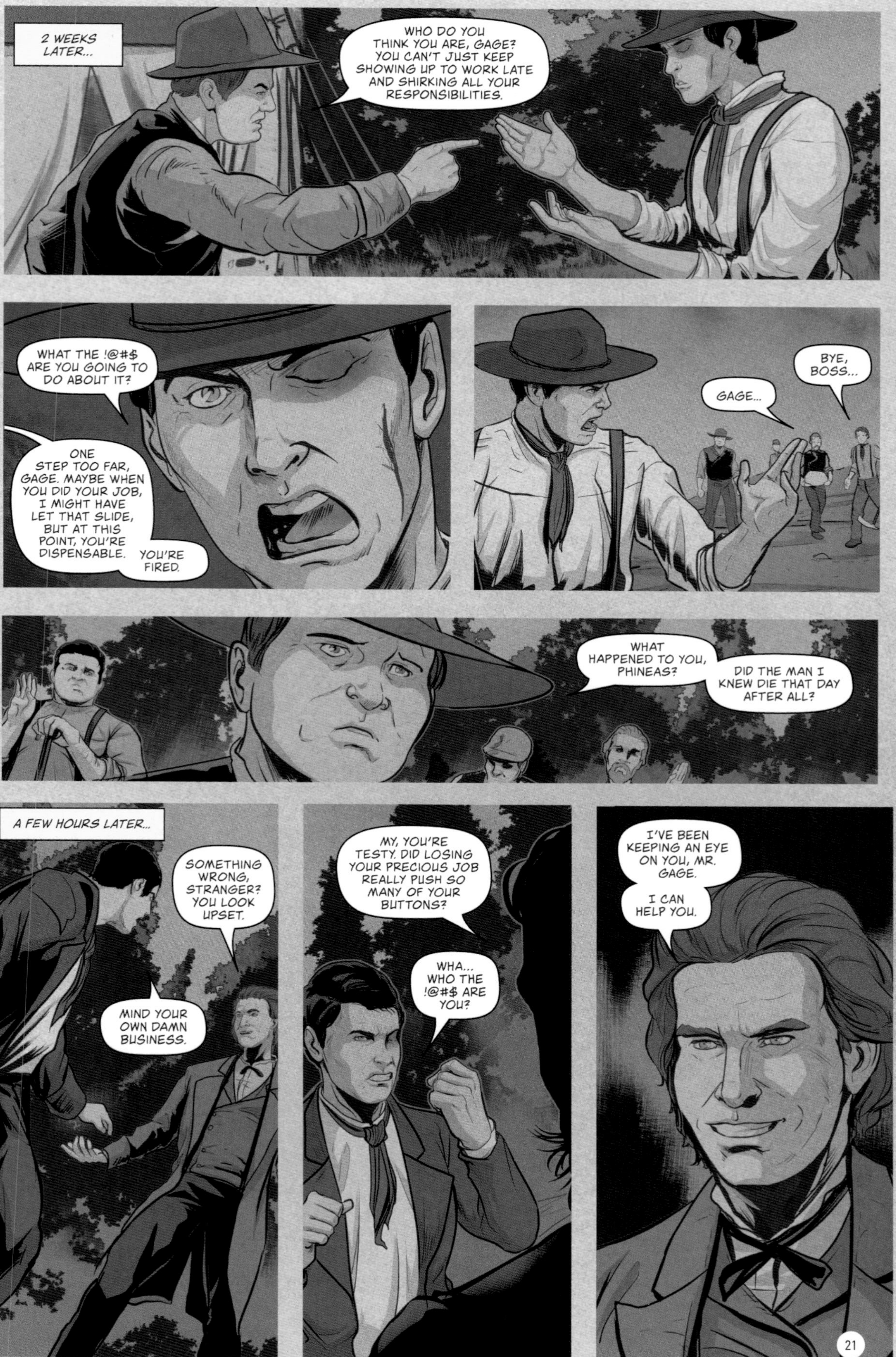
2 WEEKS LATER...
WHO DO YOU THINK YOU ARE, GAGE? YOU CAN'T JUST KEEP SHOWING UP TO WORK LATE AND SHIRKING ALL YOUR RESPONSIBILITIES.
WHAT THE !@#$ ARE YOU GOING TO DO ABOUT IT?
ONE STEP TOO FAR, GAGE. MAYBE WHEN YOU DID YOUR JOB, I MIGHT HAVE LET THAT SLIDE, BUT AT THIS POINT, YOU'RE DISPENSABLE.
YOU'RE FIRED.
GAGE...
BYE, BOSS...
WHAT HAPPENED TO YOU, PHINEAS?
DID THE MAN I KNEW DIE THAT DAY AFTER ALL?
A FEW HOURS LATER...
SOMETHING WRONG, STRANGER? YOU LOOK UPSET.
MIND YOUR OWN DAMN BUSINESS.
MY, YOU'RE TESTY. DID LOSING YOUR PRECIOUS JOB REALLY PUSH SO MANY OF YOUR BUTTONS?
WHA... WHO THE !@#$ ARE YOU?
I'VE BEEN KEEPING AN EYE ON YOU, MR. GAGE.
I CAN HELP YOU.

YOU SHOULD HELP YOURSELF BY GETTING THE !@#$ OUT OF MY SIGHT.

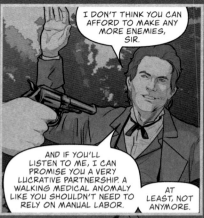

I DON'T THINK YOU CAN AFFORD TO MAKE ANY MORE ENEMIES, SIR.

AND IF YOU'LL LISTEN TO ME, I CAN PROMISE YOU A VERY LUCRATIVE PARTNERSHIP. A WALKING MEDICAL ANOMALY LIKE YOU SHOULDN'T NEED TO RELY ON MANUAL LABOR.

AT LEAST, NOT ANYMORE.

...

LATER THAT WEEK...

LADIES AND GENTLEMEN, BEFORE YOU STANDS A MAN WHO HAS FACED DOWN THE GRIM REAPER HIMSELF. A WALKING SPECTACLE WHO NEEDS NO INTRODUCTION, BUT DESERVES ONE REGARDLESS.

SOME OF YOU HAVE COME FROM AROUND THE WORLD TO WITNESS THIS WALKING MARVEL. WAS HIS SURVIVAL A SCIENTIFIC ANOMALY, OR A MODERN MIRACLE?

ONLY YOU CAN DECIDE, BUT ONE THING IS FOR CERTAIN...

...PHINEAS GAGE IS MORE THAN DESERVING OF YOUR GENEROSITY!

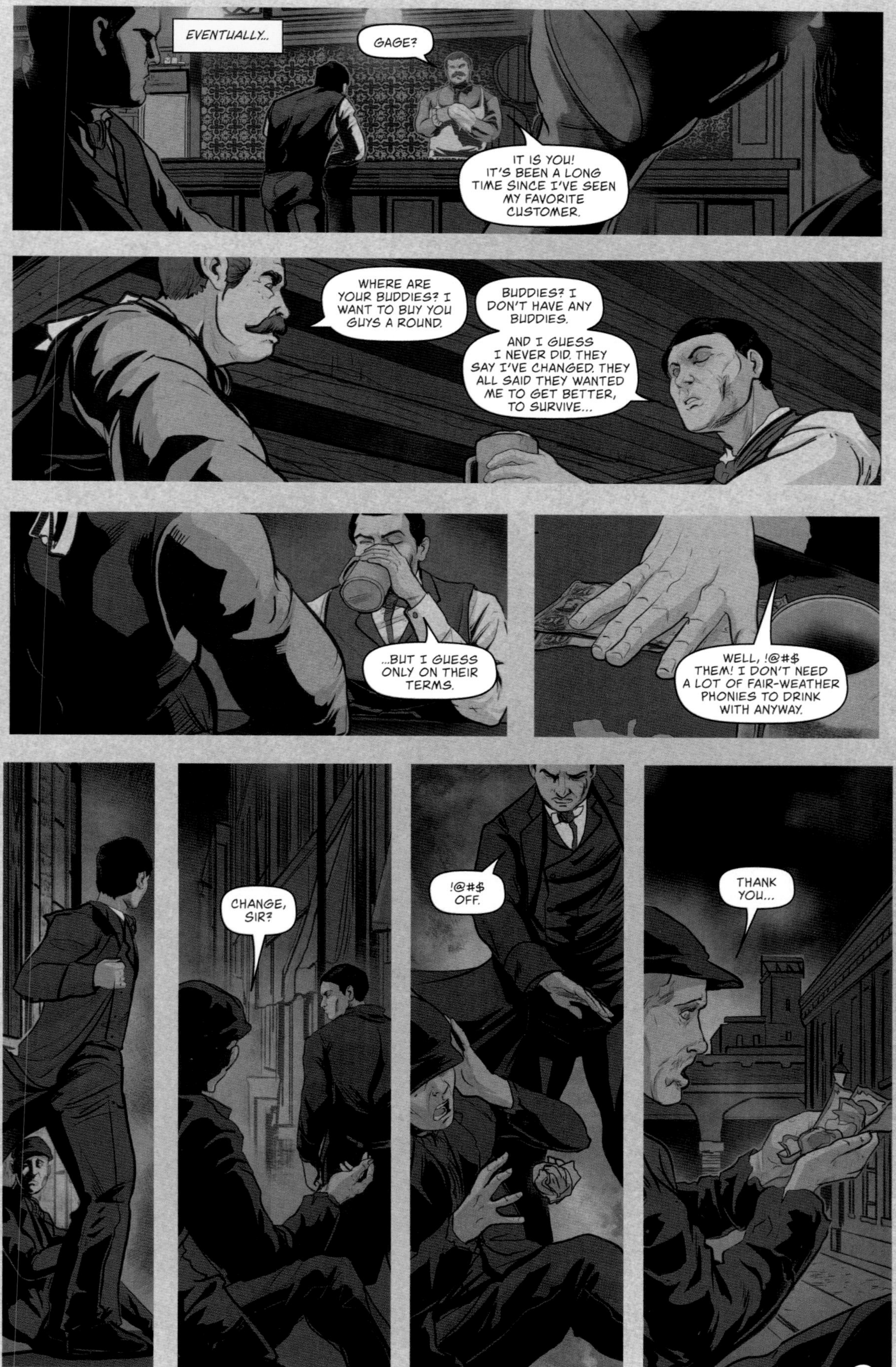
EVENTUALLY...
GAGE?
IT IS YOU! IT'S BEEN A LONG TIME SINCE I'VE SEEN MY FAVORITE CUSTOMER.
WHERE ARE YOUR BUDDIES? I WANT TO BUY YOU GUYS A ROUND.
BUDDIES? I DON'T HAVE ANY BUDDIES.
AND I GUESS I NEVER DID. THEY SAY I'VE CHANGED. THEY ALL SAID THEY WANTED ME TO GET BETTER, TO SURVIVE...
...BUT I GUESS ONLY ON THEIR TERMS.
WELL, !@#$ THEM! I DON'T NEED A LOT OF FAIR-WEATHER PHONIES TO DRINK WITH ANYWAY.
CHANGE, SIR?
!@#$ OFF.
THANK YOU...

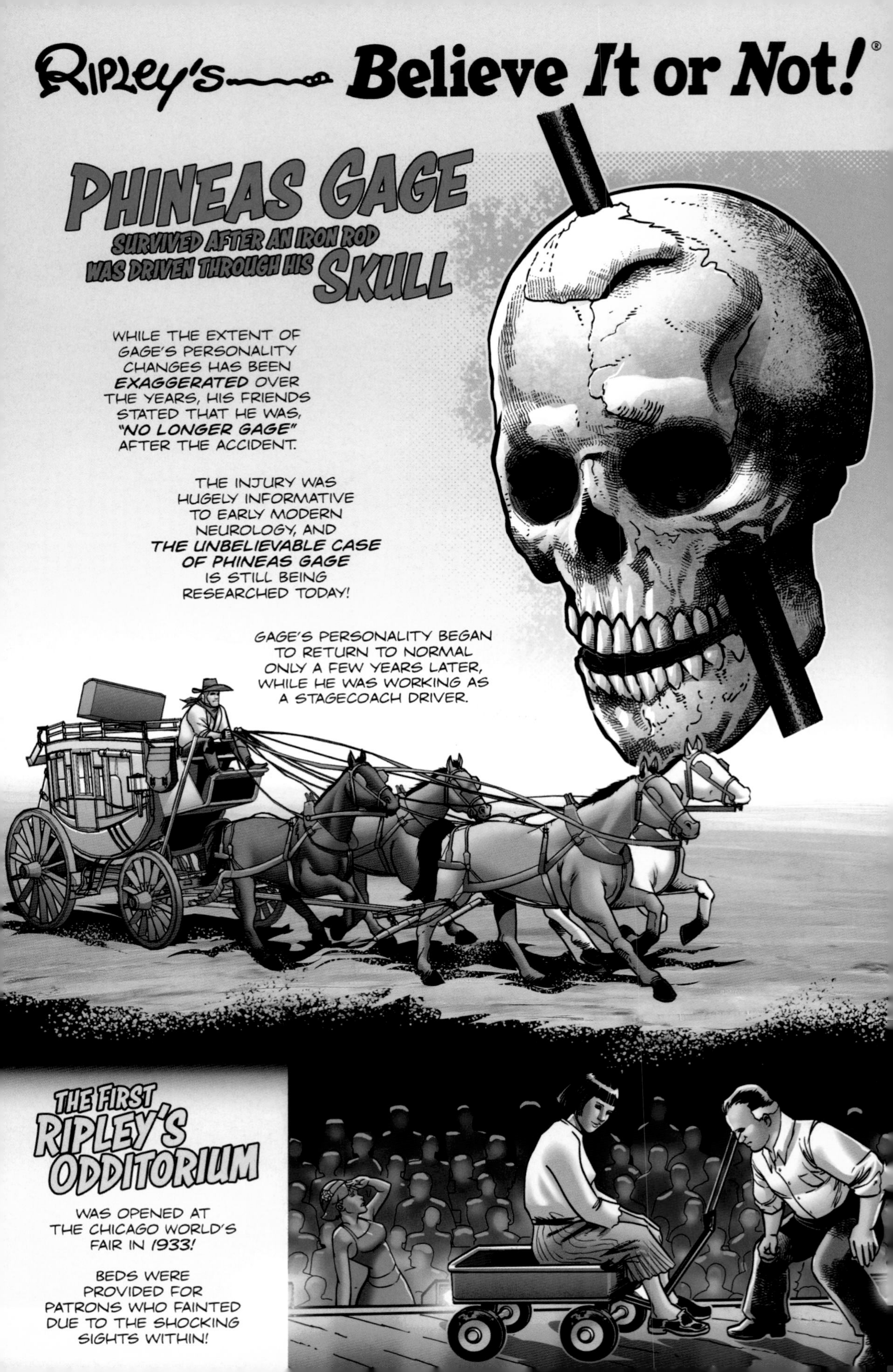
RIPLEY'S Believe It or Not!®
PHINEAS GAGE
SURVIVED AFTER AN IRON ROD WAS DRIVEN THROUGH HIS SKULL
WHILE THE EXTENT OF GAGE'S PERSONALITY CHANGES HAS BEEN EXAGGERATED OVER THE YEARS, HIS FRIENDS STATED THAT HE WAS, "NO LONGER GAGE" AFTER THE ACCIDENT.
THE INJURY WAS HUGELY INFORMATIVE TO EARLY MODERN NEUROLOGY, AND THE UNBELIEVABLE CASE OF PHINEAS GAGE IS STILL BEING RESEARCHED TODAY!
GAGE'S PERSONALITY BEGAN TO RETURN TO NORMAL ONLY A FEW YEARS LATER, WHILE HE WAS WORKING AS A STAGECOACH DRIVER.
THE FIRST RIPLEY'S ODDITORIUM
WAS OPENED AT THE CHICAGO WORLD'S FAIR IN 1933!
BEDS WERE PROVIDED FOR PATRONS WHO FAINTED DUE TO THE SHOCKING SIGHTS WITHIN!

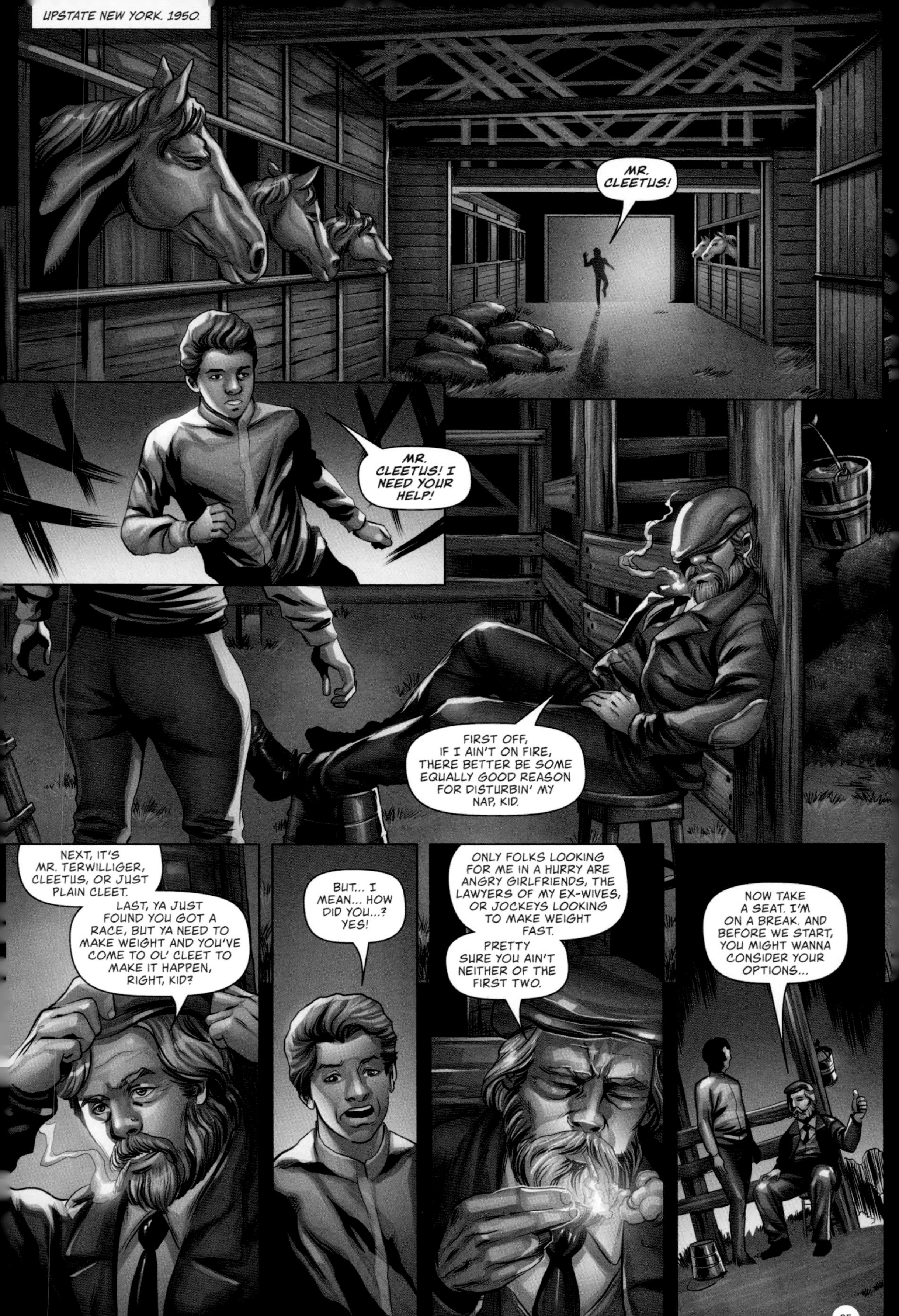
UPSTATE NEW YORK. 1950.
MR. CLEETUS!
MR. CLEETUS! I NEED YOUR HELP!
FIRST OFF, IF I AIN'T ON FIRE, THERE BETTER BE SOME EQUALLY GOOD REASON FOR DISTURBIN' MY NAP, KID.
NEXT, IT'S MR. TERWILLIGER, CLEETUS, OR JUST PLAIN CLEET.
LAST, YA JUST FOUND YOU GOT A RACE, BUT YA NEED TO MAKE WEIGHT AND YOU'VE COME TO OL' CLEET TO MAKE IT HAPPEN, RIGHT, KID?
BUT... I MEAN... HOW DID YOU...? YES!
ONLY FOLKS LOOKING FOR ME IN A HURRY ARE ANGRY GIRLFRIENDS, THE LAWYERS OF MY EX-WIVES, OR JOCKEYS LOOKING TO MAKE WEIGHT FAST.
PRETTY SURE YOU AIN'T NEITHER OF THE FIRST TWO.
NOW TAKE A SEAT. I'M ON A BREAK. AND BEFORE WE START, YOU MIGHT WANNA CONSIDER YOUR OPTIONS...

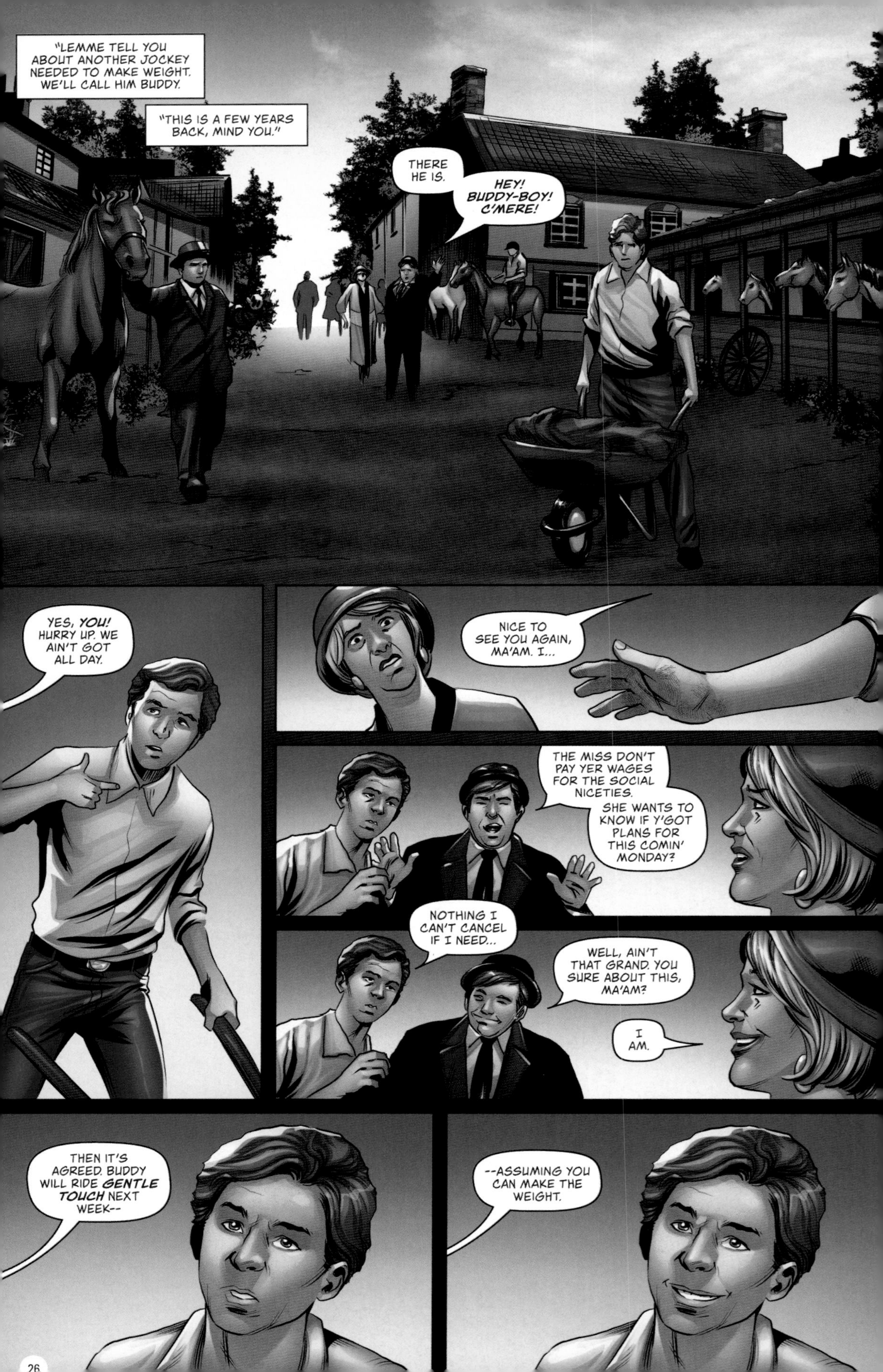
"LEMME TELL YOU ABOUT ANOTHER JOCKEY NEEDED TO MAKE WEIGHT. WE'LL CALL HIM BUDDY.
"THIS IS A FEW YEARS BACK, MIND YOU."
THERE HE IS.
HEY! BUDDY-BOY! C'MERE!
YES, YOU! HURRY UP. WE AIN'T GOT ALL DAY.
NICE TO SEE YOU AGAIN, MA'AM. I...
THE MISS DON'T PAY YER WAGES FOR THE SOCIAL NICETIES.
SHE WANTS TO KNOW IF Y'GOT PLANS FOR THIS COMIN' MONDAY?
NOTHING I CAN'T CANCEL IF I NEED...
WELL, AIN'T THAT GRAND. YOU SURE ABOUT THIS, MA'AM?
I AM.
THEN IT'S AGREED. BUDDY WILL RIDE GENTLE TOUCH NEXT WEEK--
--ASSUMING YOU CAN MAKE THE WEIGHT.

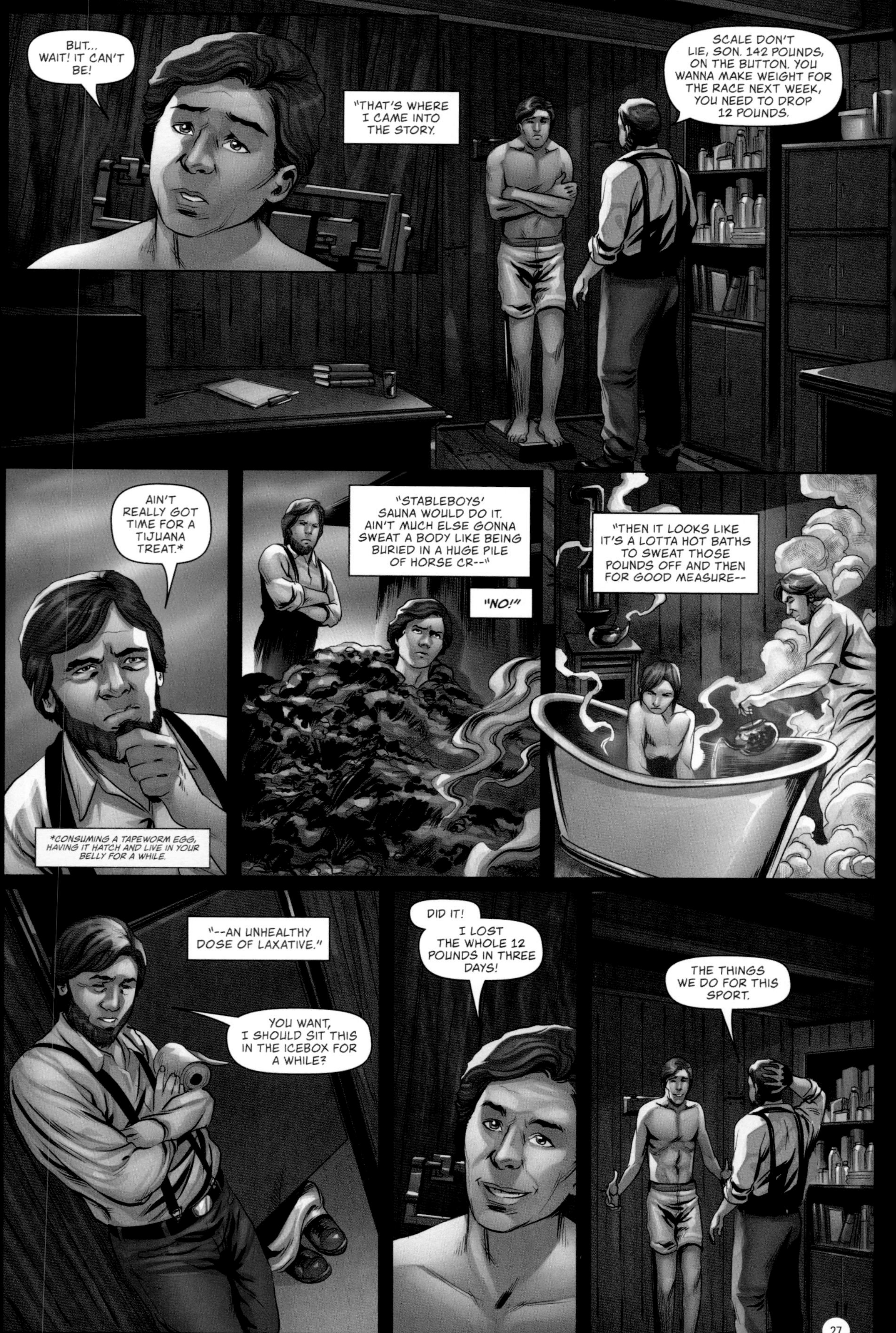
BUT... WAIT! IT CAN'T BE!
"THAT'S WHERE I CAME INTO THE STORY.
SCALE DON'T LIE, SON. 142 POUNDS, ON THE BUTTON. YOU WANNA MAKE WEIGHT FOR THE RACE NEXT WEEK, YOU NEED TO DROP 12 POUNDS.
AIN'T REALLY GOT TIME FOR A TIJUANA TREAT.*
*CONSUMING A TAPEWORM EGG, HAVING IT HATCH AND LIVE IN YOUR BELLY FOR A WHILE.
"STABLEBOYS' SAUNA WOULD DO IT. AIN'T MUCH ELSE GONNA SWEAT A BODY LIKE BEING BURIED IN A HUGE PILE OF HORSE CR--"
"NO!"
"THEN IT LOOKS LIKE IT'S A LOTTA HOT BATHS TO SWEAT THOSE POUNDS OFF AND THEN FOR GOOD MEASURE--
"--AN UNHEALTHY DOSE OF LAXATIVE."
YOU WANT, I SHOULD SIT THIS IN THE ICEBOX FOR A WHILE?
DID IT!
I LOST THE WHOLE 12 POUNDS IN THREE DAYS!
THE THINGS WE DO FOR THIS SPORT.

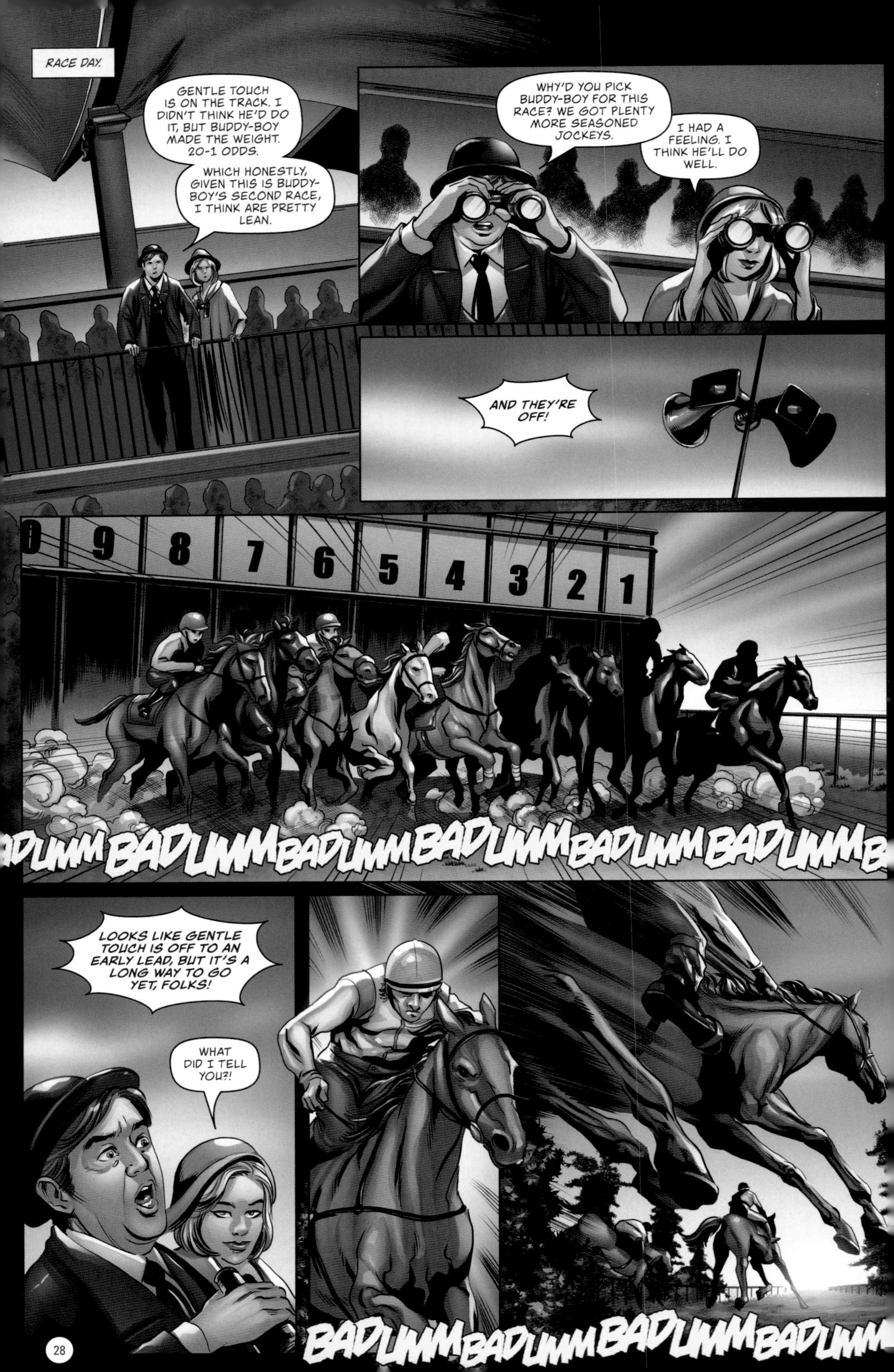
RACE DAY.
GENTLE TOUCH IS ON THE TRACK. I DIDN'T THINK HE'D DO IT, BUT BUDDY-BOY MADE THE WEIGHT. 20-1 ODDS.
WHICH HONESTLY, GIVEN THIS IS BUDDY-BOY'S SECOND RACE, I THINK ARE PRETTY LEAN.
WHY'D YOU PICK BUDDY-BOY FOR THIS RACE? WE GOT PLENTY MORE SEASONED JOCKEYS.
I HAD A FEELING. I THINK HE'LL DO WELL.
AND THEY'RE OFF!
9 8 7 6 5 4 3 2 1
BADUMM BADUMM BADUMM BADUMM BADUMM BADUMM
LOOKS LIKE GENTLE TOUCH IS OFF TO AN EARLY LEAD, BUT IT'S A LONG WAY TO GO YET, FOLKS!
WHAT DID I TELL YOU?!
BADUMM BADUMM BADUMM BADUMM

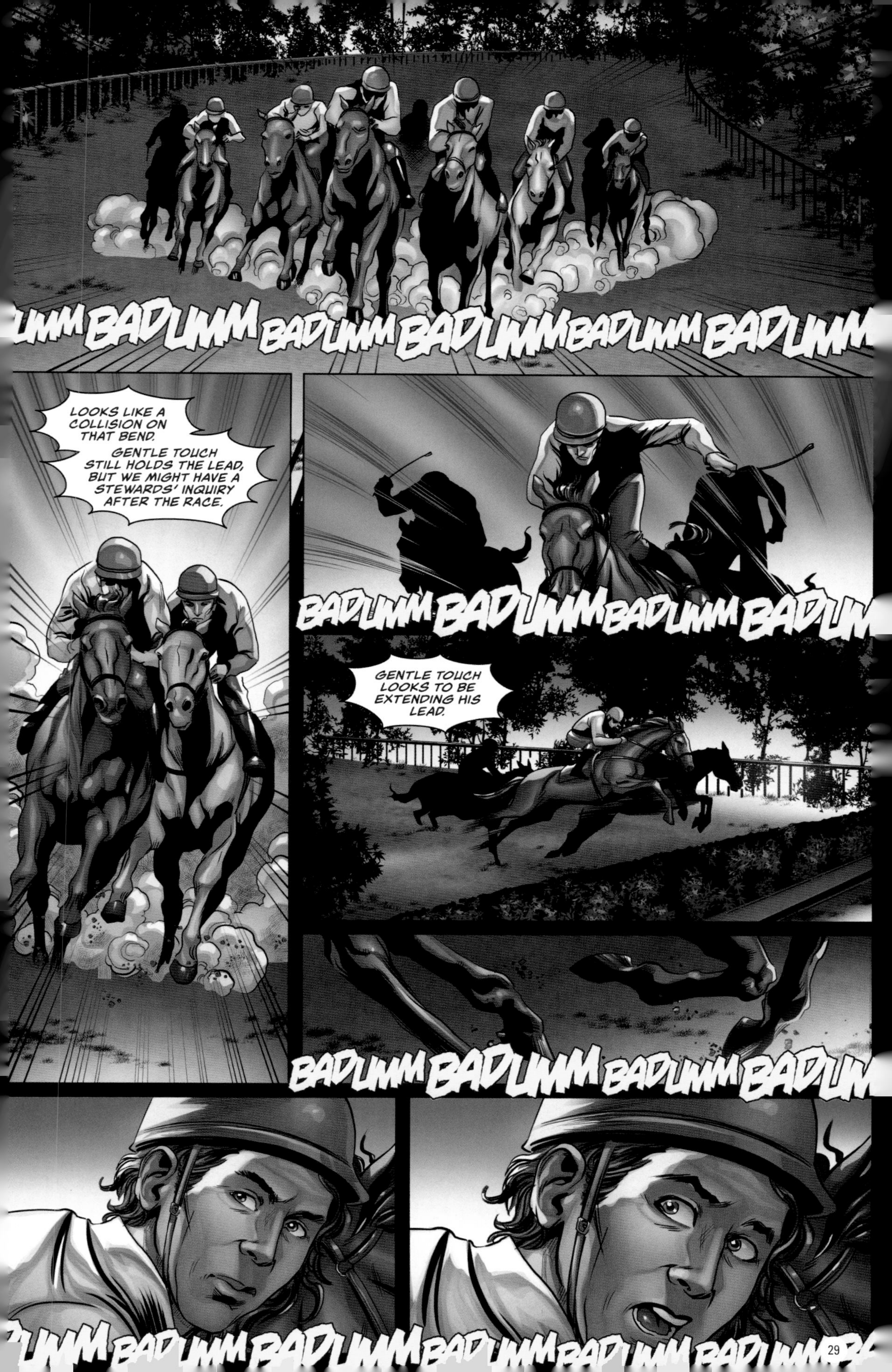
UMM BADUMM BADUMM BADUMM BADUMM BADUMM
LOOKS LIKE A COLLISION ON THAT BEND.
GENTLE TOUCH STILL HOLDS THE LEAD, BUT WE MIGHT HAVE A STEWARDS' INQUIRY AFTER THE RACE.
BADUMM BADUMM BADUMM BADU
GENTLE TOUCH LOOKS TO BE EXTENDING HIS LEAD.
BADUMM BADUMM BADUMM BADU
UMM BADUMM BADUMM BADUMM BADUMM BA

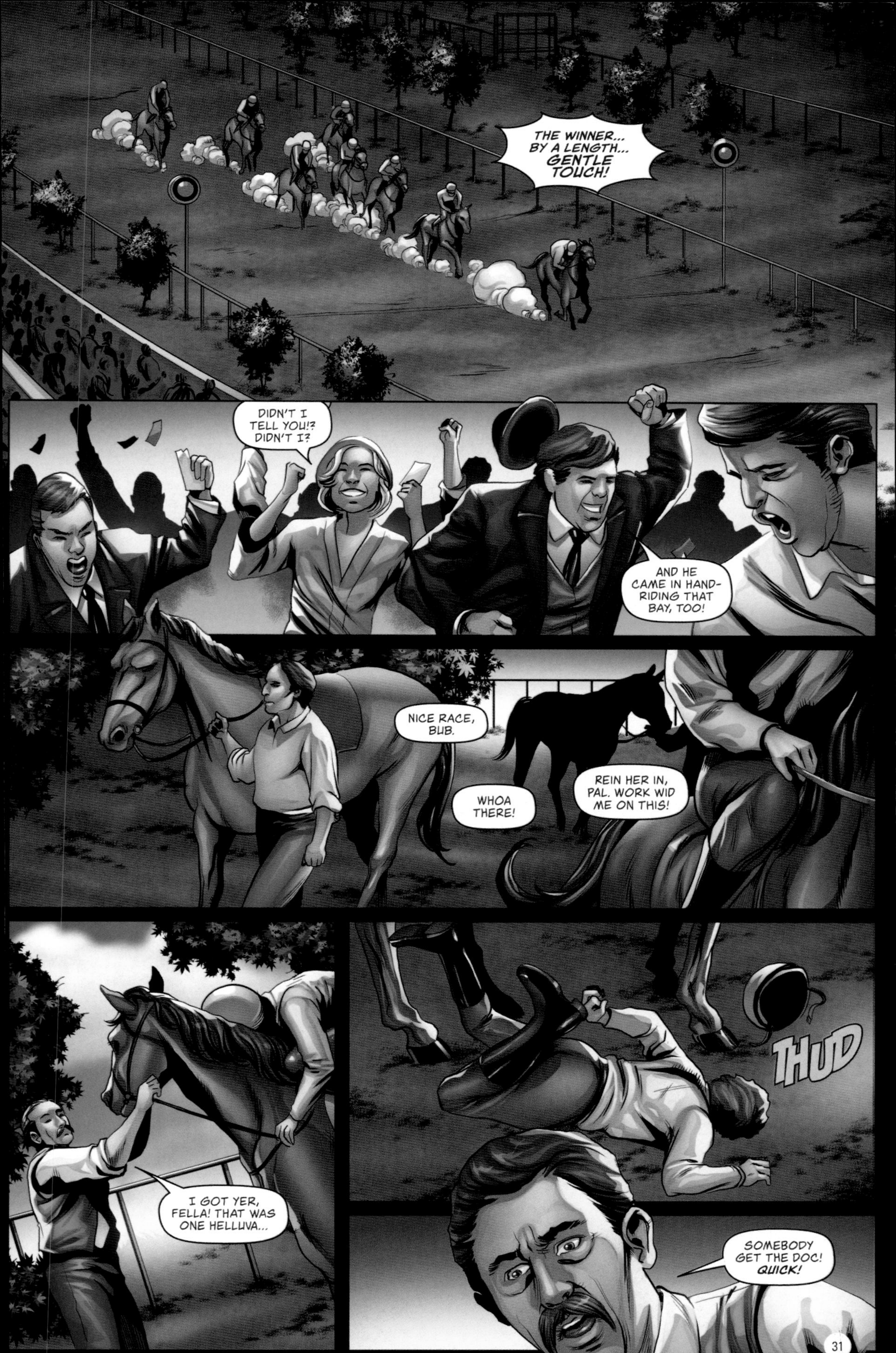

THE WINNER... BY A LENGTH... GENTLE TOUCH!
DIDN'T I TELL YOU!? DIDN'T I?
AND HE CAME IN HAND-RIDING THAT BAY, TOO!
NICE RACE, BUB.
WHOA THERE!
REIN HER IN, PAL. WORK WID ME ON THIS!
I GOT YER, FELLA! THAT WAS ONE HELLUVA...
THUD
SOMEBODY GET THE DOC! QUICK!

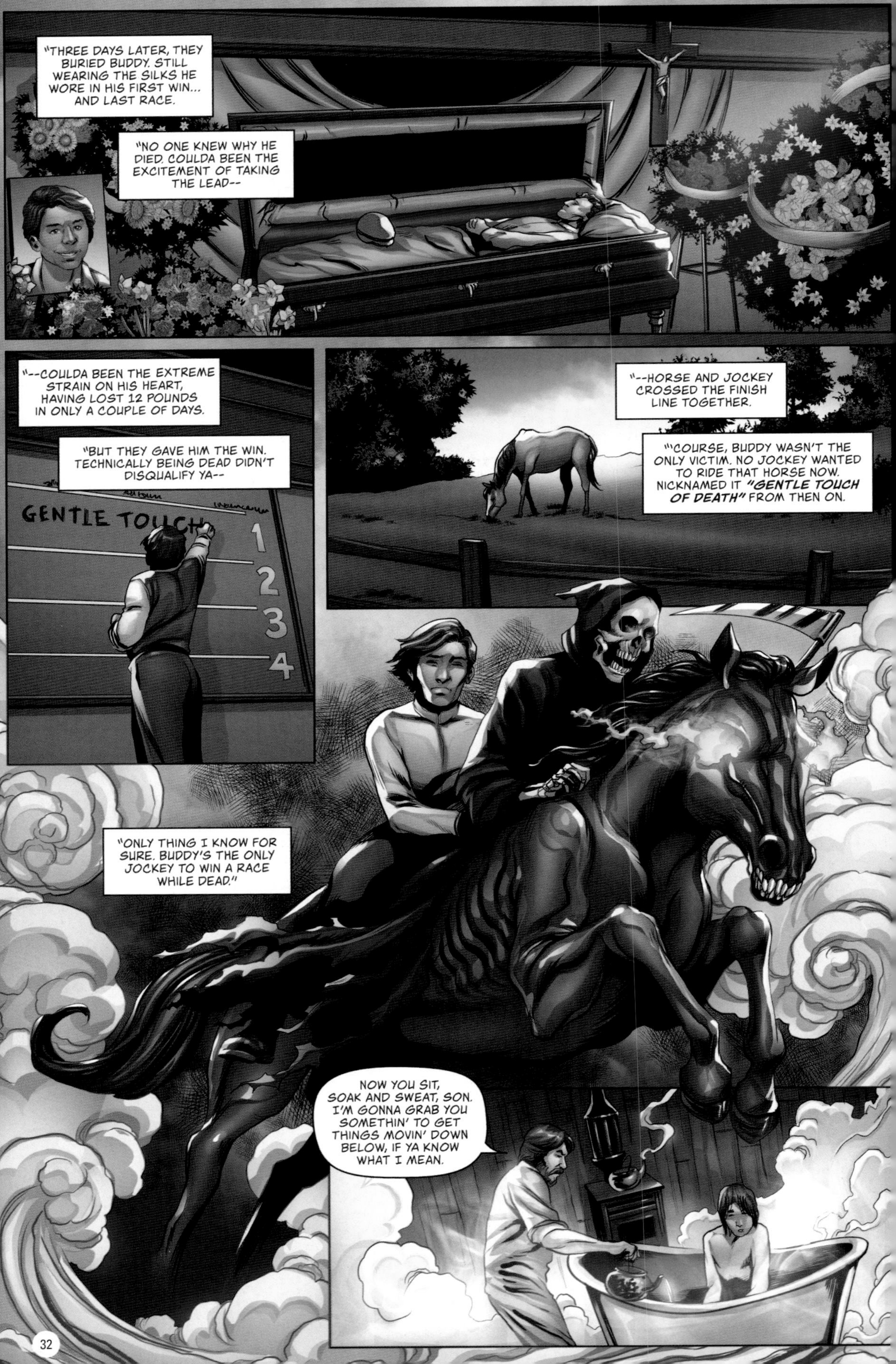
"THREE DAYS LATER, THEY BURIED BUDDY. STILL WEARING THE SILKS HE WORE IN HIS FIRST WIN... AND LAST RACE.
"NO ONE KNEW WHY HE DIED. COULDA BEEN THE EXCITEMENT OF TAKING THE LEAD--
"--COULDA BEEN THE EXTREME STRAIN ON HIS HEART, HAVING LOST 12 POUNDS IN ONLY A COUPLE OF DAYS.
"BUT THEY GAVE HIM THE WIN. TECHNICALLY BEING DEAD DIDN'T DISQUALIFY YA--
GENTLE TOUCH
1
2
3
4
"--HORSE AND JOCKEY CROSSED THE FINISH LINE TOGETHER.
"COURSE, BUDDY WASN'T THE ONLY VICTIM. NO JOCKEY WANTED TO RIDE THAT HORSE NOW. NICKNAMED IT *"GENTLE TOUCH OF DEATH"* FROM THEN ON.
"ONLY THING I KNOW FOR SURE. BUDDY'S THE ONLY JOCKEY TO WIN A RACE WHILE DEAD."
NOW YOU SIT, SOAK AND SWEAT, SON. I'M GONNA GRAB YOU SOMETHIN' TO GET THINGS MOVIN' DOWN BELOW, IF YA KNOW WHAT I MEAN.

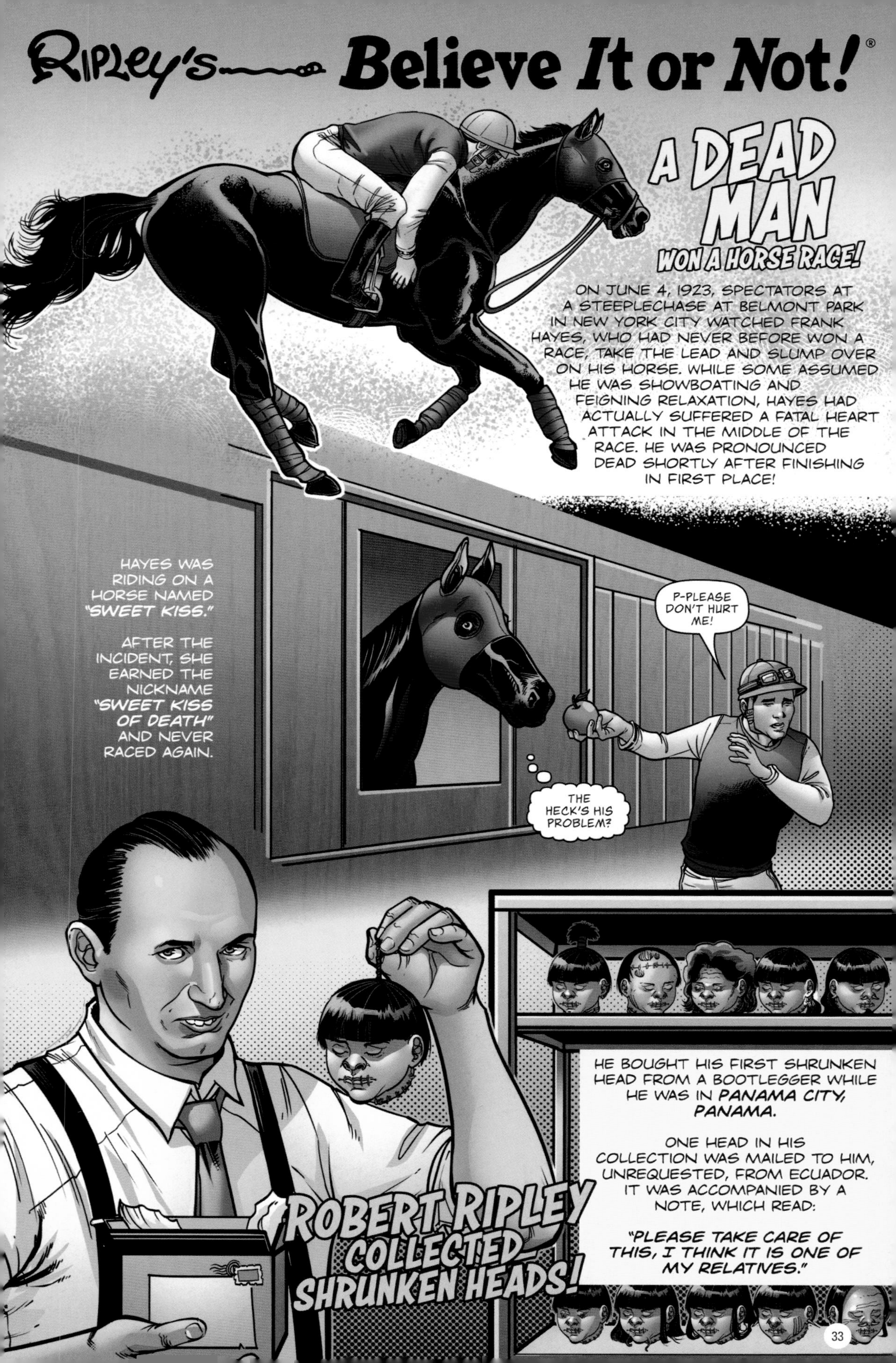
RIPLEY'S Believe It or Not!®
A DEAD MAN WON A HORSE RACE!
ON JUNE 4, 1923, SPECTATORS AT A STEEPLECHASE AT BELMONT PARK IN NEW YORK CITY WATCHED FRANK HAYES, WHO HAD NEVER BEFORE WON A RACE, TAKE THE LEAD AND SLUMP OVER ON HIS HORSE. WHILE SOME ASSUMED HE WAS SHOWBOATING AND FEIGNING RELAXATION, HAYES HAD ACTUALLY SUFFERED A FATAL HEART ATTACK IN THE MIDDLE OF THE RACE. HE WAS PRONOUNCED DEAD SHORTLY AFTER FINISHING IN FIRST PLACE!
HAYES WAS RIDING ON A HORSE NAMED *"SWEET KISS."*
AFTER THE INCIDENT, SHE EARNED THE NICKNAME *"SWEET KISS OF DEATH"* AND NEVER RACED AGAIN.
P-PLEASE DON'T HURT ME!
THE HECK'S HIS PROBLEM?
ROBERT RIPLEY COLLECTED SHRUNKEN HEADS!
HE BOUGHT HIS FIRST SHRUNKEN HEAD FROM A BOOTLEGGER WHILE HE WAS IN *PANAMA CITY, PANAMA.*
ONE HEAD IN HIS COLLECTION WAS MAILED TO HIM, UNREQUESTED, FROM ECUADOR. IT WAS ACCOMPANIED BY A NOTE, WHICH READ:
"PLEASE TAKE CARE OF THIS, I THINK IT IS ONE OF MY RELATIVES."

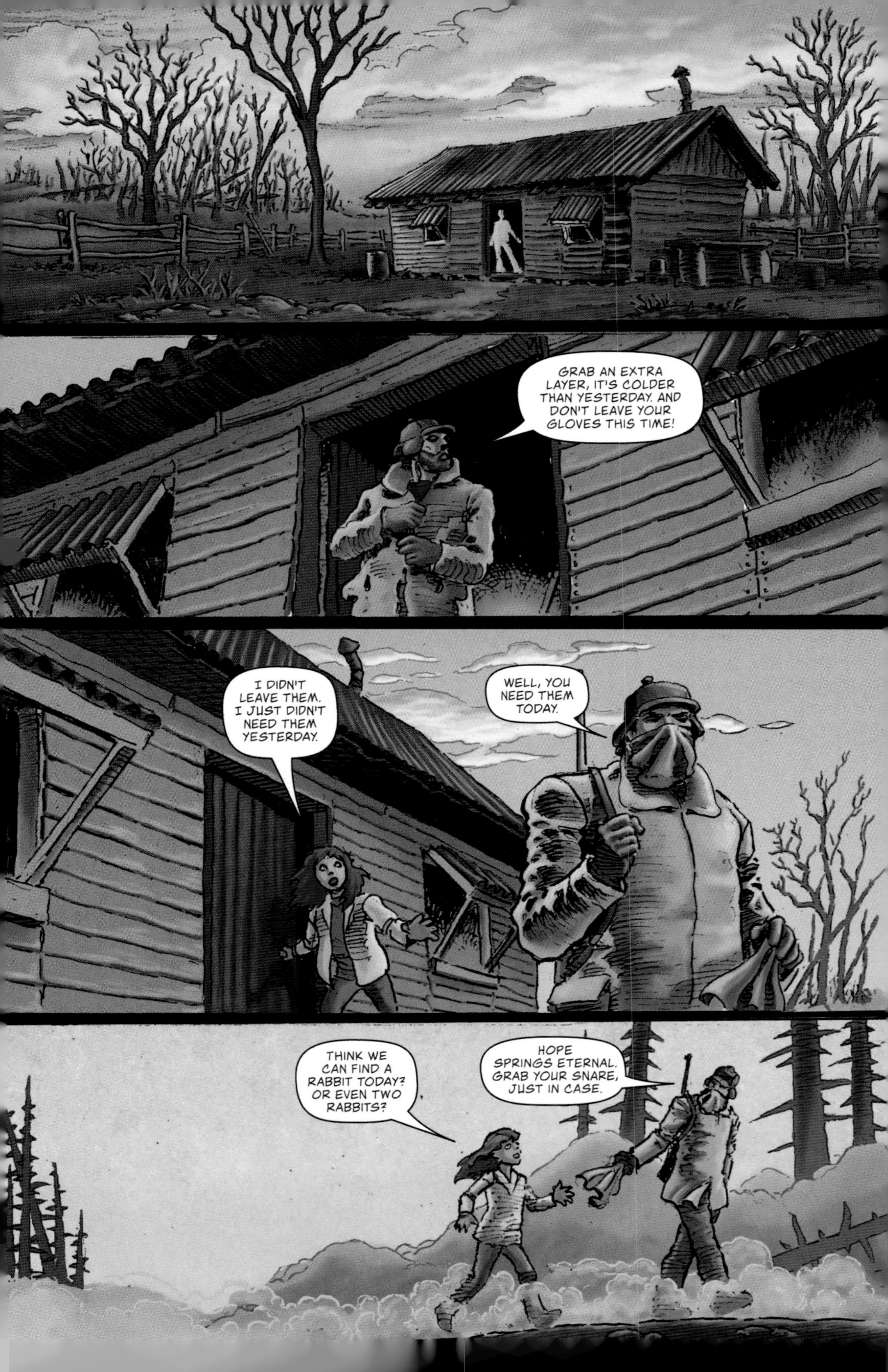
GRAB AN EXTRA LAYER, IT'S COLDER THAN YESTERDAY. AND DON'T LEAVE YOUR GLOVES THIS TIME!
I DIDN'T LEAVE THEM. I JUST DIDN'T NEED THEM YESTERDAY.
WELL, YOU NEED THEM TODAY.
THINK WE CAN FIND A RABBIT TODAY? OR EVEN TWO RABBITS?
HOPE SPRINGS ETERNAL. GRAB YOUR SNARE, JUST IN CASE.

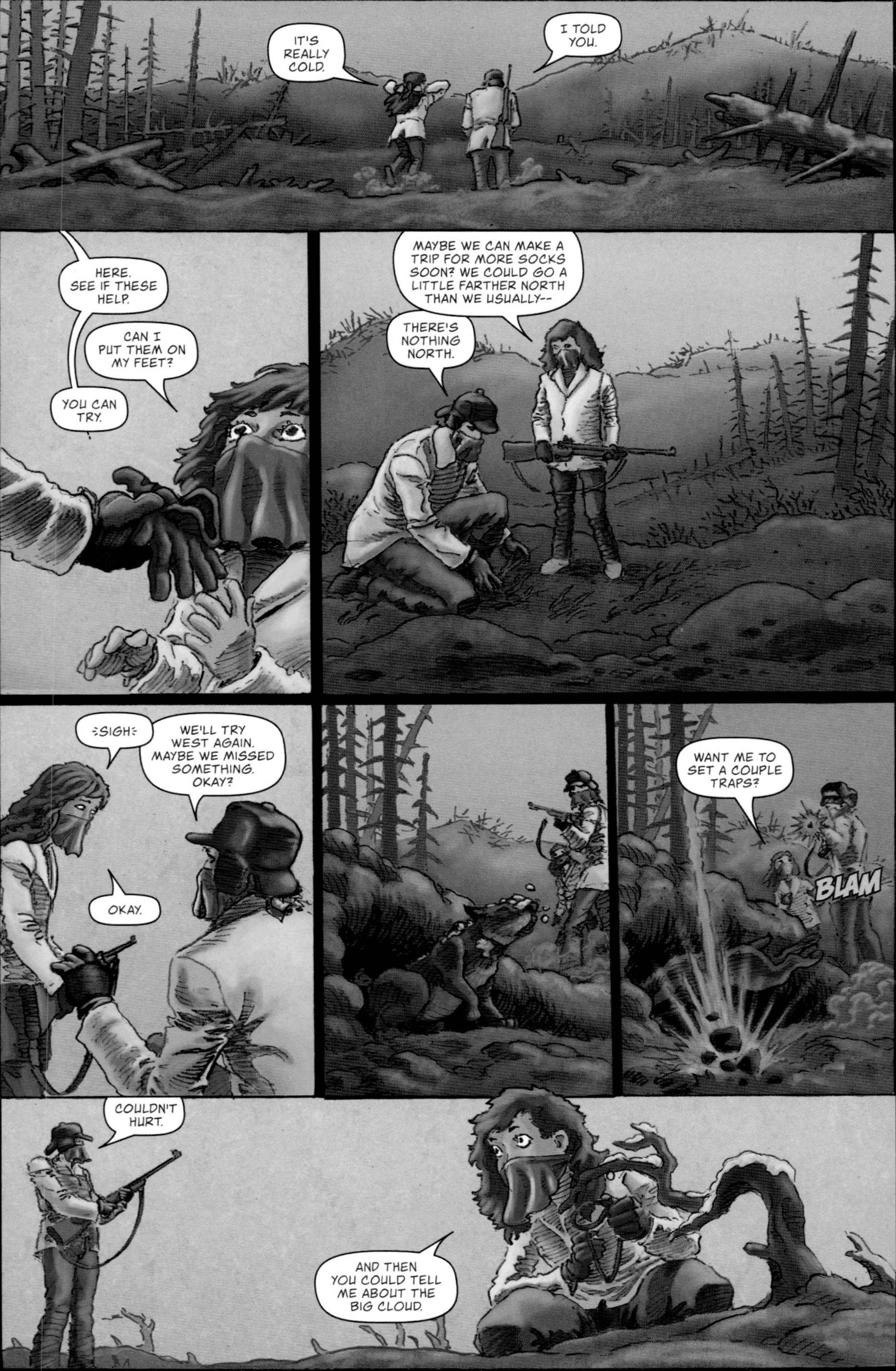

IT'S REALLY COLD.
I TOLD YOU.
HERE. SEE IF THESE HELP.
CAN I PUT THEM ON MY FEET?
YOU CAN TRY.
MAYBE WE CAN MAKE A TRIP FOR MORE SOCKS SOON? WE COULD GO A LITTLE FARTHER NORTH THAN WE USUALLY--
THERE'S NOTHING NORTH.
SIGH
WE'LL TRY WEST AGAIN. MAYBE WE MISSED SOMETHING. OKAY?
OKAY.
WANT ME TO SET A COUPLE TRAPS?
BLAM
COULDN'T HURT.
AND THEN YOU COULD TELL ME ABOUT THE BIG CLOUD.

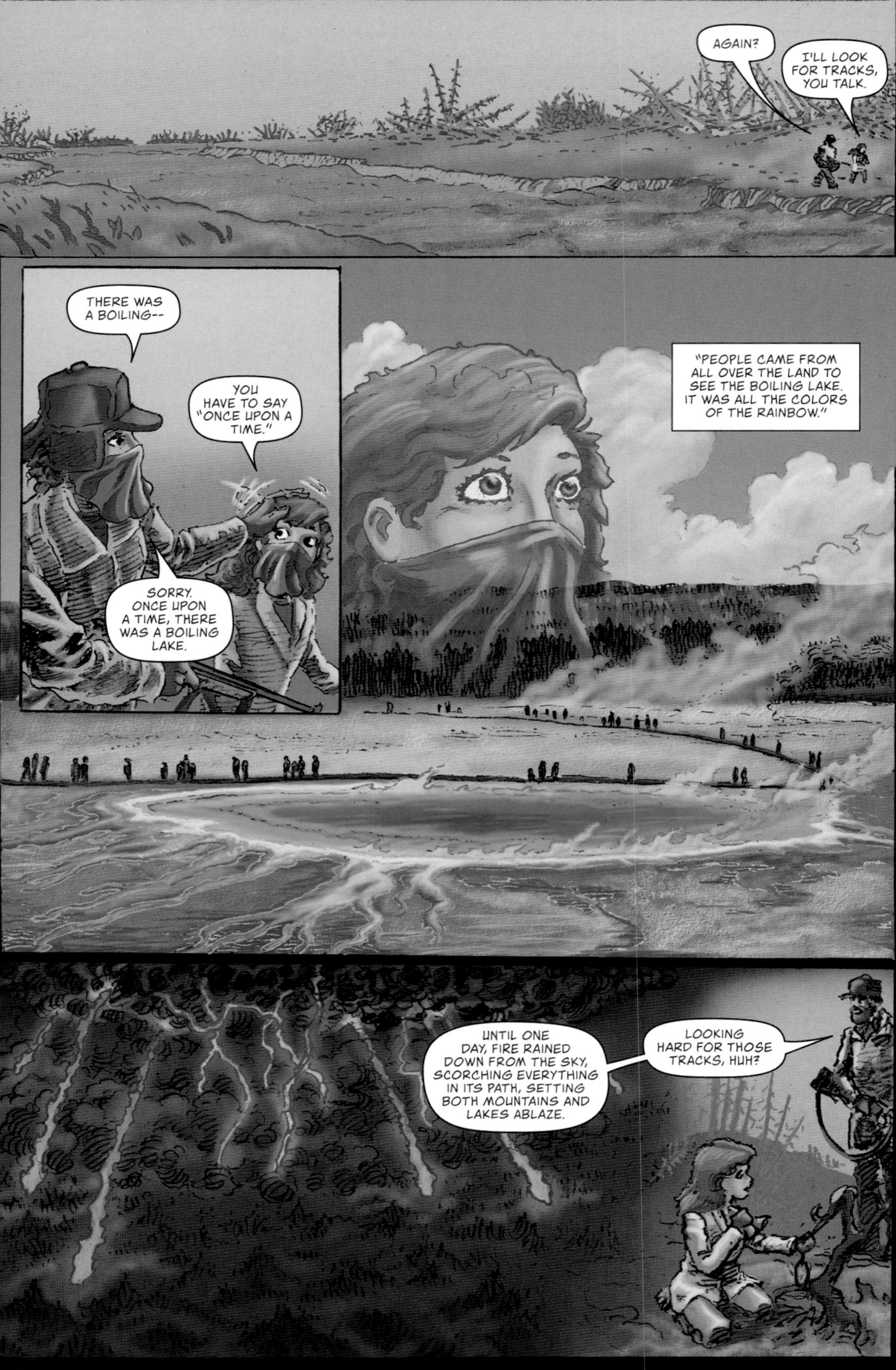
AGAIN?
I'LL LOOK FOR TRACKS, YOU TALK.
THERE WAS A BOILING--
YOU HAVE TO SAY "ONCE UPON A TIME."
SORRY. ONCE UPON A TIME, THERE WAS A BOILING LAKE.
"PEOPLE CAME FROM ALL OVER THE LAND TO SEE THE BOILING LAKE. IT WAS ALL THE COLORS OF THE RAINBOW."
UNTIL ONE DAY, FIRE RAINED DOWN FROM THE SKY, SCORCHING EVERYTHING IN ITS PATH, SETTING BOTH MOUNTAINS AND LAKES ABLAZE.
LOOKING HARD FOR THOSE TRACKS, HUH?

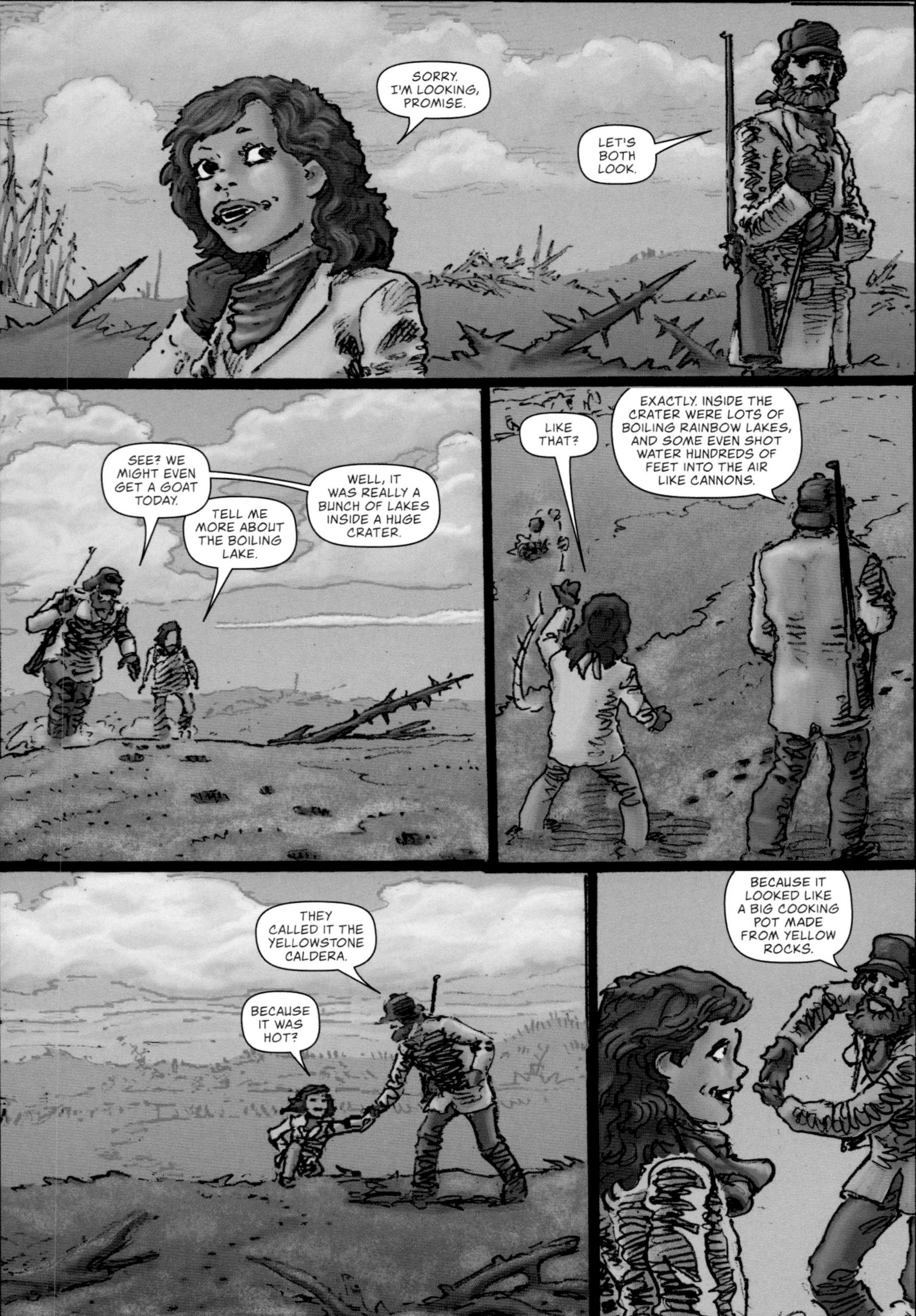
SORRY. I'M LOOKING, PROMISE.
LET'S BOTH LOOK.
SEE? WE MIGHT EVEN GET A GOAT TODAY.
WELL, IT WAS REALLY A BUNCH OF LAKES INSIDE A HUGE CRATER.
TELL ME MORE ABOUT THE BOILING LAKE.
LIKE THAT?
EXACTLY. INSIDE THE CRATER WERE LOTS OF BOILING RAINBOW LAKES, AND SOME EVEN SHOT WATER HUNDREDS OF FEET INTO THE AIR LIKE CANNONS.
THEY CALLED IT THE YELLOWSTONE CALDERA.
BECAUSE IT WAS HOT?
BECAUSE IT LOOKED LIKE A BIG COOKING POT MADE FROM YELLOW ROCKS.

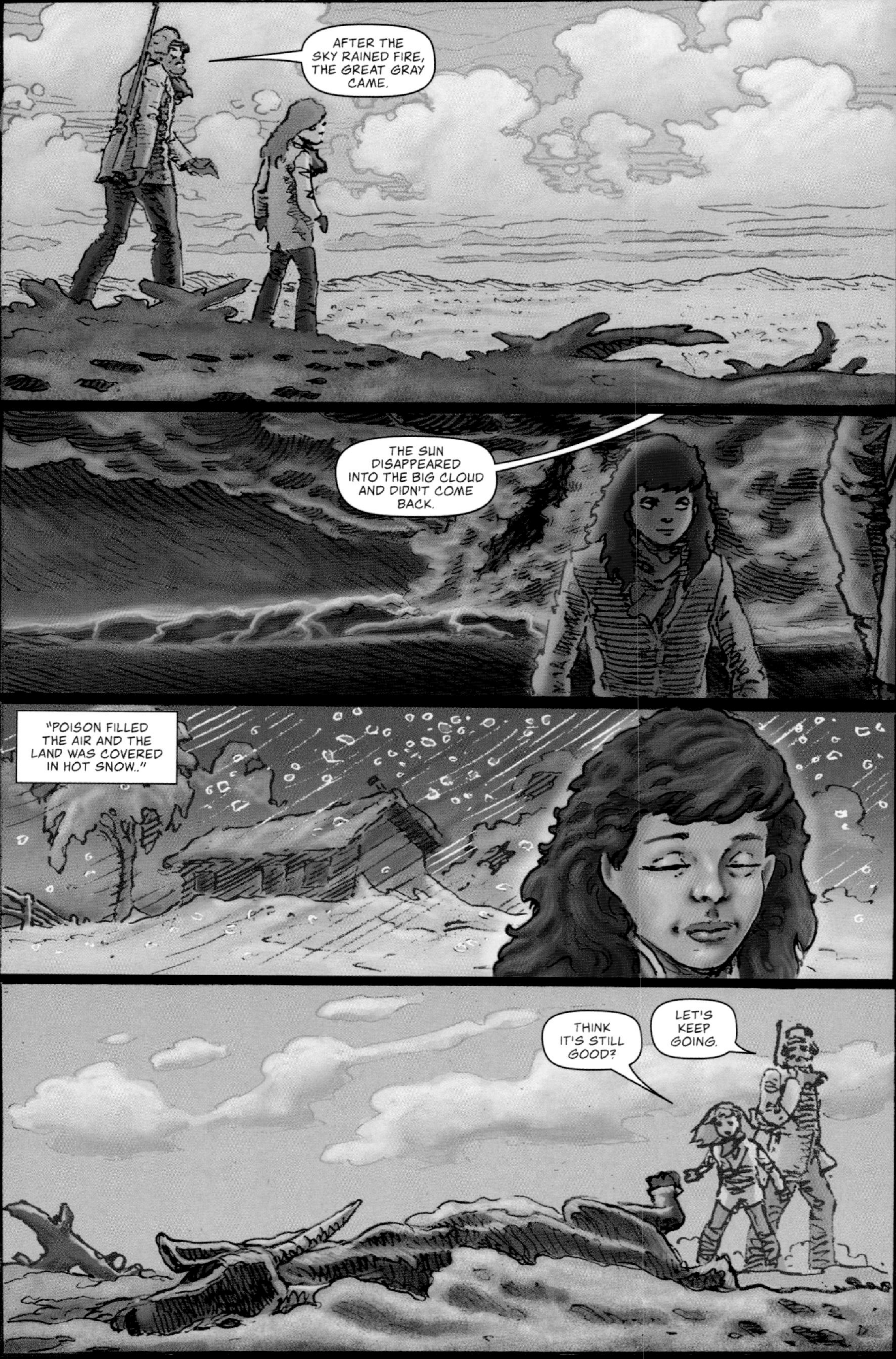
AFTER THE SKY RAINED FIRE, THE GREAT GRAY CAME.
THE SUN DISAPPEARED INTO THE BIG CLOUD AND DIDN'T COME BACK.
"POISON FILLED THE AIR AND THE LAND WAS COVERED IN HOT SNOW.."
LET'S KEEP GOING.
THINK IT'S STILL GOOD?

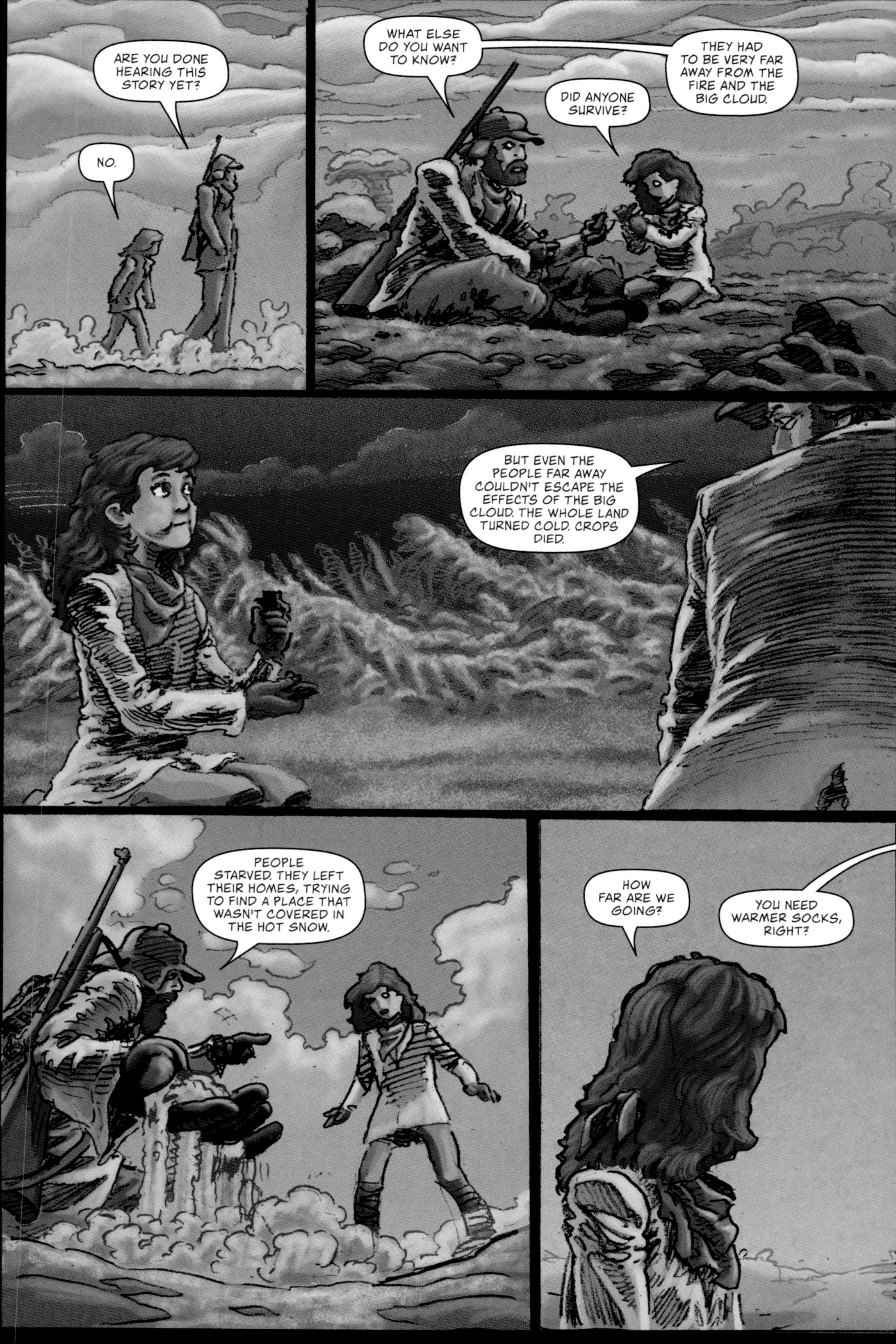
ARE YOU DONE HEARING THIS STORY YET?
NO.
WHAT ELSE DO YOU WANT TO KNOW?
DID ANYONE SURVIVE?
THEY HAD TO BE VERY FAR AWAY FROM THE FIRE AND THE BIG CLOUD.
BUT EVEN THE PEOPLE FAR AWAY COULDN'T ESCAPE THE EFFECTS OF THE BIG CLOUD. THE WHOLE LAND TURNED COLD. CROPS DIED.
PEOPLE STARVED. THEY LEFT THEIR HOMES, TRYING TO FIND A PLACE THAT WASN'T COVERED IN THE HOT SNOW.
HOW FAR ARE WE GOING?
YOU NEED WARMER SOCKS, RIGHT?

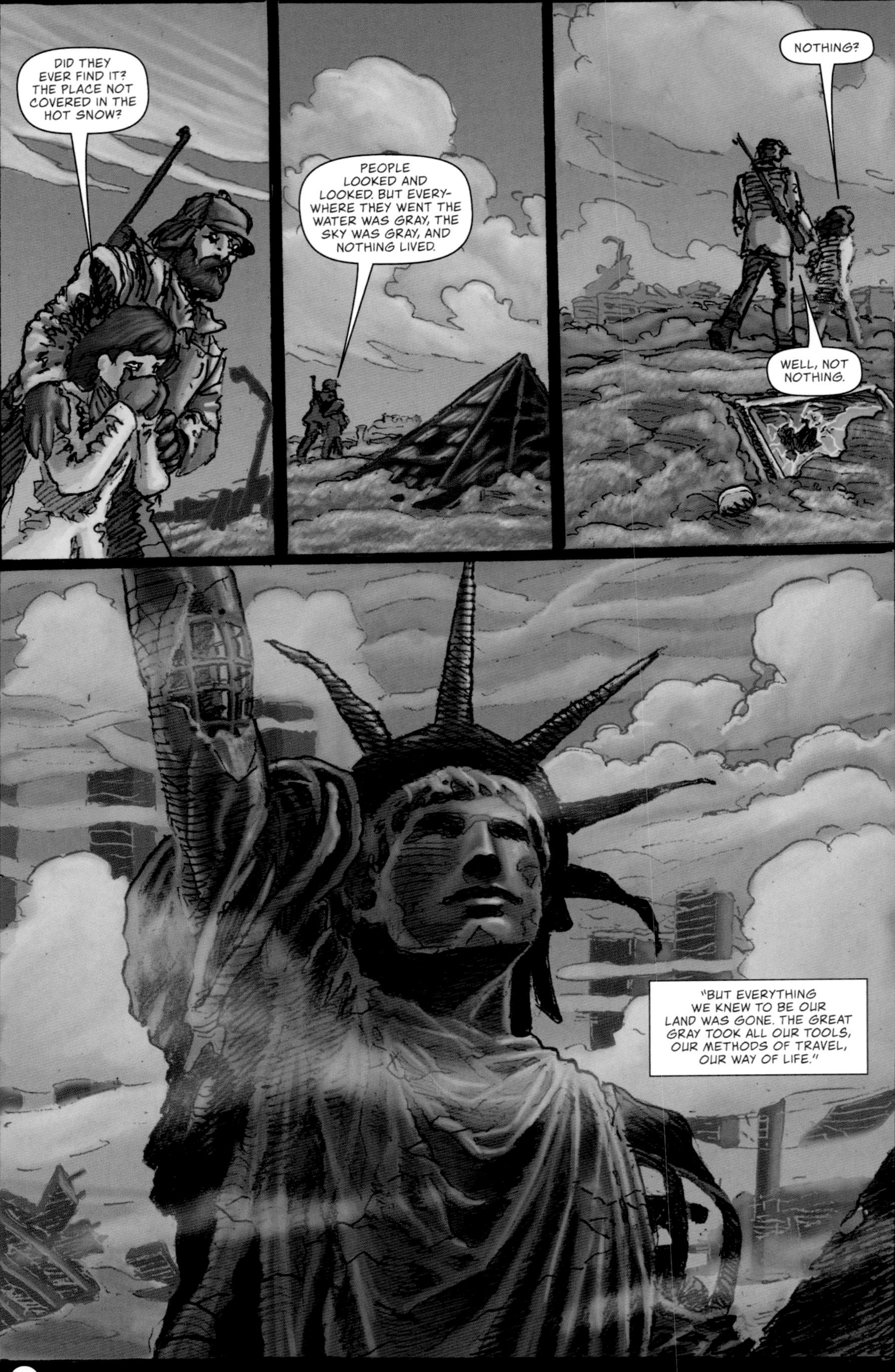
DID THEY EVER FIND IT? THE PLACE NOT COVERED IN THE HOT SNOW?
PEOPLE LOOKED AND LOOKED. BUT EVERY-WHERE THEY WENT THE WATER WAS GRAY, THE SKY WAS GRAY, AND NOTHING LIVED.
NOTHING?
WELL, NOT NOTHING.
"BUT EVERYTHING WE KNEW TO BE OUR LAND WAS GONE. THE GREAT GRAY TOOK ALL OUR TOOLS, OUR METHODS OF TRAVEL, OUR WAY OF LIFE."

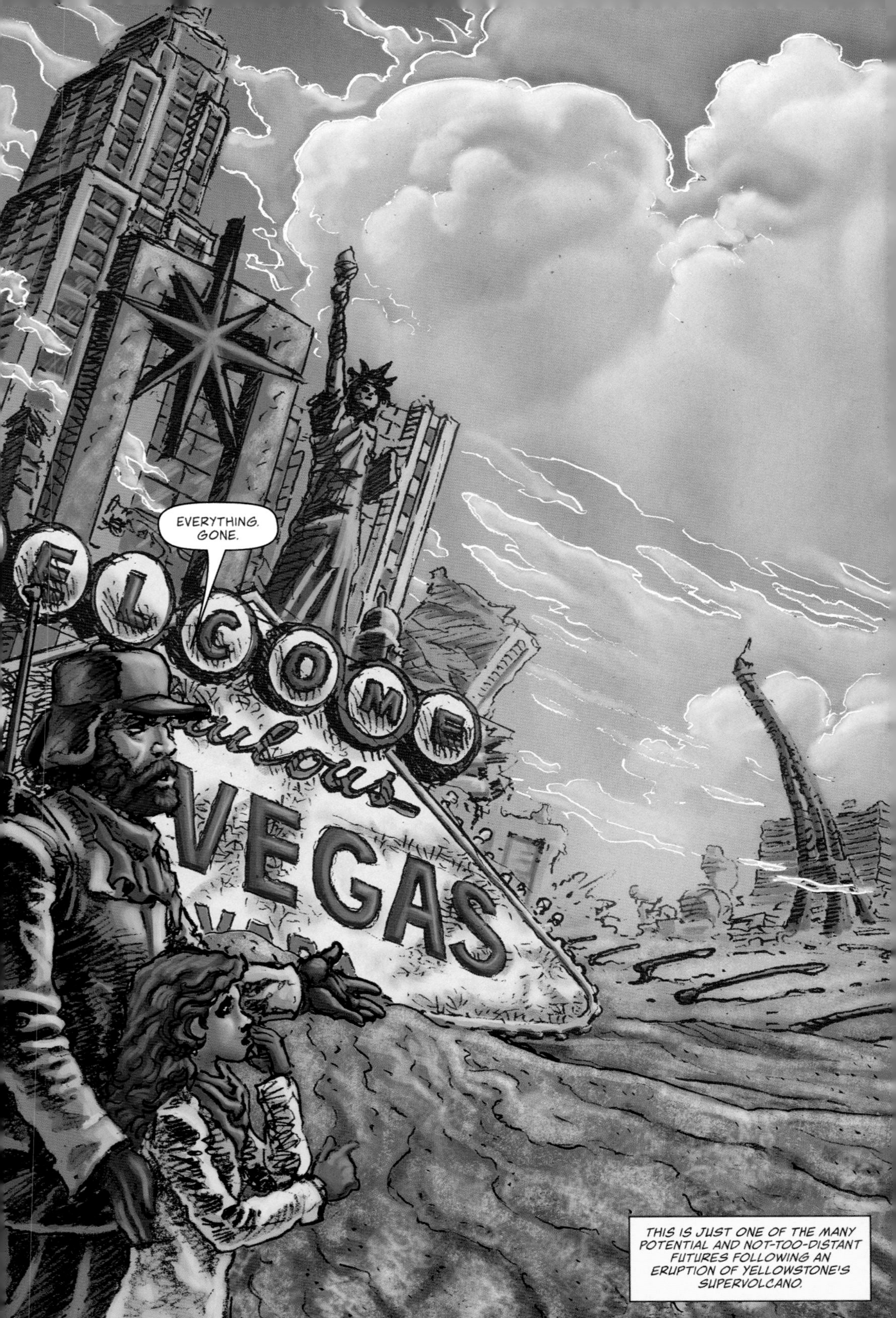
EVERYTHING. GONE.
ELCOME
VEGAS
THIS IS JUST ONE OF THE MANY POTENTIAL AND NOT-TOO-DISTANT FUTURES FOLLOWING AN ERUPTION OF YELLOWSTONE'S SUPERVOLCANO.

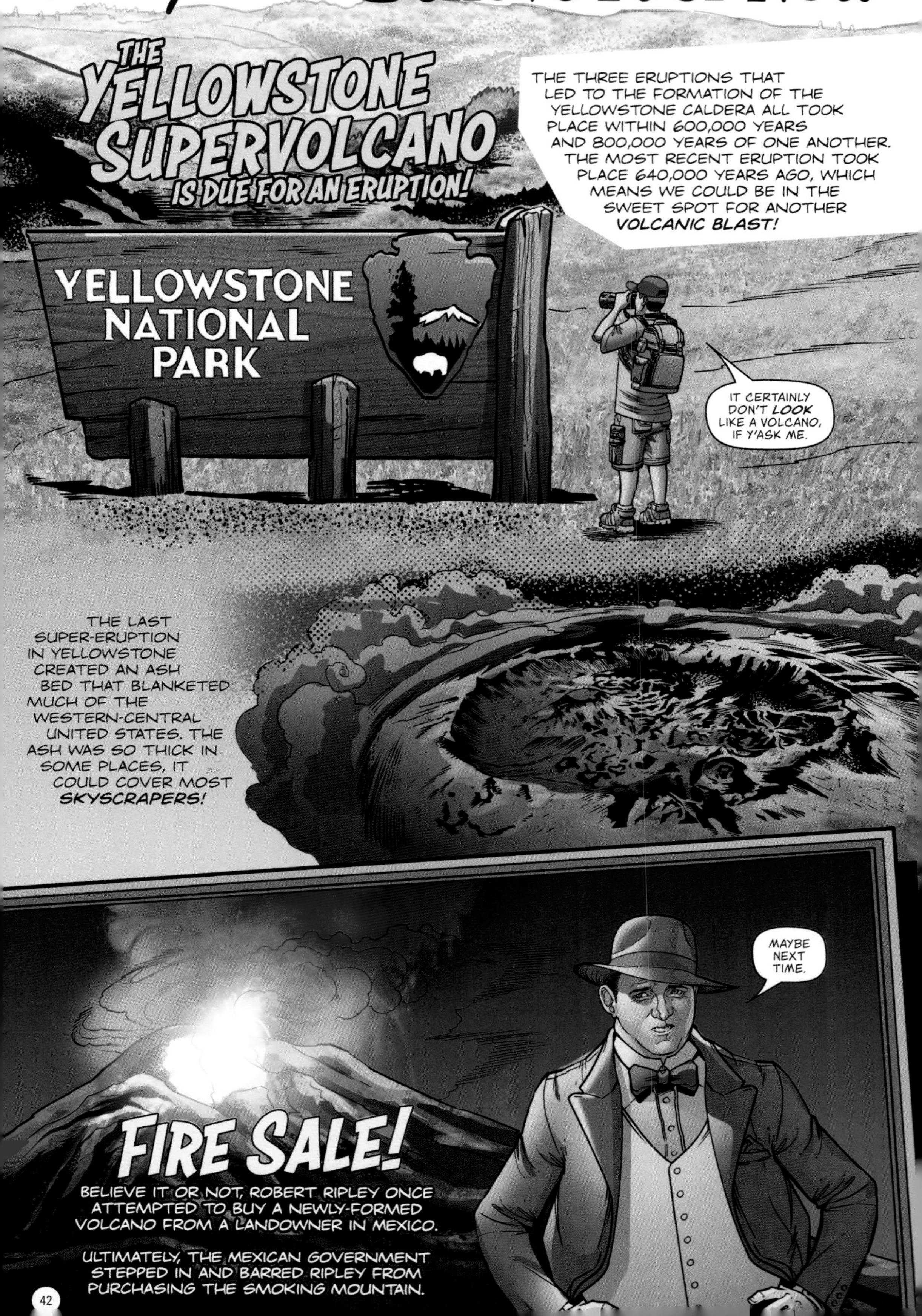
THE YELLOWSTONE SUPERVOLCANO IS DUE FOR AN ERUPTION!
THE THREE ERUPTIONS THAT LED TO THE FORMATION OF THE YELLOWSTONE CALDERA ALL TOOK PLACE WITHIN 600,000 YEARS AND 800,000 YEARS OF ONE ANOTHER. THE MOST RECENT ERUPTION TOOK PLACE 640,000 YEARS AGO, WHICH MEANS WE COULD BE IN THE SWEET SPOT FOR ANOTHER *VOLCANIC BLAST!*
YELLOWSTONE NATIONAL PARK
IT CERTAINLY DON'T *LOOK* LIKE A VOLCANO, IF Y'ASK ME.
THE LAST SUPER-ERUPTION IN YELLOWSTONE CREATED AN ASH BED THAT BLANKETED MUCH OF THE WESTERN-CENTRAL UNITED STATES. THE ASH WAS SO THICK IN SOME PLACES, IT COULD COVER MOST *SKYSCRAPERS!*
MAYBE NEXT TIME.
FIRE SALE!
BELIEVE IT OR NOT, ROBERT RIPLEY ONCE ATTEMPTED TO BUY A NEWLY-FORMED VOLCANO FROM A LANDOWNER IN MEXICO.
ULTIMATELY, THE MEXICAN GOVERNMENT STEPPED IN AND BARRED RIPLEY FROM PURCHASING THE SMOKING MOUNTAIN.

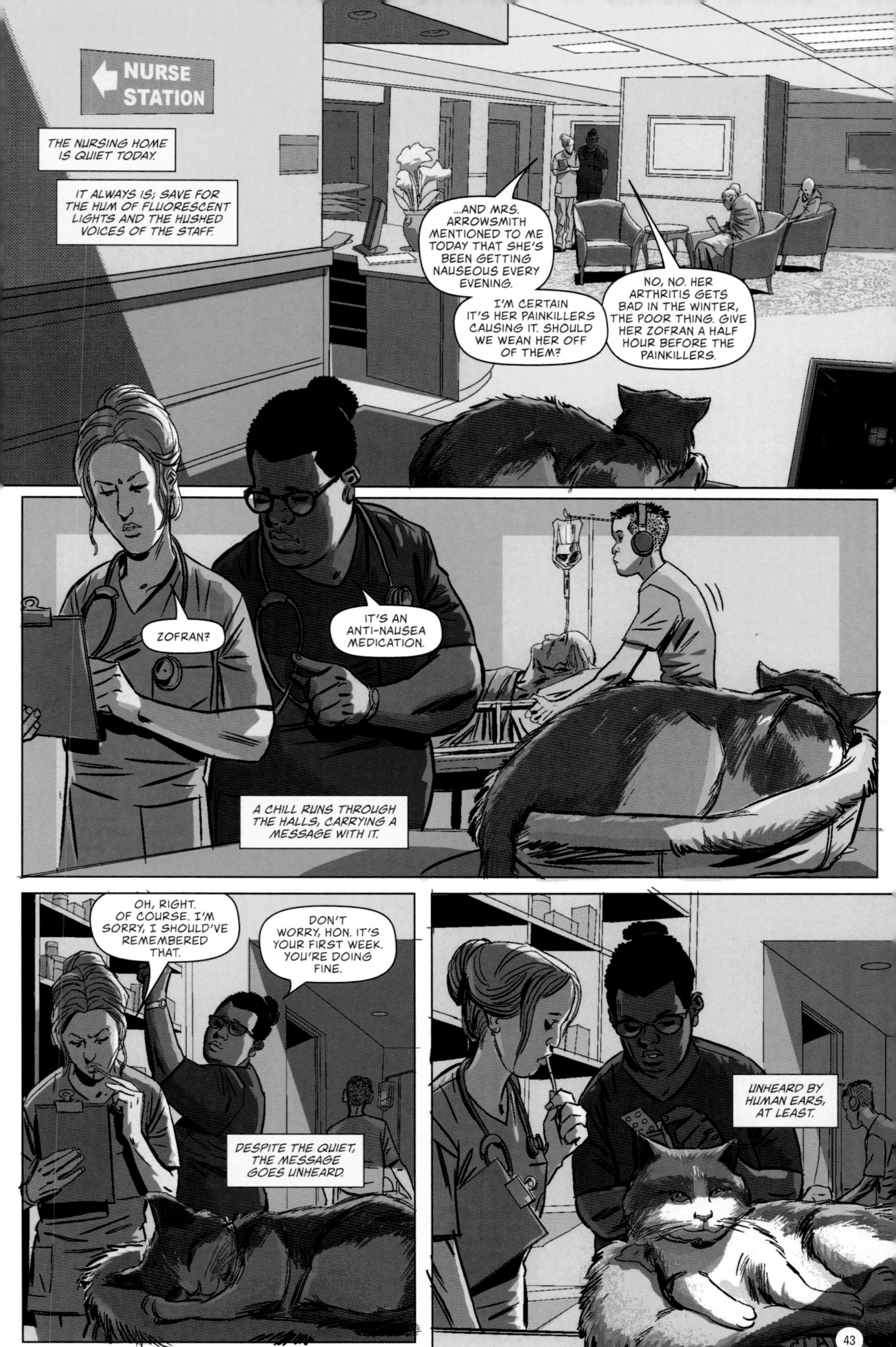
NURSE STATION
THE NURSING HOME IS QUIET TODAY.
IT ALWAYS IS; SAVE FOR THE HUM OF FLUORESCENT LIGHTS AND THE HUSHED VOICES OF THE STAFF.
...AND MRS. ARROWSMITH MENTIONED TO ME TODAY THAT SHE'S BEEN GETTING NAUSEOUS EVERY EVENING.
I'M CERTAIN IT'S HER PAINKILLERS CAUSING IT. SHOULD WE WEAN HER OFF OF THEM?
NO, NO. HER ARTHRITIS GETS BAD IN THE WINTER, THE POOR THING. GIVE HER ZOFRAN A HALF HOUR BEFORE THE PAINKILLERS.
ZOFRAN?
IT'S AN ANTI-NAUSEA MEDICATION.
A CHILL RUNS THROUGH THE HALLS, CARRYING A MESSAGE WITH IT.
OH, RIGHT. OF COURSE. I'M SORRY, I SHOULD'VE REMEMBERED THAT.
DON'T WORRY, HON. IT'S YOUR FIRST WEEK. YOU'RE DOING FINE.
DESPITE THE QUIET, THE MESSAGE GOES UNHEARD.
UNHEARD BY HUMAN EARS, AT LEAST.

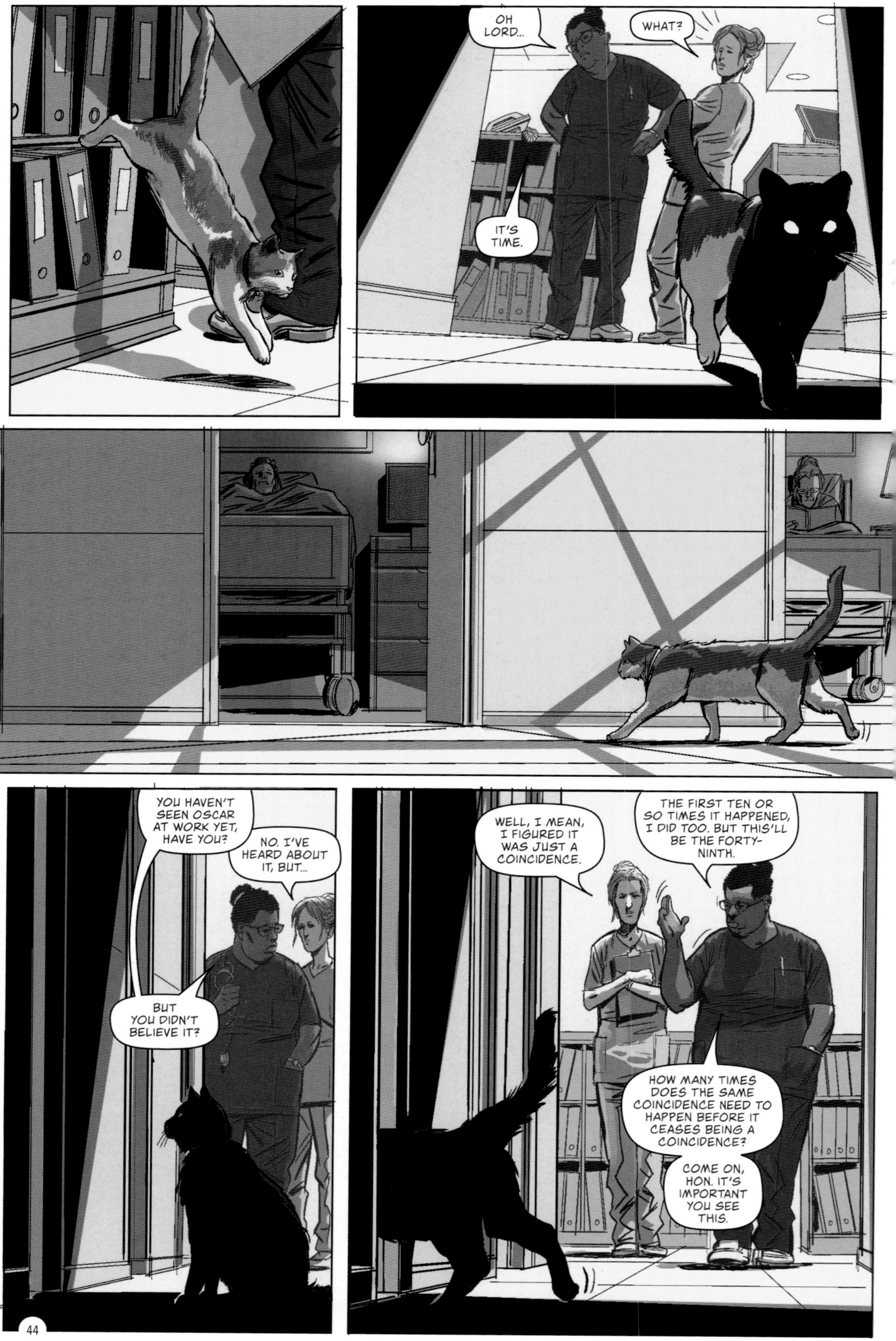
OH LORD...
WHAT?
IT'S TIME.
YOU HAVEN'T SEEN OSCAR AT WORK YET, HAVE YOU?
NO. I'VE HEARD ABOUT IT, BUT...
BUT YOU DIDN'T BELIEVE IT?
WELL, I MEAN, I FIGURED IT WAS JUST A COINCIDENCE.
THE FIRST TEN OR SO TIMES IT HAPPENED, I DID TOO. BUT THIS'LL BE THE FORTY-NINTH.
HOW MANY TIMES DOES THE SAME COINCIDENCE NEED TO HAPPEN BEFORE IT CEASES BEING A COINCIDENCE?
COME ON, HON. IT'S IMPORTANT YOU SEE THIS.

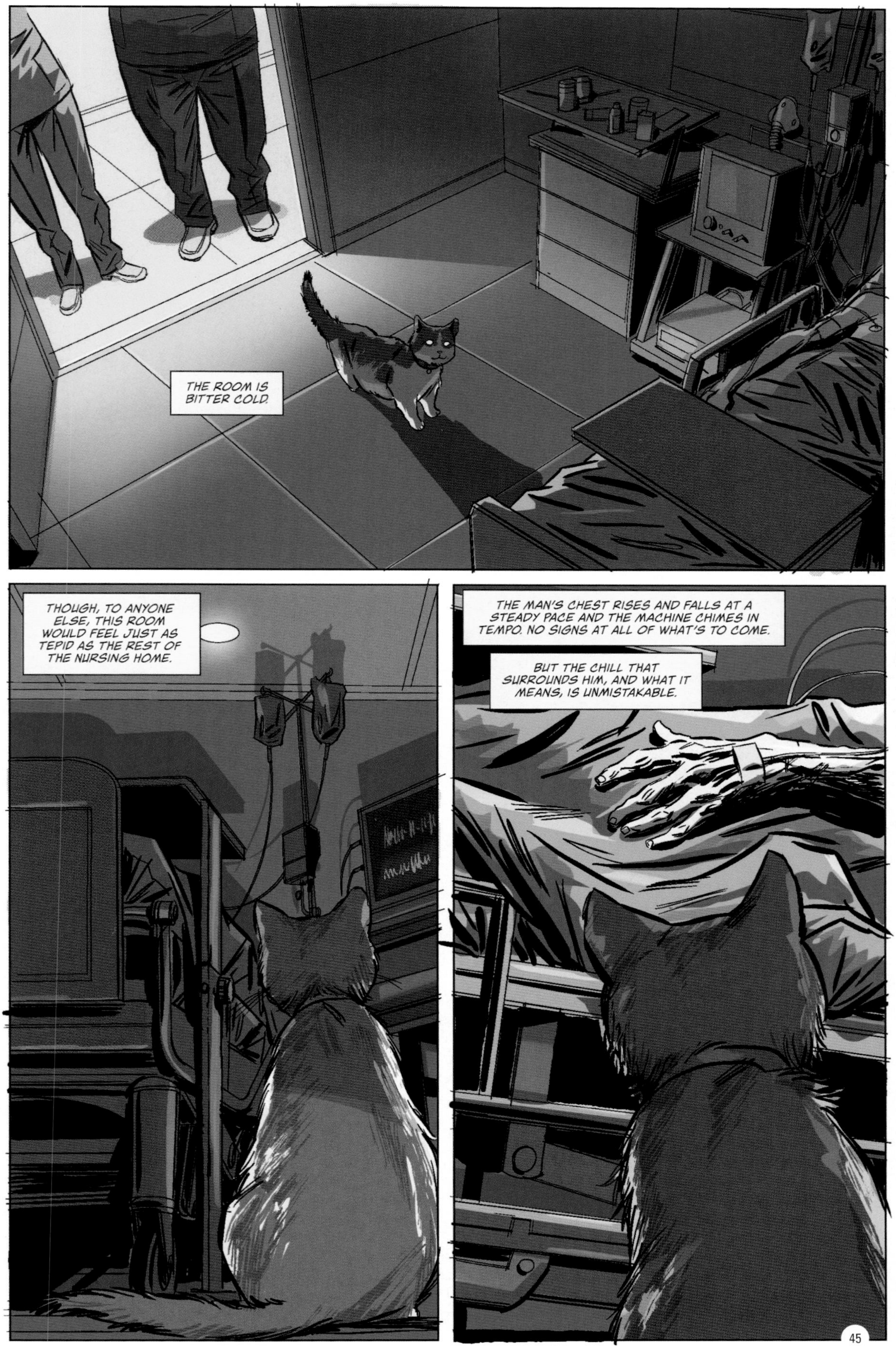
THE ROOM IS BITTER COLD.
THOUGH, TO ANYONE ELSE, THIS ROOM WOULD FEEL JUST AS TEPID AS THE REST OF THE NURSING HOME.
THE MAN'S CHEST RISES AND FALLS AT A STEADY PACE AND THE MACHINE CHIMES IN TEMPO. NO SIGNS AT ALL OF WHAT'S TO COME.
BUT THE CHILL THAT SURROUNDS HIM, AND WHAT IT MEANS, IS UNMISTAKABLE.

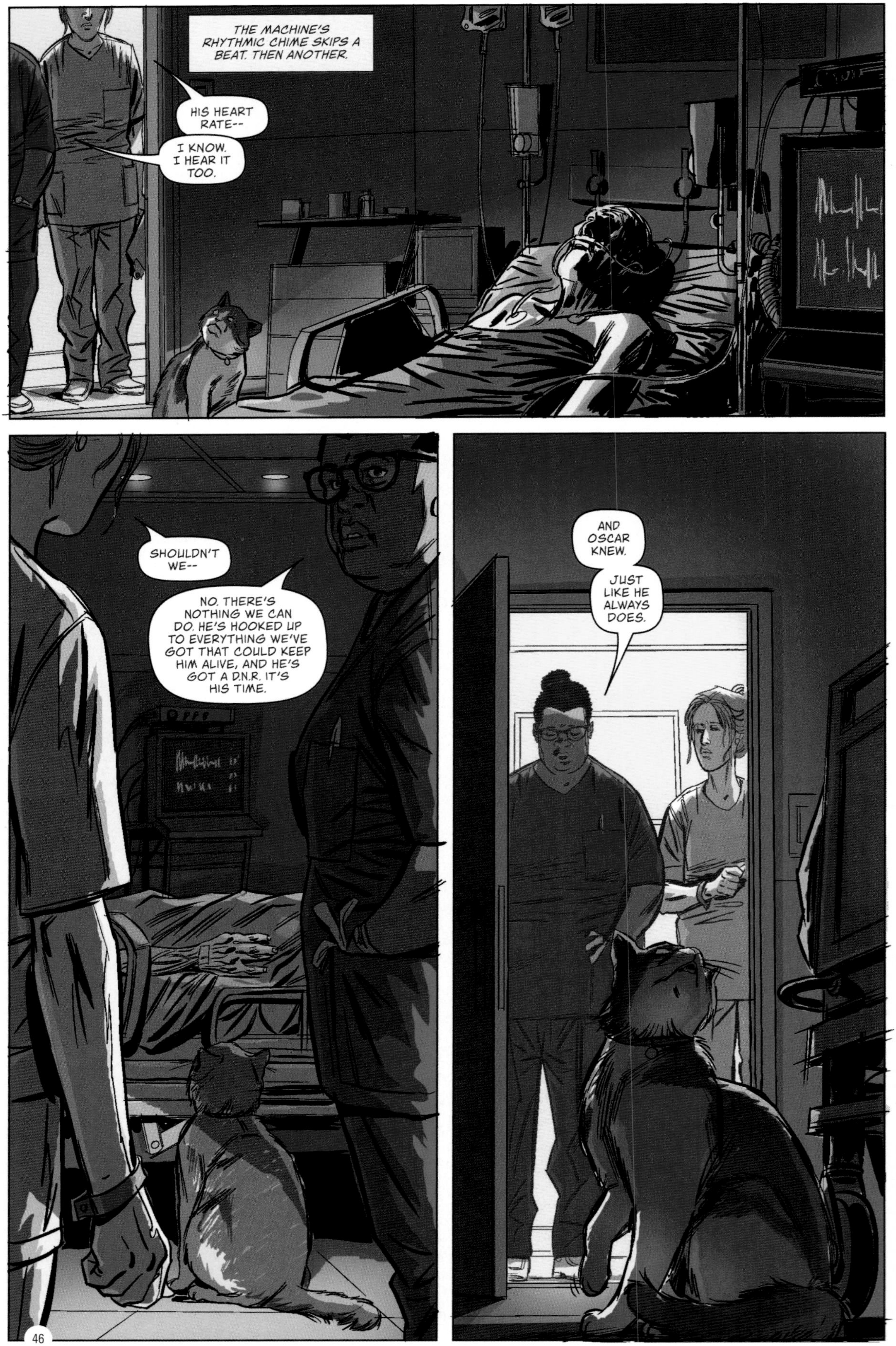
THE MACHINE'S RHYTHMIC CHIME SKIPS A BEAT. THEN ANOTHER.
HIS HEART RATE--
I KNOW. I HEAR IT TOO.
SHOULDN'T WE--
NO. THERE'S NOTHING WE CAN DO. HE'S HOOKED UP TO EVERYTHING WE'VE GOT THAT COULD KEEP HIM ALIVE, AND HE'S GOT A D.N.R. IT'S HIS TIME.
AND OSCAR KNEW.
JUST LIKE HE ALWAYS DOES.

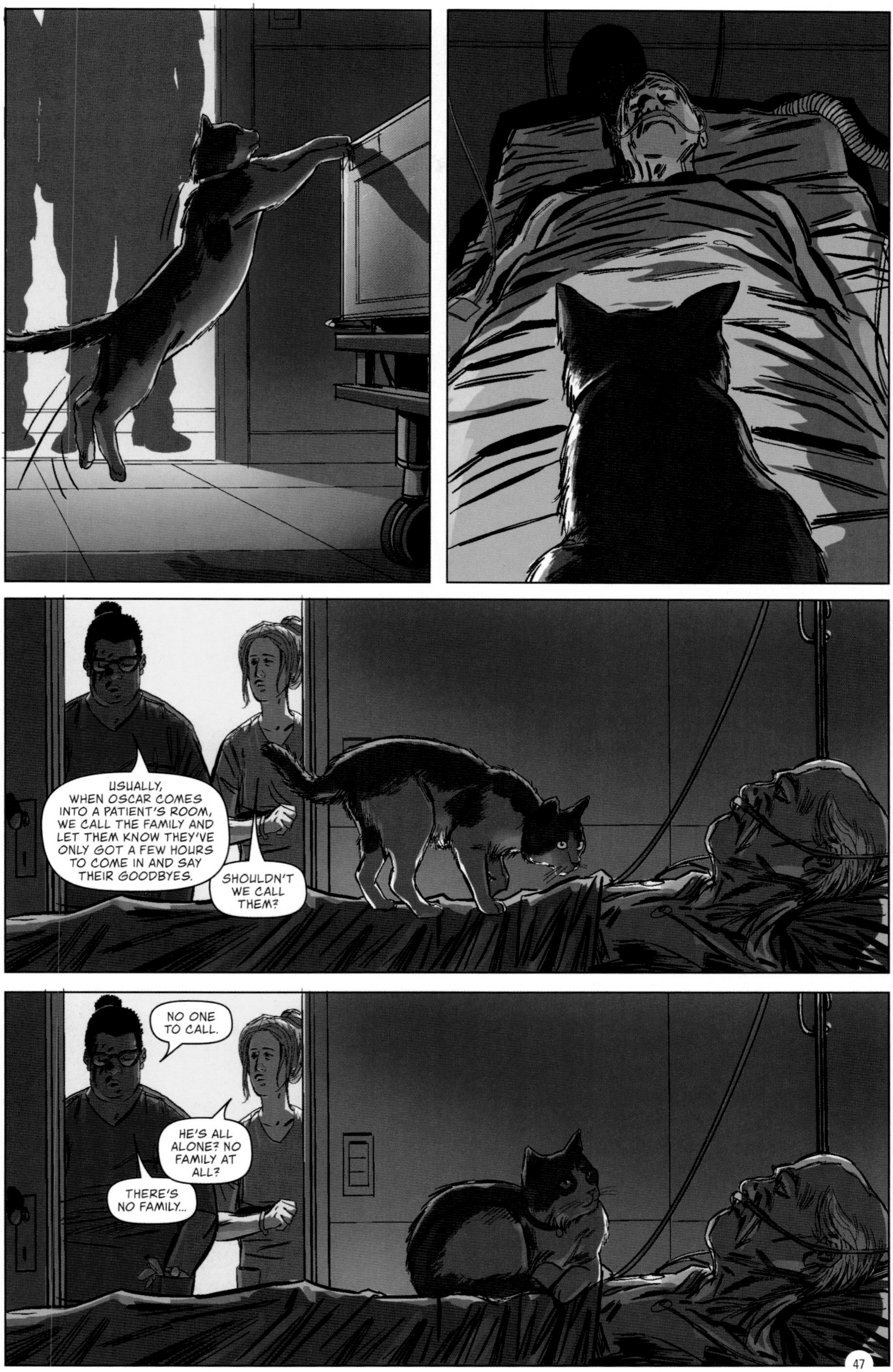
USUALLY, WHEN OSCAR COMES INTO A PATIENT'S ROOM, WE CALL THE FAMILY AND LET THEM KNOW THEY'VE ONLY GOT A FEW HOURS TO COME IN AND SAY THEIR GOODBYES.
SHOULDN'T WE CALL THEM?
NO ONE TO CALL.
HE'S ALL ALONE? NO FAMILY AT ALL?
THERE'S NO FAMILY...

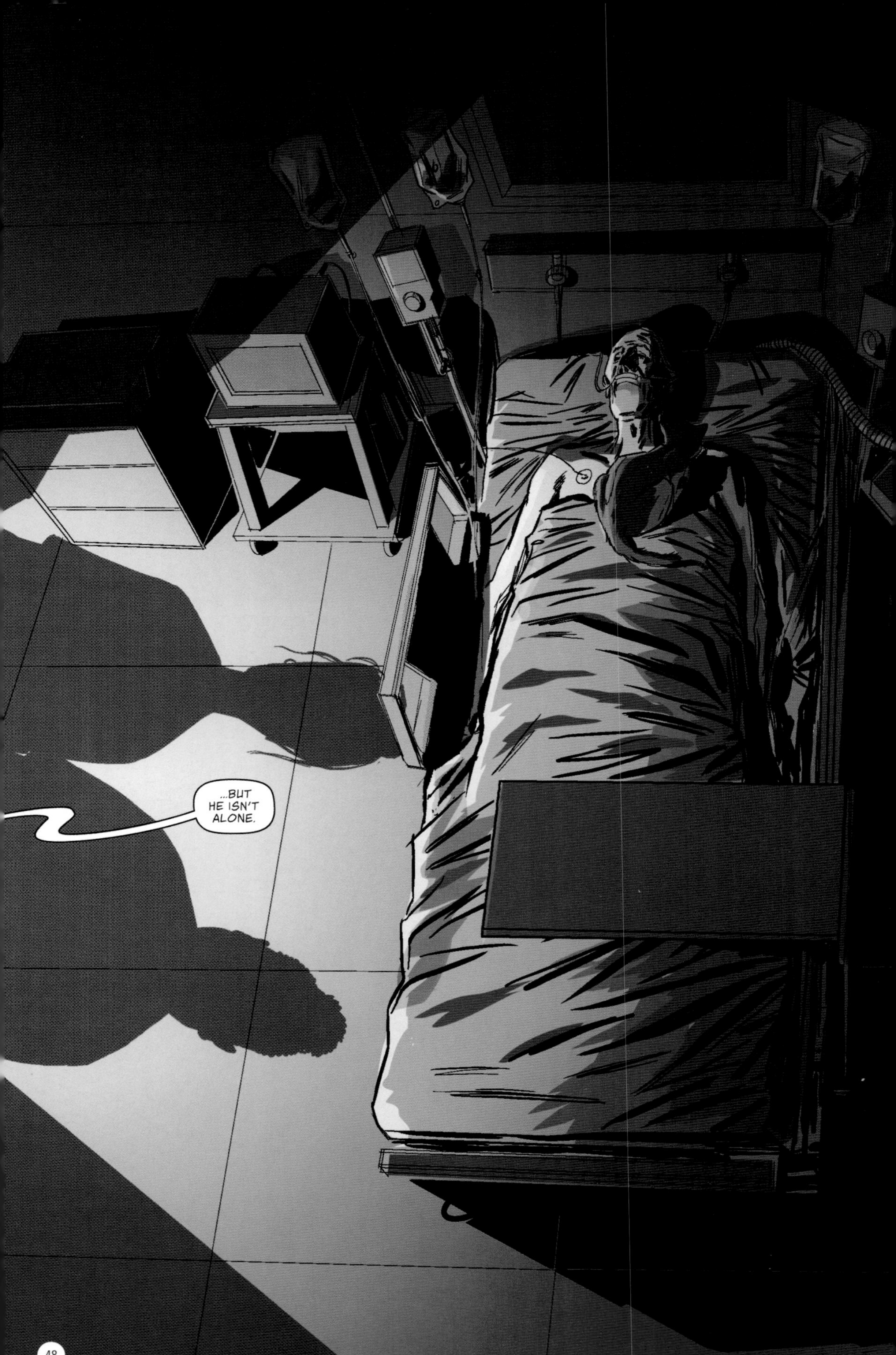
...BUT HE ISN'T ALONE.

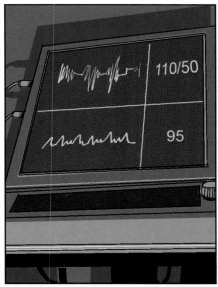

HIS CHEST HEAVES AND SHUDDERS AS THE END BEGINS.

A FRAIL HAND, WRACKED WITH TREMORS, REACHES OUT.

WHAT HE'S REACHING FOR IS ANYONE'S GUESS.

BUT WHAT HE FINDS IS A COMFORTING PRESENCE.

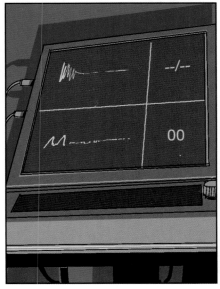

AND, JUST LIKE THAT...

...THE MAN IS GONE.

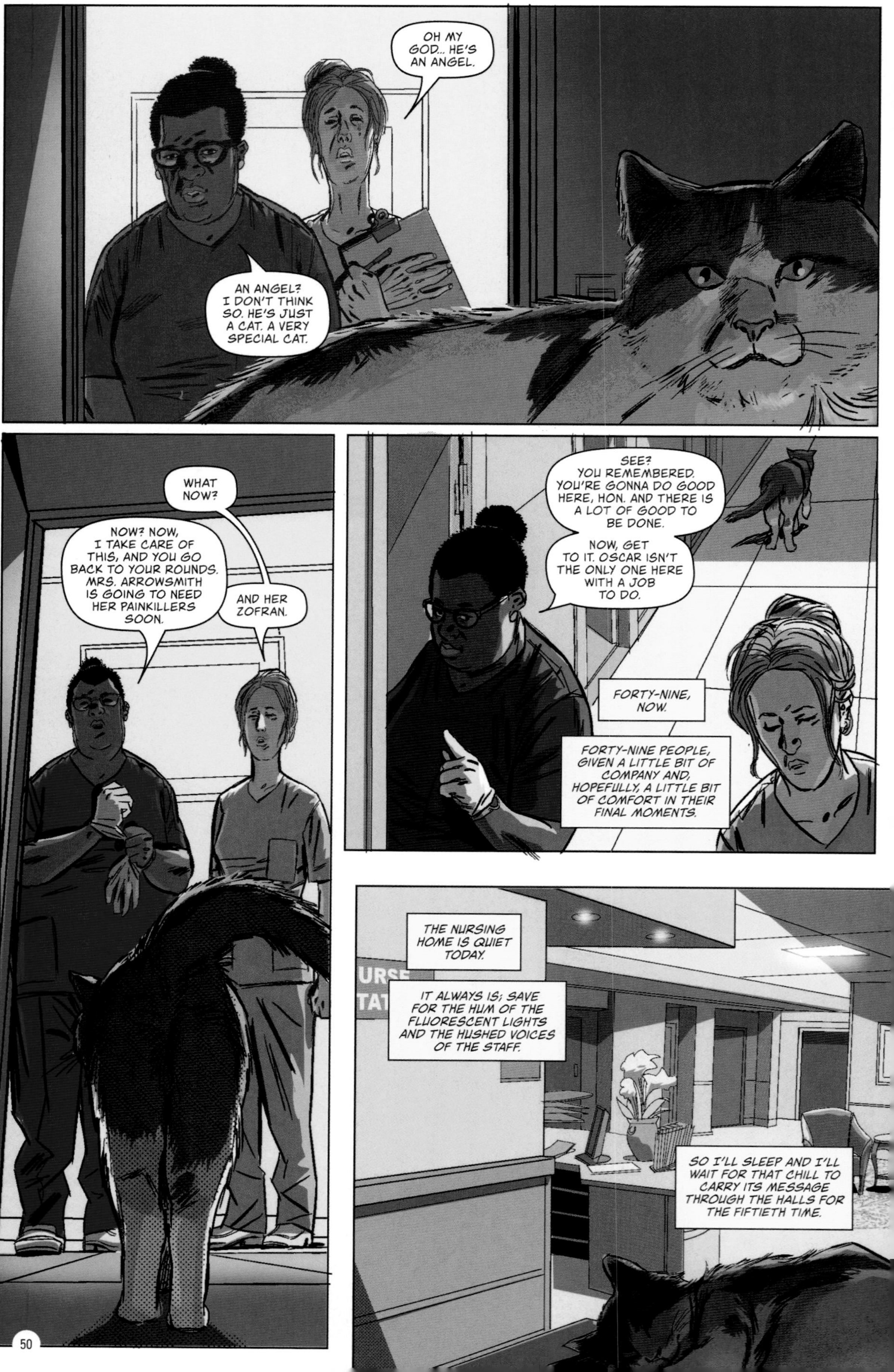
OH MY GOD... HE'S AN ANGEL.
AN ANGEL? I DON'T THINK SO. HE'S JUST A CAT. A VERY SPECIAL CAT.
WHAT NOW?
NOW? NOW, I TAKE CARE OF THIS, AND YOU GO BACK TO YOUR ROUNDS. MRS. ARROWSMITH IS GOING TO NEED HER PAINKILLERS SOON.
AND HER ZOFRAN.
SEE? YOU REMEMBERED. YOU'RE GONNA DO GOOD HERE, HON. AND THERE IS A LOT OF GOOD TO BE DONE.
NOW, GET TO IT. OSCAR ISN'T THE ONLY ONE HERE WITH A JOB TO DO.
FORTY-NINE, NOW.
FORTY-NINE PEOPLE, GIVEN A LITTLE BIT OF COMPANY AND, HOPEFULLY, A LITTLE BIT OF COMFORT IN THEIR FINAL MOMENTS.
THE NURSING HOME IS QUIET TODAY.
IT ALWAYS IS; SAVE FOR THE HUM OF THE FLUORESCENT LIGHTS AND THE HUSHED VOICES OF THE STAFF.
SO I'LL SLEEP AND I'LL WAIT FOR THAT CHILL TO CARRY ITS MESSAGE THROUGH THE HALLS FOR THE FIFTIETH TIME.

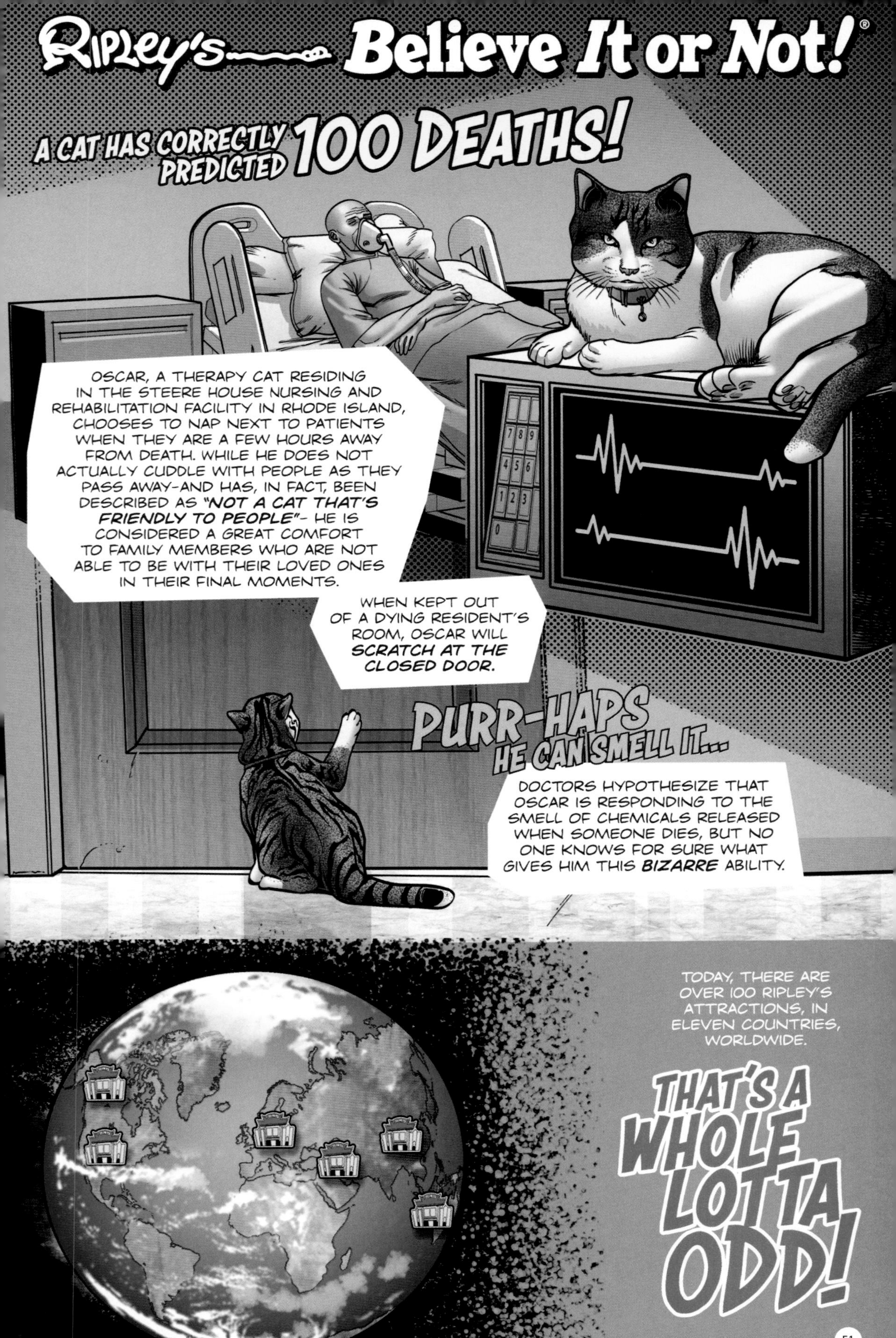
Ripley's Believe It or Not!®
A CAT HAS CORRECTLY PREDICTED 100 DEATHS!
OSCAR, A THERAPY CAT RESIDING IN THE STEERE HOUSE NURSING AND REHABILITATION FACILITY IN RHODE ISLAND, CHOOSES TO NAP NEXT TO PATIENTS WHEN THEY ARE A FEW HOURS AWAY FROM DEATH. WHILE HE DOES NOT ACTUALLY CUDDLE WITH PEOPLE AS THEY PASS AWAY–AND HAS, IN FACT, BEEN DESCRIBED AS "NOT A CAT THAT'S FRIENDLY TO PEOPLE"– HE IS CONSIDERED A GREAT COMFORT TO FAMILY MEMBERS WHO ARE NOT ABLE TO BE WITH THEIR LOVED ONES IN THEIR FINAL MOMENTS.
7 8 9
4 5 6
1 2 3
0
WHEN KEPT OUT OF A DYING RESIDENT'S ROOM, OSCAR WILL SCRATCH AT THE CLOSED DOOR.
PURR-HAPS HE CAN SMELL IT...
DOCTORS HYPOTHESIZE THAT OSCAR IS RESPONDING TO THE SMELL OF CHEMICALS RELEASED WHEN SOMEONE DIES, BUT NO ONE KNOWS FOR SURE WHAT GIVES HIM THIS BIZARRE ABILITY.
TODAY, THERE ARE OVER 100 RIPLEY'S ATTRACTIONS, IN ELEVEN COUNTRIES, WORLDWIDE.
THAT'S A WHOLE LOTTA ODD!

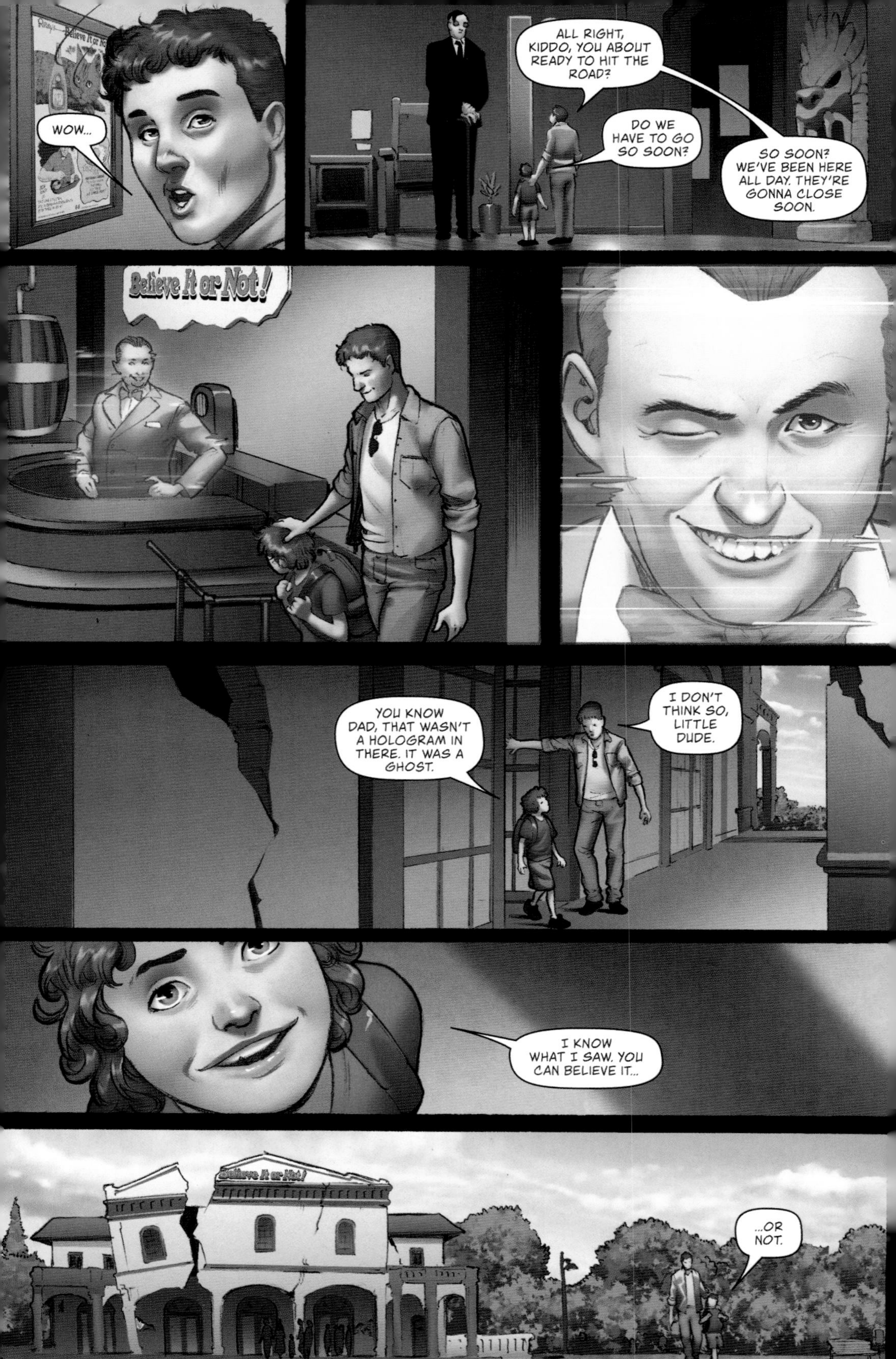

WOW...
ALL RIGHT, KIDDO, YOU ABOUT READY TO HIT THE ROAD?
DO WE HAVE TO GO SO SOON?
SO SOON? WE'VE BEEN HERE ALL DAY. THEY'RE GONNA CLOSE SOON.
Believe It or Not!
YOU KNOW DAD, THAT WASN'T A HOLOGRAM IN THERE. IT WAS A GHOST.
I DON'T THINK SO, LITTLE DUDE.
I KNOW WHAT I SAW. YOU CAN BELIEVE IT...
Believe It or Not!
...OR NOT.

Ripley's Believe It or Not!

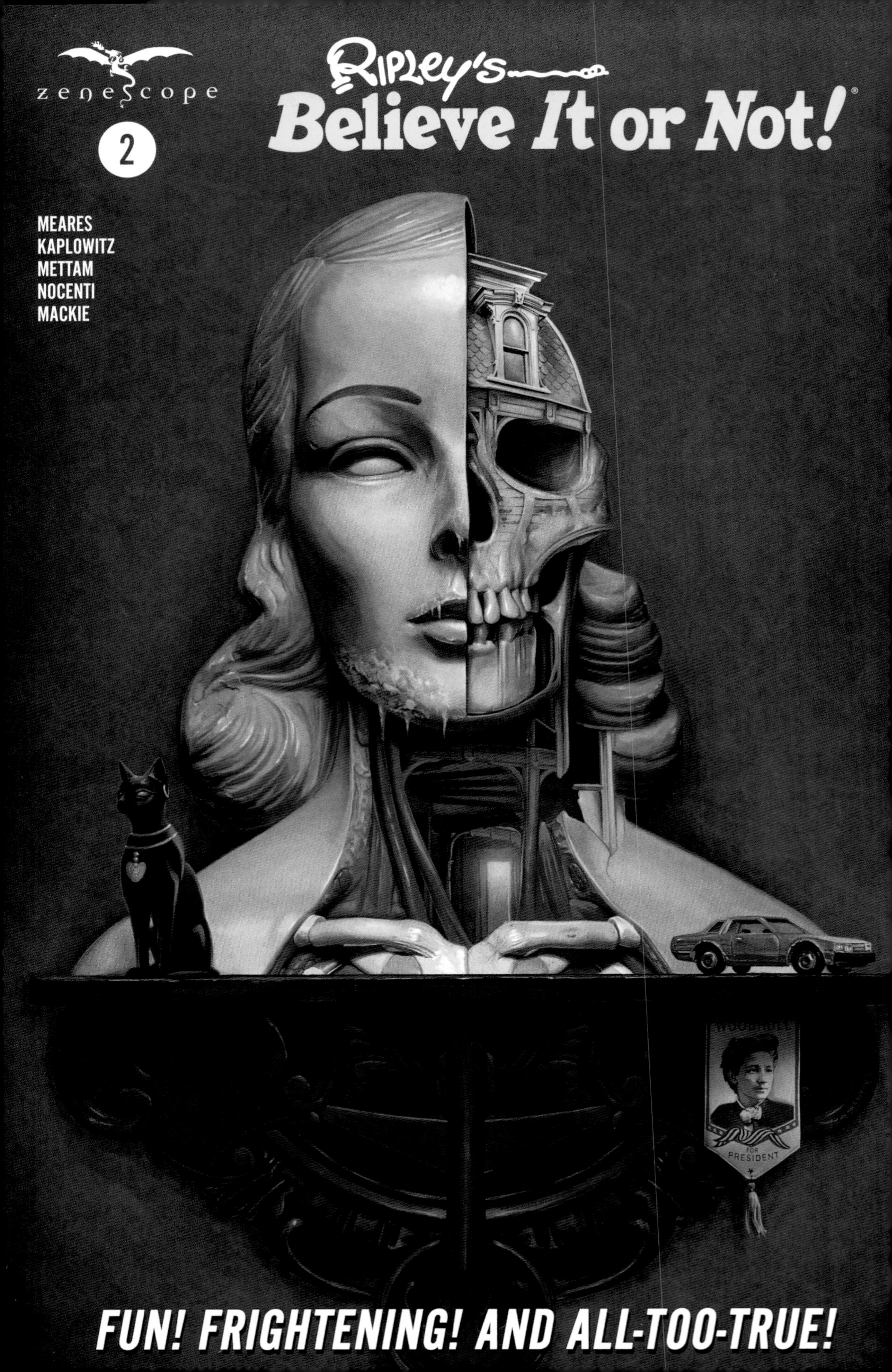
zenescope
2
Ripley's
Believe It or Not!®
MEARES
KAPLOWITZ
METTAM
NOCENTI
MACKIE
FOR
PRESIDENT
FUN! FRIGHTENING! AND ALL-TOO-TRUE!

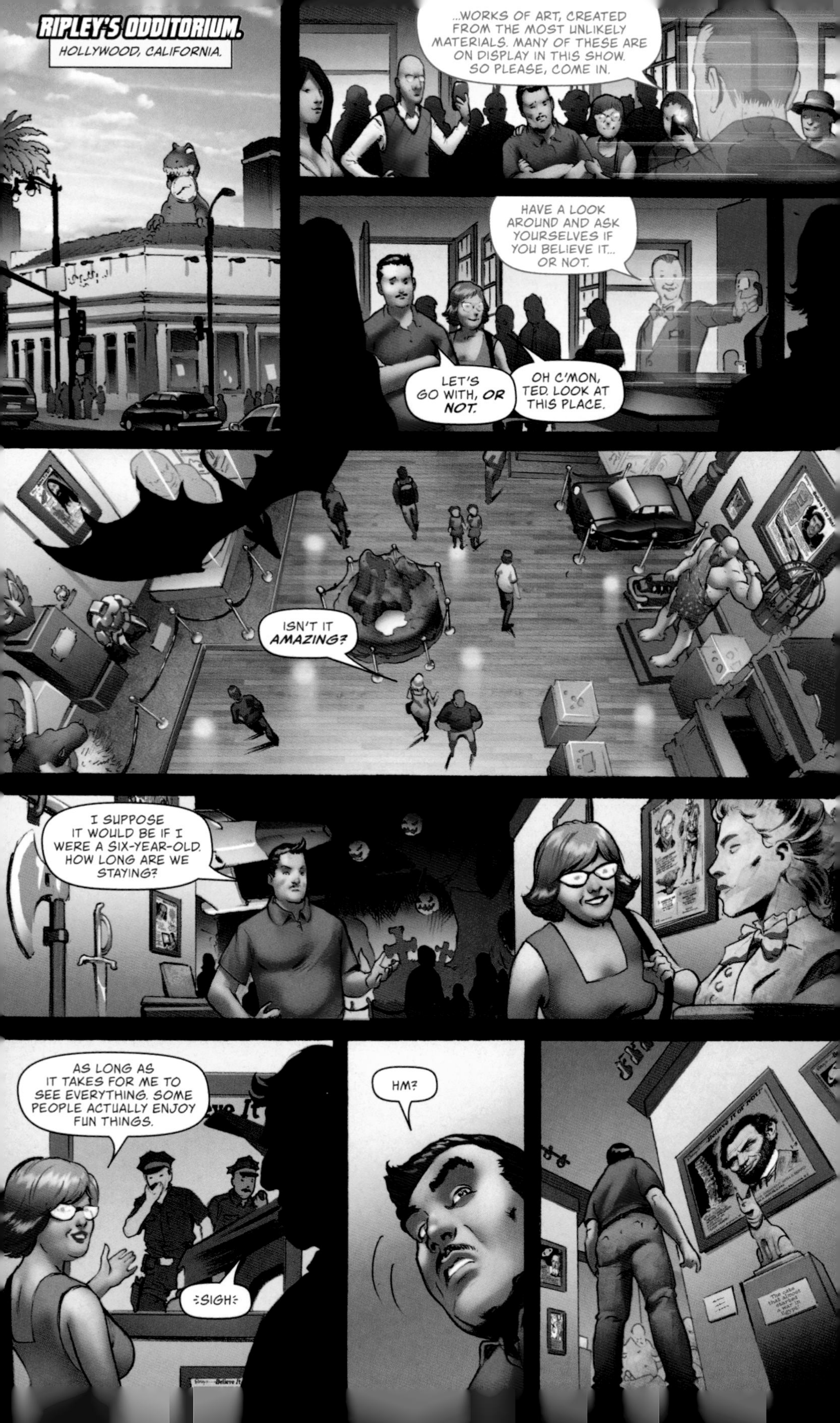
RIPLEY'S ODDITORIUM.
HOLLYWOOD, CALIFORNIA.
...WORKS OF ART, CREATED FROM THE MOST UNLIKELY MATERIALS. MANY OF THESE ARE ON DISPLAY IN THIS SHOW. SO PLEASE, COME IN.
HAVE A LOOK AROUND AND ASK YOURSELVES IF YOU BELIEVE IT... OR NOT.
LET'S GO WITH, *OR NOT.*
OH C'MON, TED. LOOK AT THIS PLACE.
ISN'T IT *AMAZING?*
I SUPPOSE IT WOULD BE IF I WERE A SIX-YEAR-OLD. HOW LONG ARE WE STAYING?
AS LONG AS IT TAKES FOR ME TO SEE EVERYTHING. SOME PEOPLE ACTUALLY ENJOY FUN THINGS.
SIGH
HM?

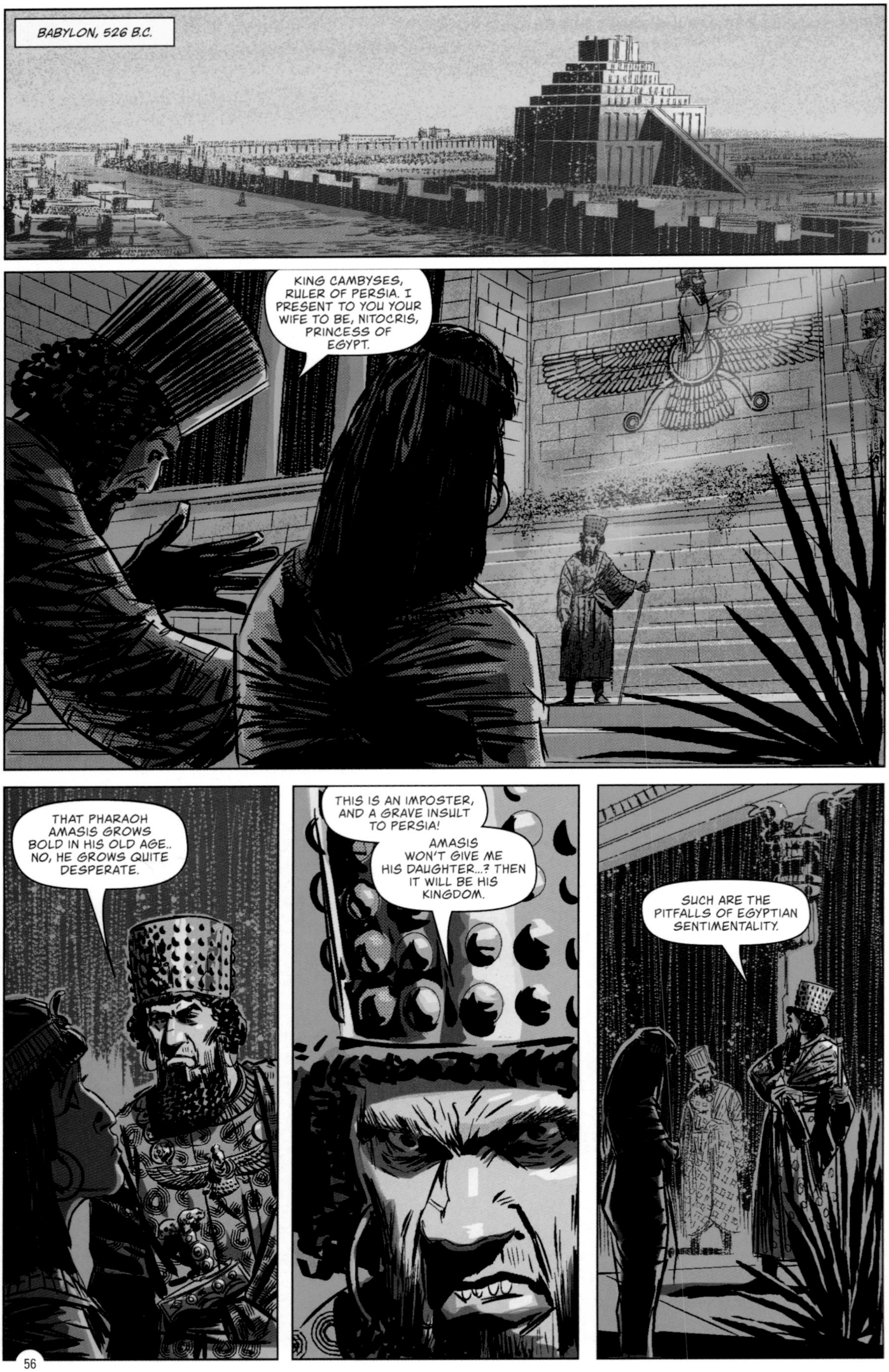
BABYLON, 526 B.C.
KING CAMBYSES, RULER OF PERSIA. I PRESENT TO YOU YOUR WIFE TO BE, NITOCRIS, PRINCESS OF EGYPT.
THAT PHARAOH AMASIS GROWS BOLD IN HIS OLD AGE.. NO, HE GROWS QUITE DESPERATE.
THIS IS AN IMPOSTER, AND A GRAVE INSULT TO PERSIA!
AMASIS WON'T GIVE ME HIS DAUGHTER...? THEN IT WILL BE HIS KINGDOM.
SUCH ARE THE PITFALLS OF EGYPTIAN SENTIMENTALITY.

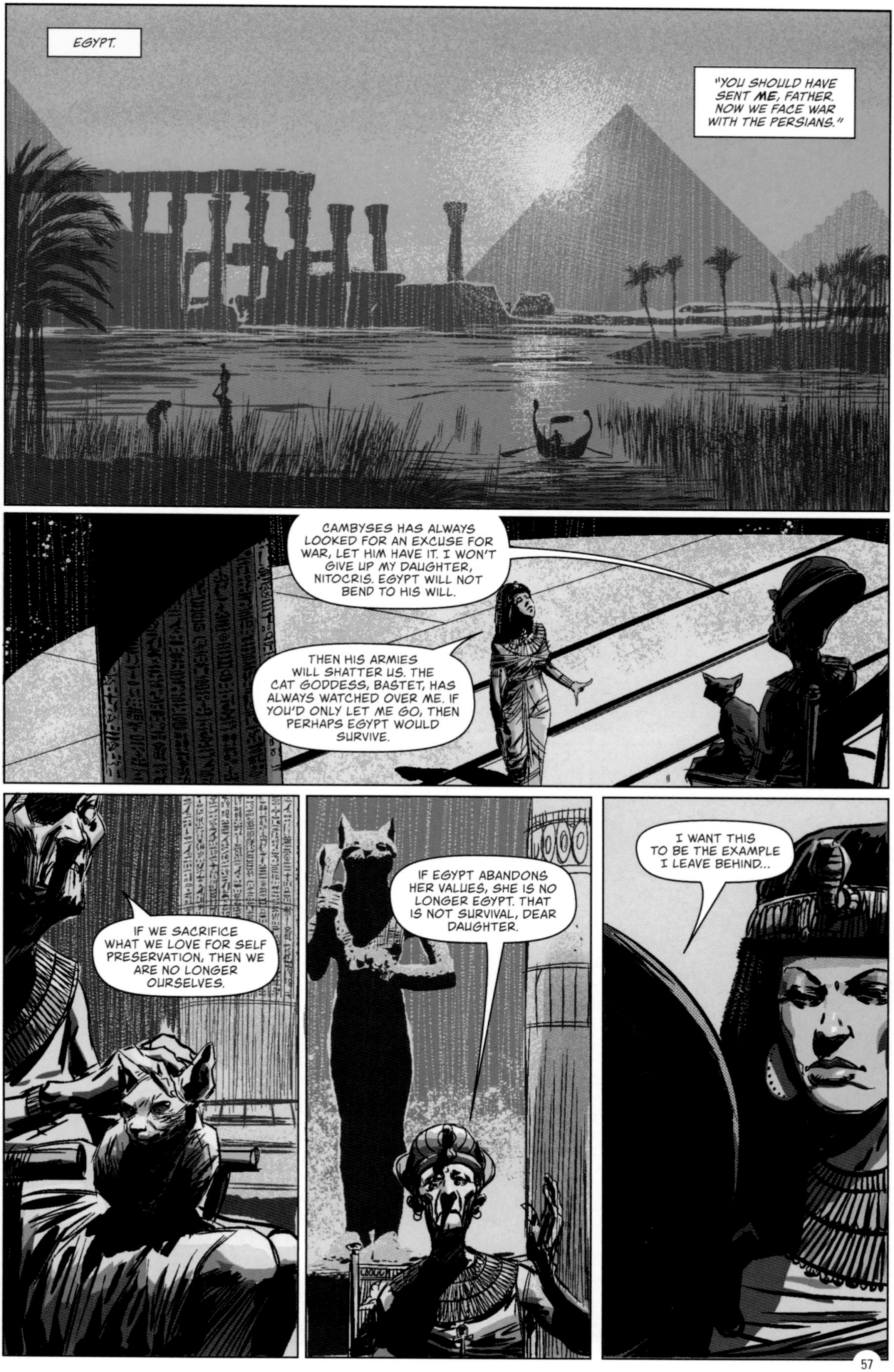
EGYPT.
"YOU SHOULD HAVE SENT ME, FATHER. NOW WE FACE WAR WITH THE PERSIANS."
CAMBYSES HAS ALWAYS LOOKED FOR AN EXCUSE FOR WAR, LET HIM HAVE IT. I WON'T GIVE UP MY DAUGHTER, NITOCRIS. EGYPT WILL NOT BEND TO HIS WILL.
THEN HIS ARMIES WILL SHATTER US. THE CAT GODDESS, BASTET, HAS ALWAYS WATCHED OVER ME. IF YOU'D ONLY LET ME GO, THEN PERHAPS EGYPT WOULD SURVIVE.
IF WE SACRIFICE WHAT WE LOVE FOR SELF PRESERVATION, THEN WE ARE NO LONGER OURSELVES.
IF EGYPT ABANDONS HER VALUES, SHE IS NO LONGER EGYPT. THAT IS NOT SURVIVAL, DEAR DAUGHTER.
I WANT THIS TO BE THE EXAMPLE I LEAVE BEHIND...

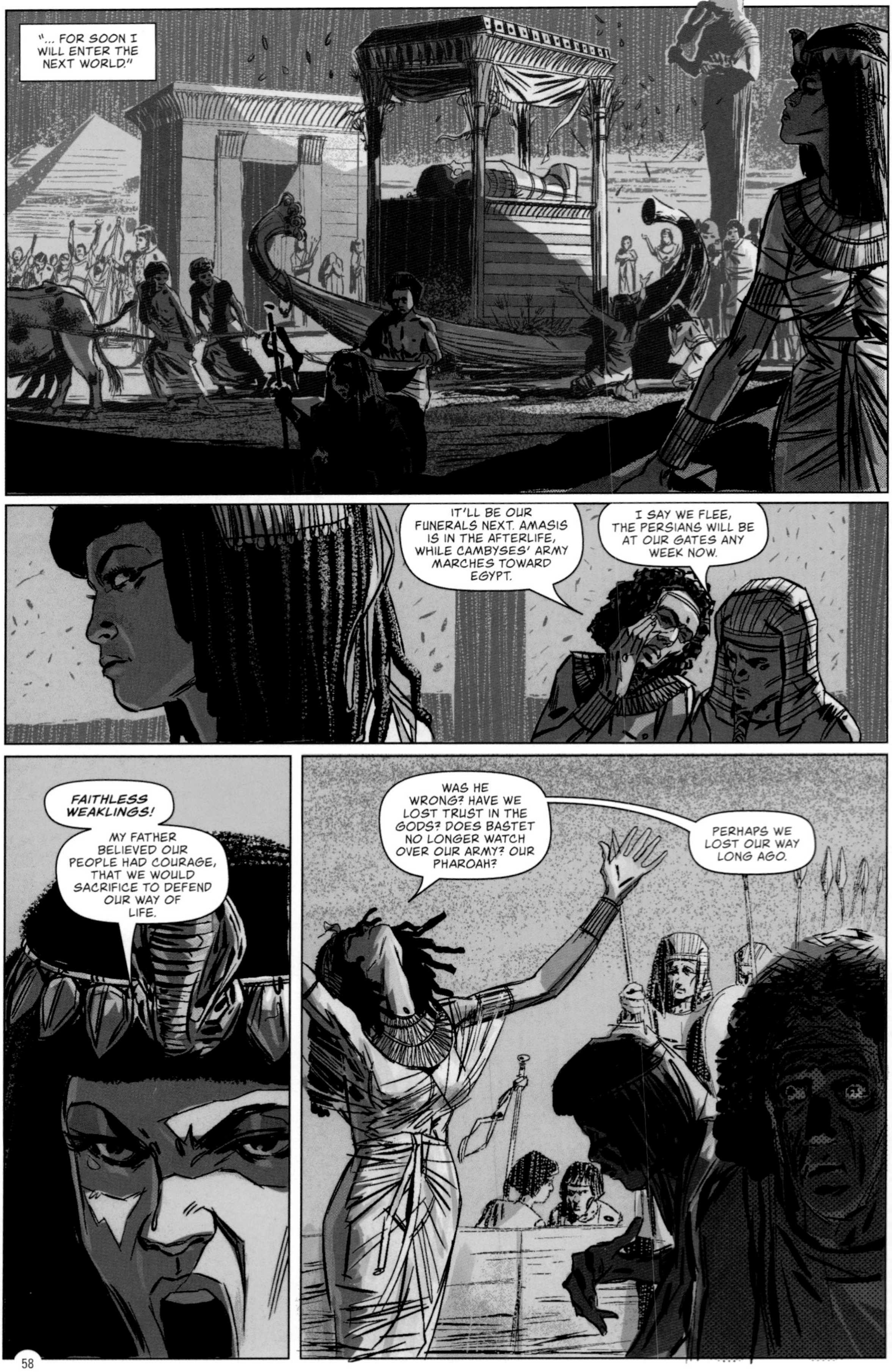
"... FOR SOON I WILL ENTER THE NEXT WORLD."
IT'LL BE OUR FUNERALS NEXT. AMASIS IS IN THE AFTERLIFE, WHILE CAMBYSES' ARMY MARCHES TOWARD EGYPT.
I SAY WE FLEE, THE PERSIANS WILL BE AT OUR GATES ANY WEEK NOW.
FAITHLESS WEAKLINGS!
MY FATHER BELIEVED OUR PEOPLE HAD COURAGE, THAT WE WOULD SACRIFICE TO DEFEND OUR WAY OF LIFE.
WAS HE WRONG? HAVE WE LOST TRUST IN THE GODS? DOES BASTET NO LONGER WATCH OVER OUR ARMY? OUR PHAROAH?
PERHAPS WE LOST OUR WAY LONG AGO.

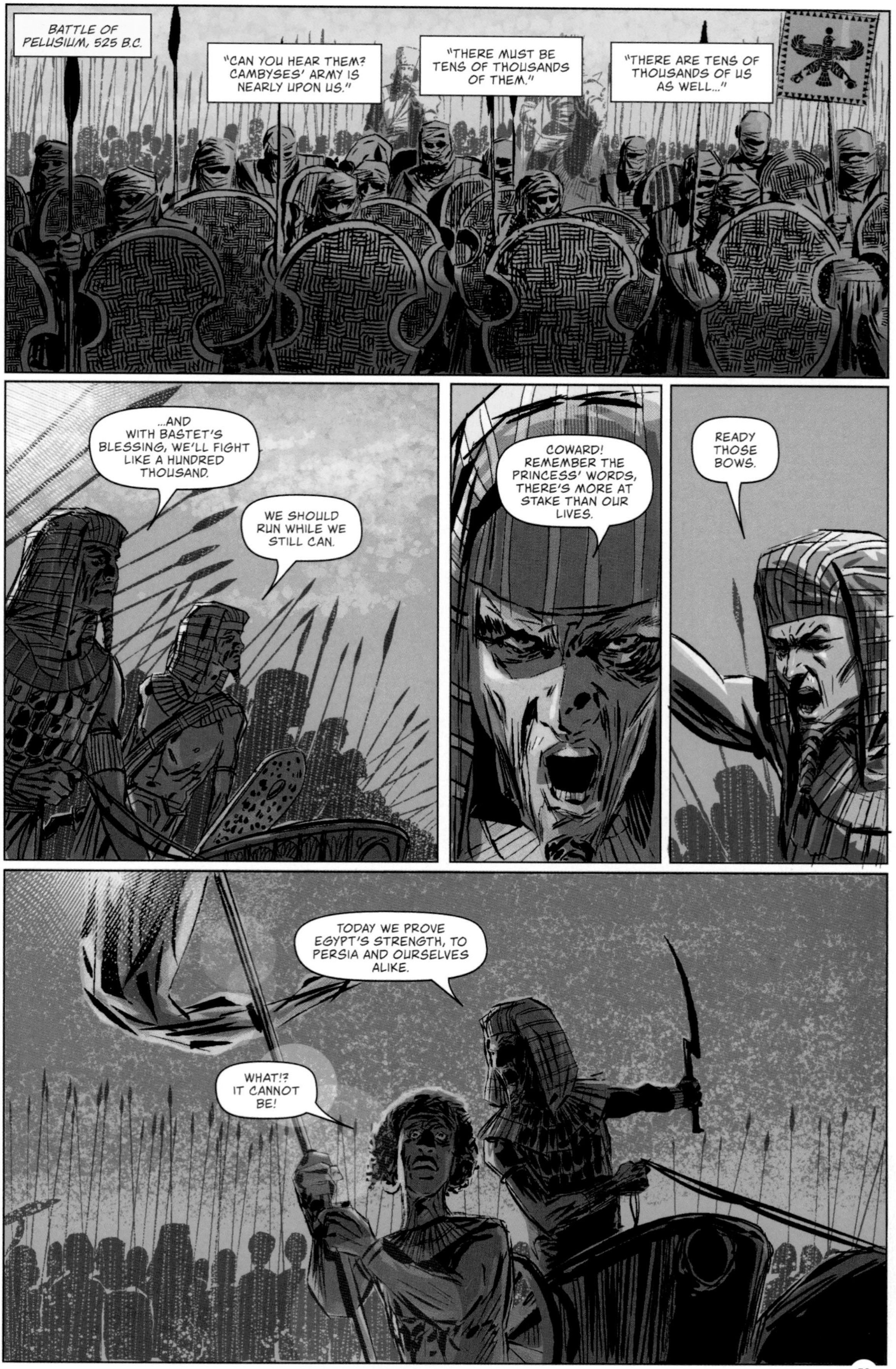
BATTLE OF PELUSIUM, 525 B.C.
"CAN YOU HEAR THEM? CAMBYSES' ARMY IS NEARLY UPON US."
"THERE MUST BE TENS OF THOUSANDS OF THEM."
"THERE ARE TENS OF THOUSANDS OF US AS WELL..."
...AND WITH BASTET'S BLESSING, WE'LL FIGHT LIKE A HUNDRED THOUSAND.
WE SHOULD RUN WHILE WE STILL CAN.
COWARD! REMEMBER THE PRINCESS' WORDS, THERE'S MORE AT STAKE THAN OUR LIVES.
READY THOSE BOWS.
TODAY WE PROVE EGYPT'S STRENGTH, TO PERSIA AND OURSELVES ALIKE.
WHAT!? IT CANNOT BE!

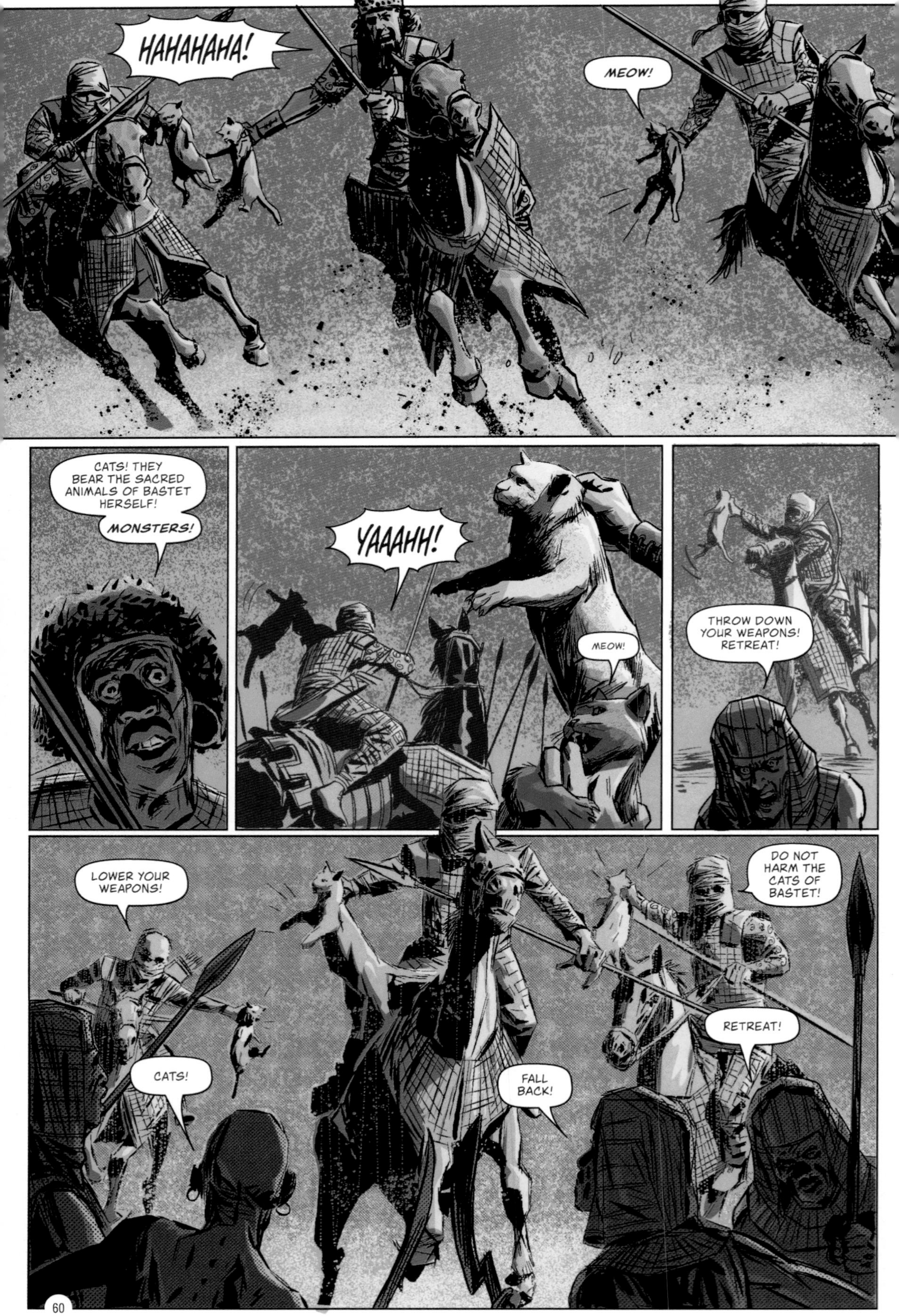
HAHAHAHA!
MEOW!
CATS! THEY BEAR THE SACRED ANIMALS OF BASTET HERSELF!
MONSTERS!
YAAAHH!
MEOW!
THROW DOWN YOUR WEAPONS! RETREAT!
LOWER YOUR WEAPONS!
DO NOT HARM THE CATS OF BASTET!
RETREAT!
CATS!
FALL BACK!

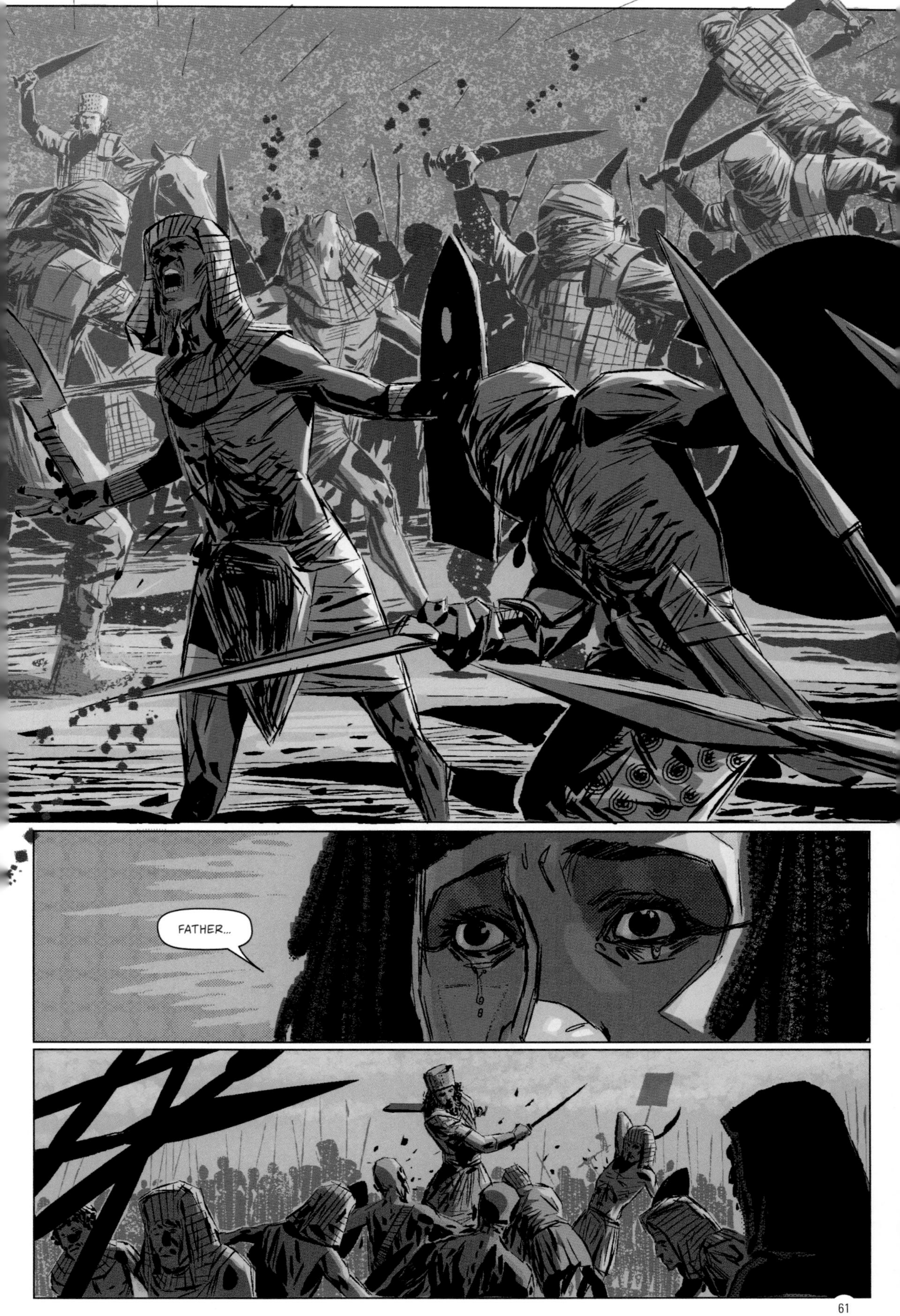
FATHER...

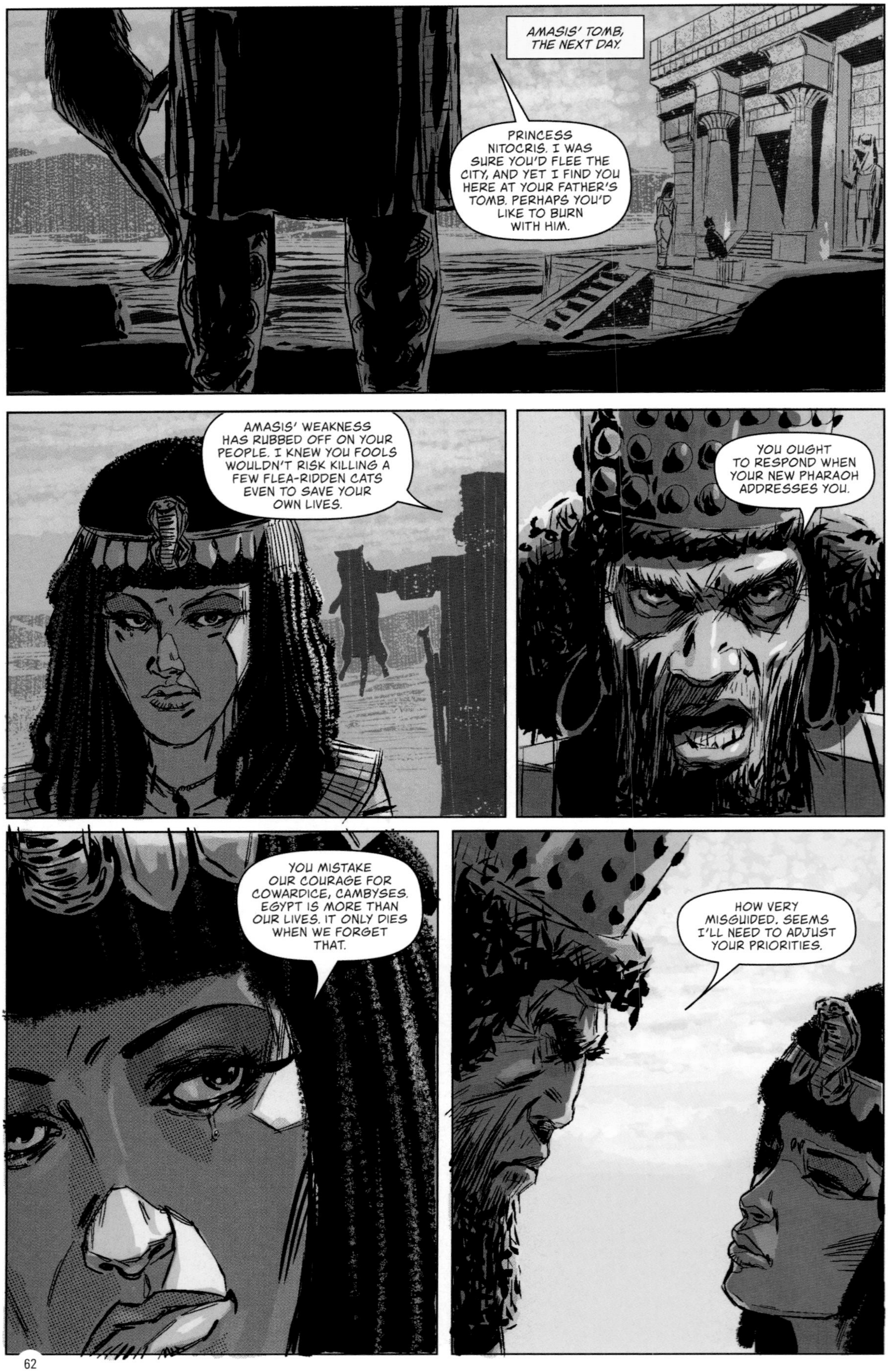

AMASIS' TOMB, THE NEXT DAY.
PRINCESS NITOCRIS. I WAS SURE YOU'D FLEE THE CITY, AND YET I FIND YOU HERE AT YOUR FATHER'S TOMB. PERHAPS YOU'D LIKE TO BURN WITH HIM.
AMASIS' WEAKNESS HAS RUBBED OFF ON YOUR PEOPLE. I KNEW YOU FOOLS WOULDN'T RISK KILLING A FEW FLEA-RIDDEN CATS EVEN TO SAVE YOUR OWN LIVES.
YOU OUGHT TO RESPOND WHEN YOUR NEW PHARAOH ADDRESSES YOU.
YOU MISTAKE OUR COURAGE FOR COWARDICE, CAMBYSES. EGYPT IS MORE THAN OUR LIVES. IT ONLY DIES WHEN WE FORGET THAT.
HOW VERY MISGUIDED. SEEMS I'LL NEED TO ADJUST YOUR PRIORITIES.

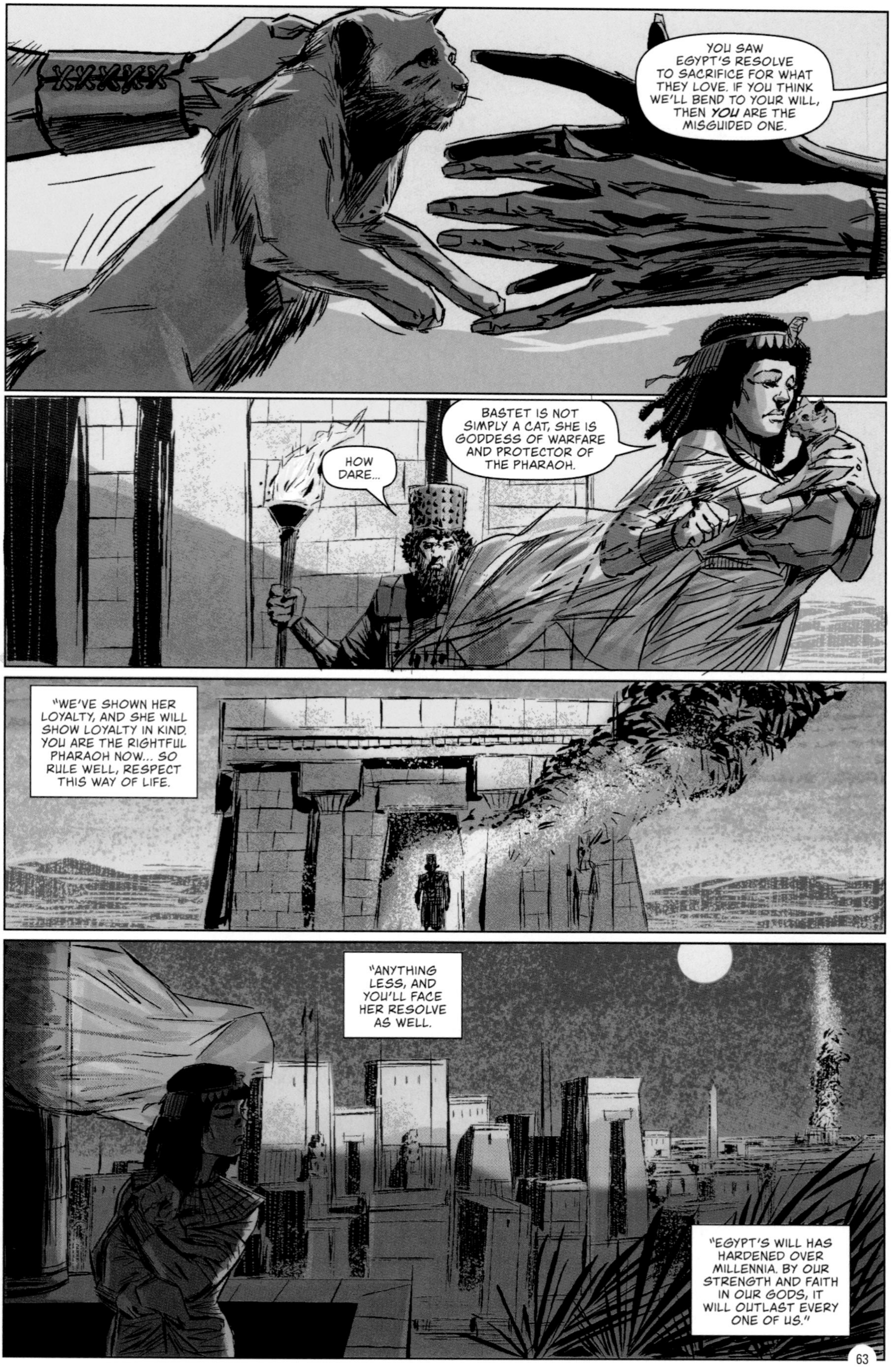
YOU SAW EGYPT'S RESOLVE TO SACRIFICE FOR WHAT THEY LOVE. IF YOU THINK WE'LL BEND TO YOUR WILL, THEN *YOU* ARE THE MISGUIDED ONE.
BASTET IS NOT SIMPLY A CAT, SHE IS GODDESS OF WARFARE AND PROTECTOR OF THE PHARAOH.
HOW DARE...
"WE'VE SHOWN HER LOYALTY, AND SHE WILL SHOW LOYALTY IN KIND. YOU ARE THE RIGHTFUL PHARAOH NOW... SO RULE WELL, RESPECT THIS WAY OF LIFE.
"ANYTHING LESS, AND YOU'LL FACE HER RESOLVE AS WELL.
"EGYPT'S WILL HAS HARDENED OVER MILLENNIA. BY OUR STRENGTH AND FAITH IN OUR GODS, IT WILL OUTLAST EVERY ONE OF US."

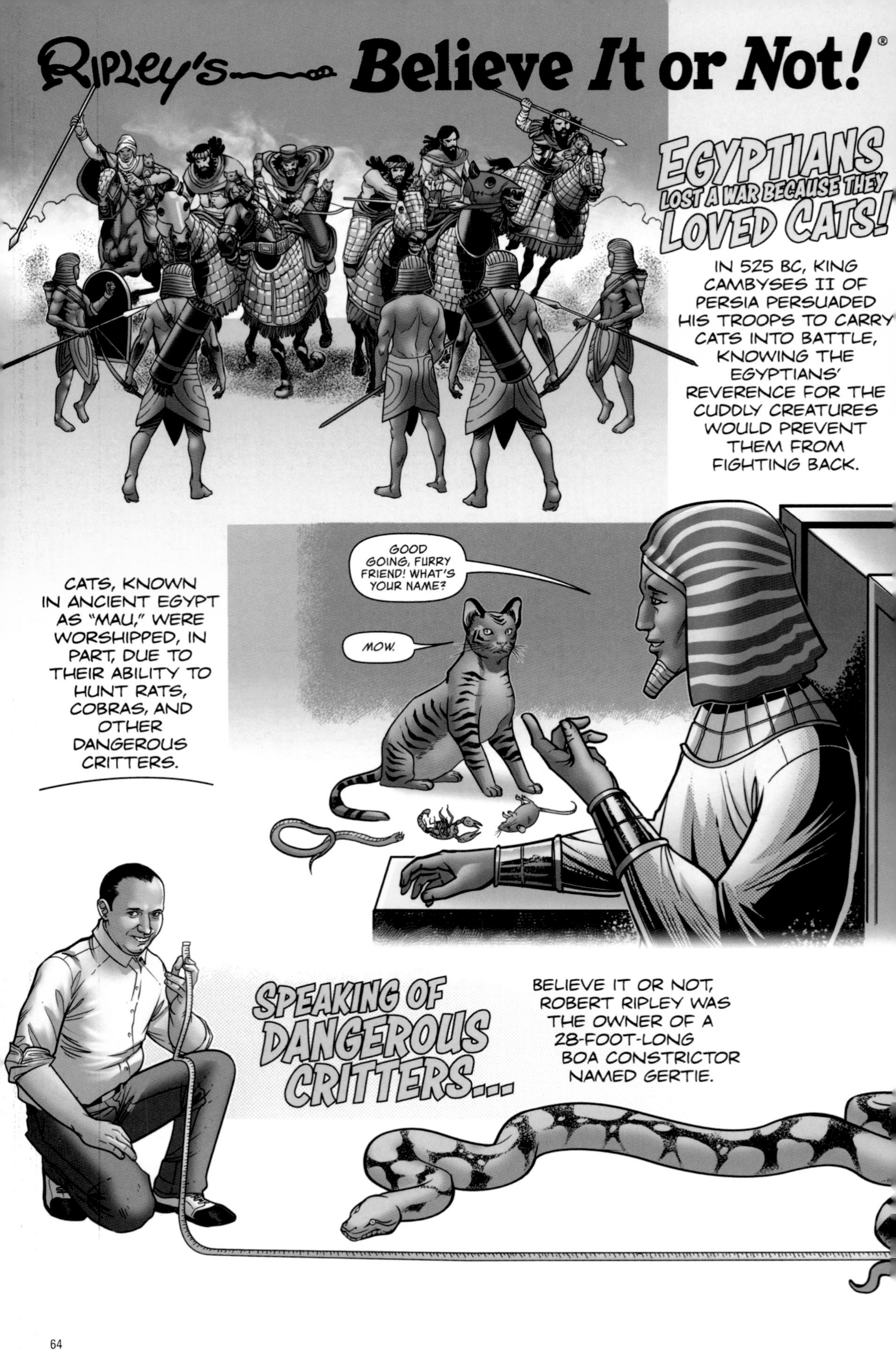

RIPLEY'S Believe It or Not!®
EGYPTIANS LOST A WAR BECAUSE THEY LOVED CATS!
IN 525 BC, KING CAMBYSES II OF PERSIA PERSUADED HIS TROOPS TO CARRY CATS INTO BATTLE, KNOWING THE EGYPTIANS' REVERENCE FOR THE CUDDLY CREATURES WOULD PREVENT THEM FROM FIGHTING BACK.
CATS, KNOWN IN ANCIENT EGYPT AS "MAU," WERE WORSHIPPED, IN PART, DUE TO THEIR ABILITY TO HUNT RATS, COBRAS, AND OTHER DANGEROUS CRITTERS.
GOOD GOING, FURRY FRIEND! WHAT'S YOUR NAME?
MOW.
SPEAKING OF DANGEROUS CRITTERS...
BELIEVE IT OR NOT, ROBERT RIPLEY WAS THE OWNER OF A 28-FOOT-LONG BOA CONSTRICTOR NAMED GERTIE.

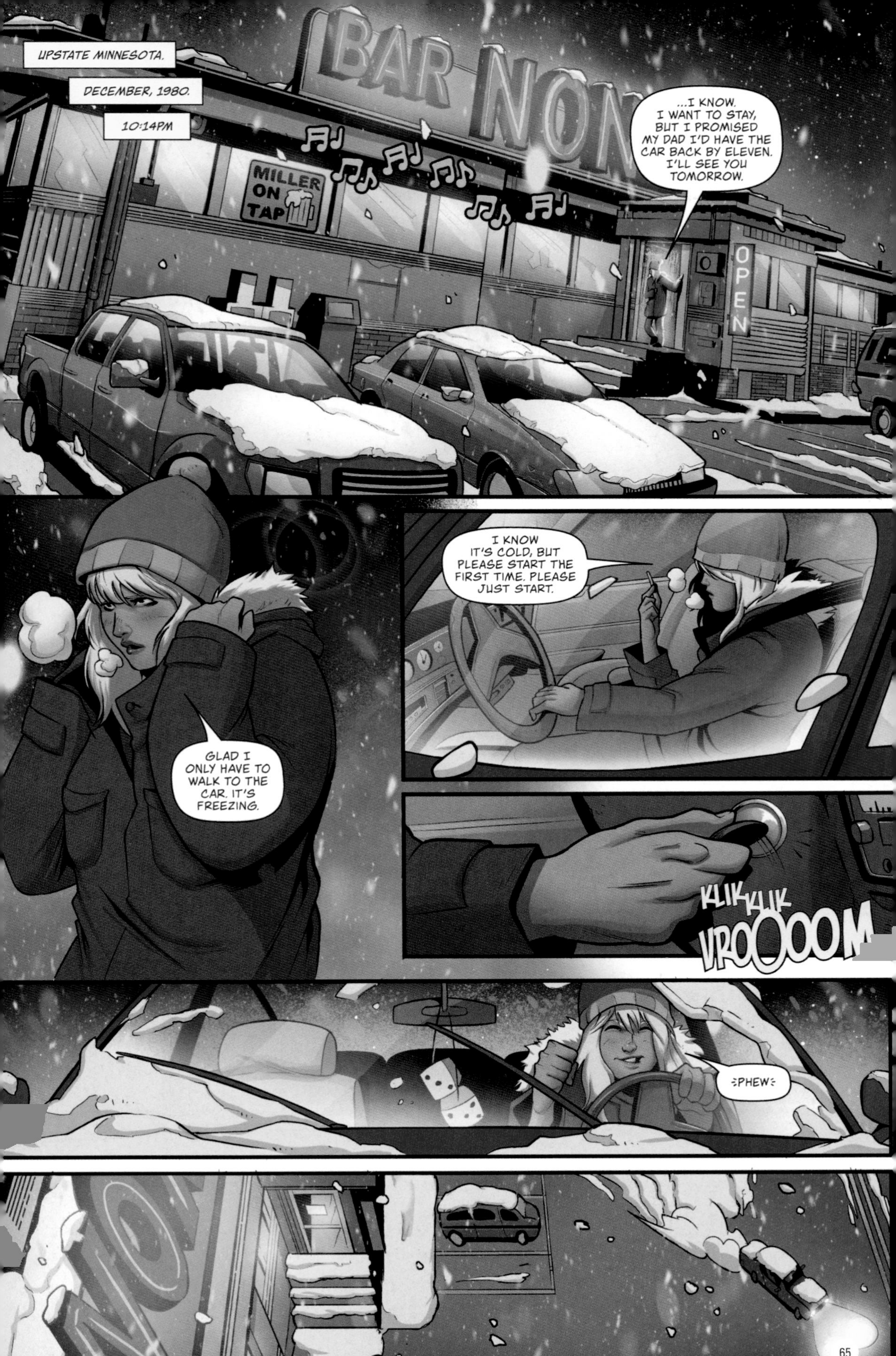
UPSTATE MINNESOTA.
DECEMBER, 1980.
10:14PM
BAR NON
MILLER ON TAP
...I KNOW. I WANT TO STAY, BUT I PROMISED MY DAD I'D HAVE THE CAR BACK BY ELEVEN. I'LL SEE YOU TOMORROW.
OPEN
GLAD I ONLY HAVE TO WALK TO THE CAR. IT'S FREEZING.
I KNOW IT'S COLD, BUT PLEASE START THE FIRST TIME. PLEASE JUST START.
KLIK KLIK
VROOOOOM
PHEW

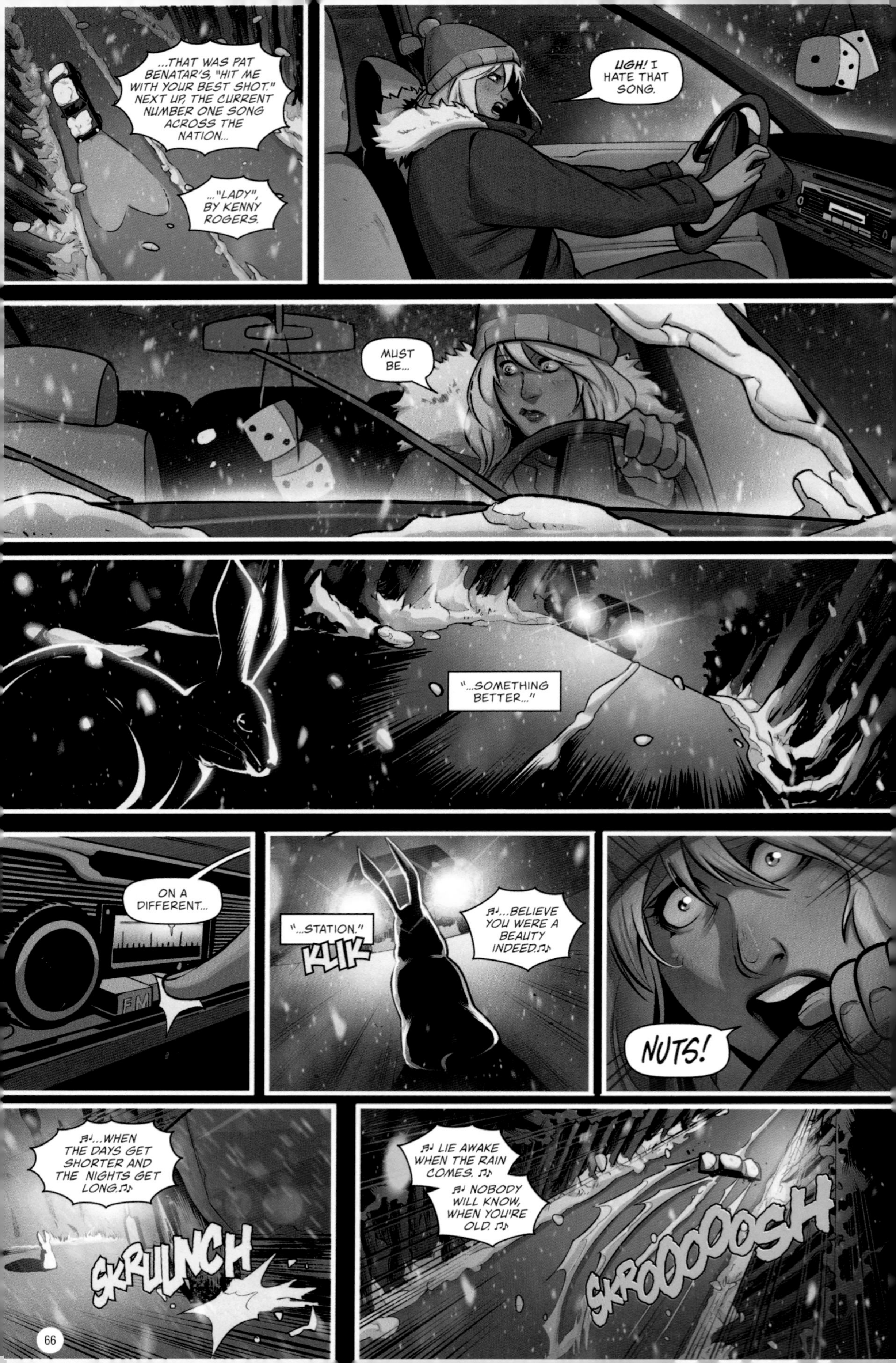
...THAT WAS PAT BENATAR'S, "HIT ME WITH YOUR BEST SHOT." NEXT UP, THE CURRENT NUMBER ONE SONG ACROSS THE NATION...
..."LADY", BY KENNY ROGERS.
UGH! I HATE THAT SONG.
MUST BE...
"...SOMETHING BETTER..."
ON A DIFFERENT...
"...STATION."
KLIK
♬♩...BELIEVE YOU WERE A BEAUTY INDEED.♫♪
NUTS!
♬♩...WHEN THE DAYS GET SHORTER AND THE NIGHTS GET LONG.♫♪
SKRUNCH
♬♩ LIE AWAKE WHEN THE RAIN COMES. ♫♪
♬♩ NOBODY WILL KNOW, WHEN YOU'RE OLD. ♫♪
SKROOOOOOSH

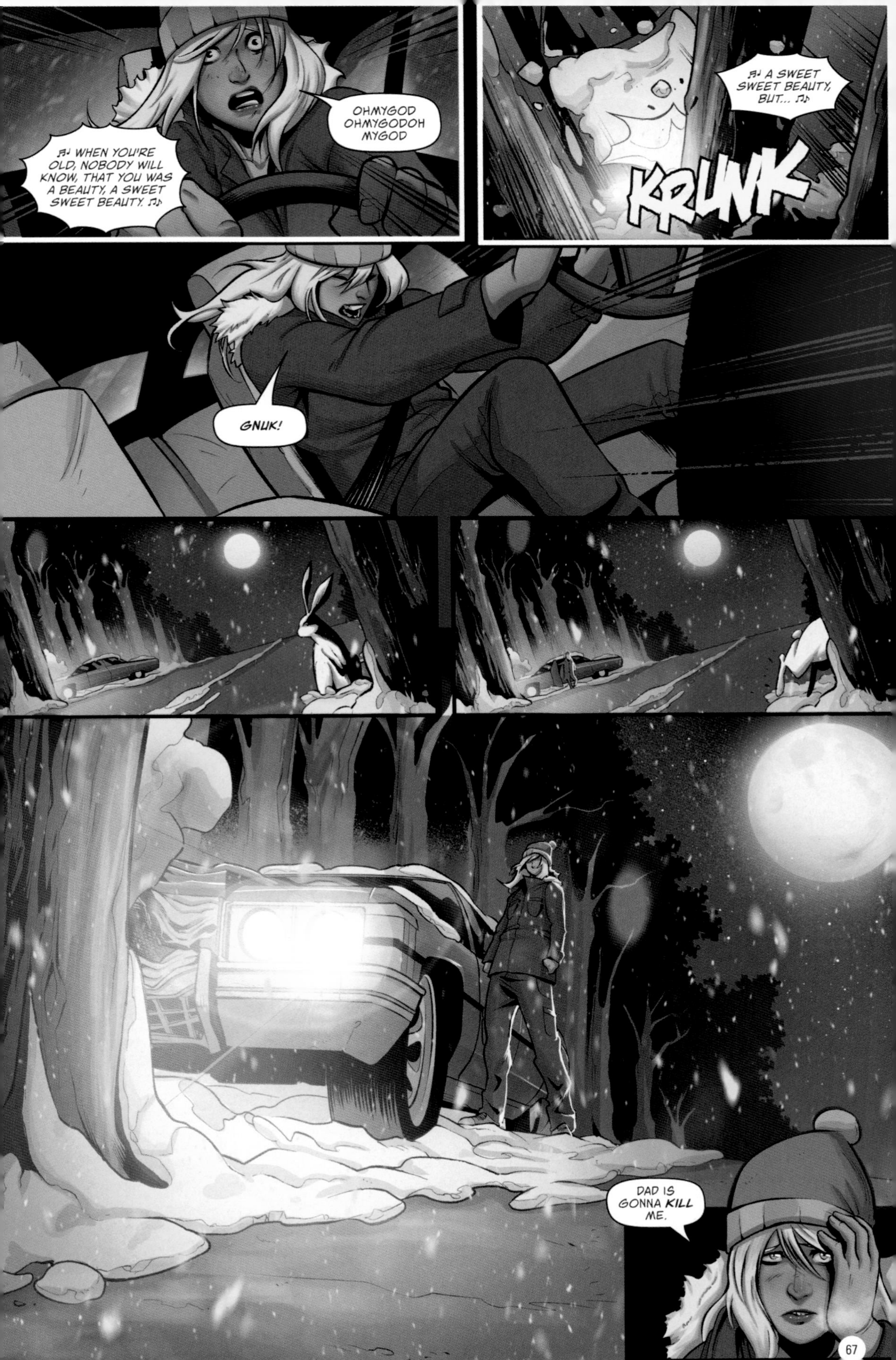
♬♩ WHEN YOU'RE OLD, NOBODY WILL KNOW, THAT YOU WAS A BEAUTY, A SWEET SWEET BEAUTY. ♫♪
OHMYGOD OHMYGODOH MYGOD
♬♩ A SWEET SWEET BEAUTY, BUT... ♫♪
KRUNK
GNUK!
DAD IS GONNA **KILL** ME.

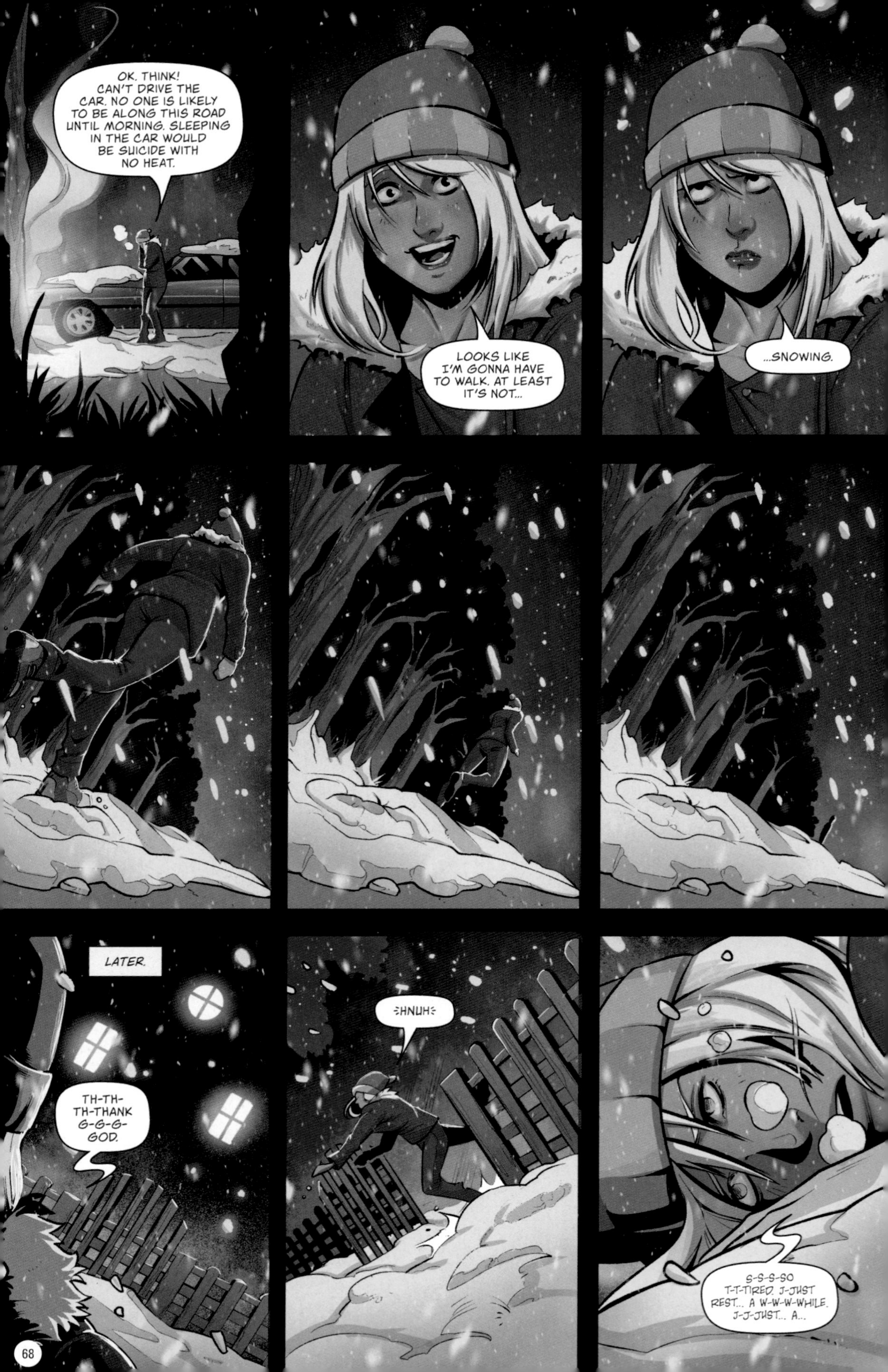
OK. THINK! CAN'T DRIVE THE CAR. NO ONE IS LIKELY TO BE ALONG THIS ROAD UNTIL MORNING. SLEEPING IN THE CAR WOULD BE SUICIDE WITH NO HEAT.
LOOKS LIKE I'M GONNA HAVE TO WALK. AT LEAST IT'S NOT...
...SNOWING.
LATER.
TH-TH-TH-THANK G-G-G-GOD.
HNUH
S-S-S-SO T-T-TIRED. J-JUST REST... A W-W-W-WHILE. J-J-JUST... A...

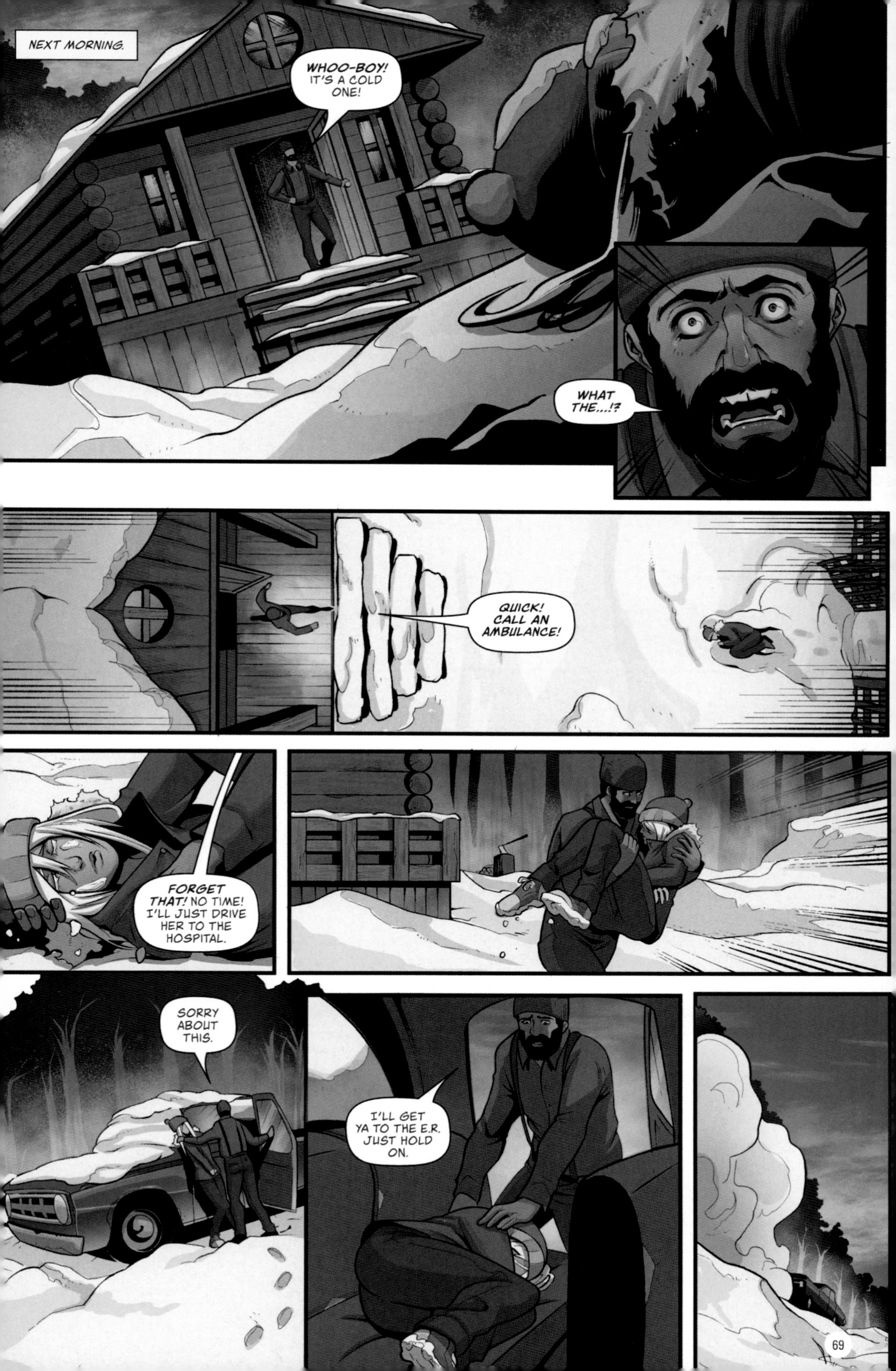
NEXT MORNING.
WHOO-BOY! IT'S A COLD ONE!
WHAT THE...!?
QUICK! CALL AN AMBULANCE!
FORGET THAT! NO TIME! I'LL JUST DRIVE HER TO THE HOSPITAL.
SORRY ABOUT THIS.
I'LL GET YA TO THE E.R. JUST HOLD ON.

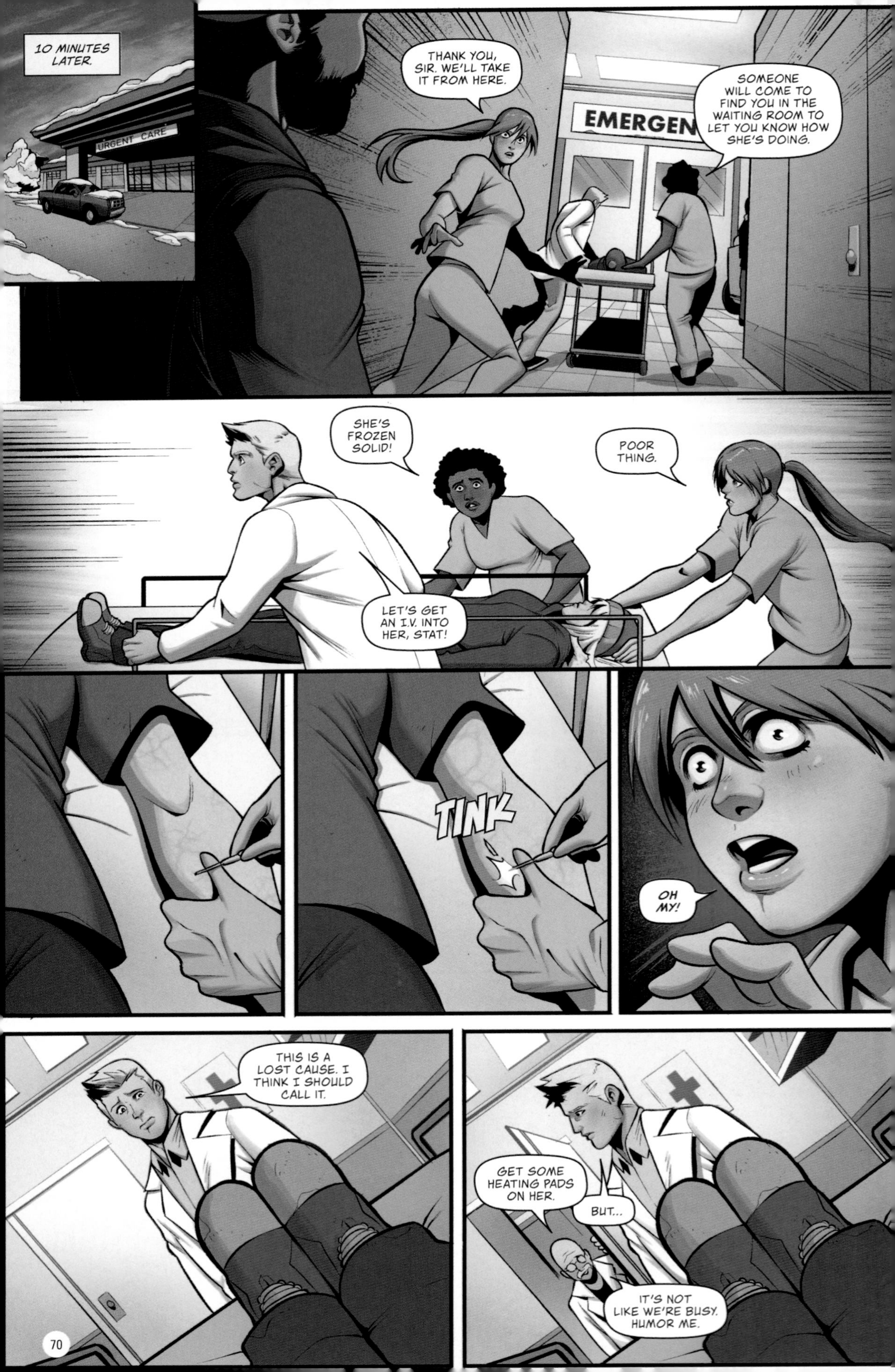

10 MINUTES LATER.
URGENT CARE
THANK YOU, SIR. WE'LL TAKE IT FROM HERE.
EMERGEN
SOMEONE WILL COME TO FIND YOU IN THE WAITING ROOM TO LET YOU KNOW HOW SHE'S DOING.
SHE'S FROZEN SOLID!
POOR THING.
LET'S GET AN I.V. INTO HER, STAT!
TINK
OH MY!
THIS IS A LOST CAUSE. I THINK I SHOULD CALL IT.
GET SOME HEATING PADS ON HER.
BUT...
IT'S NOT LIKE WE'RE BUSY. HUMOR ME.

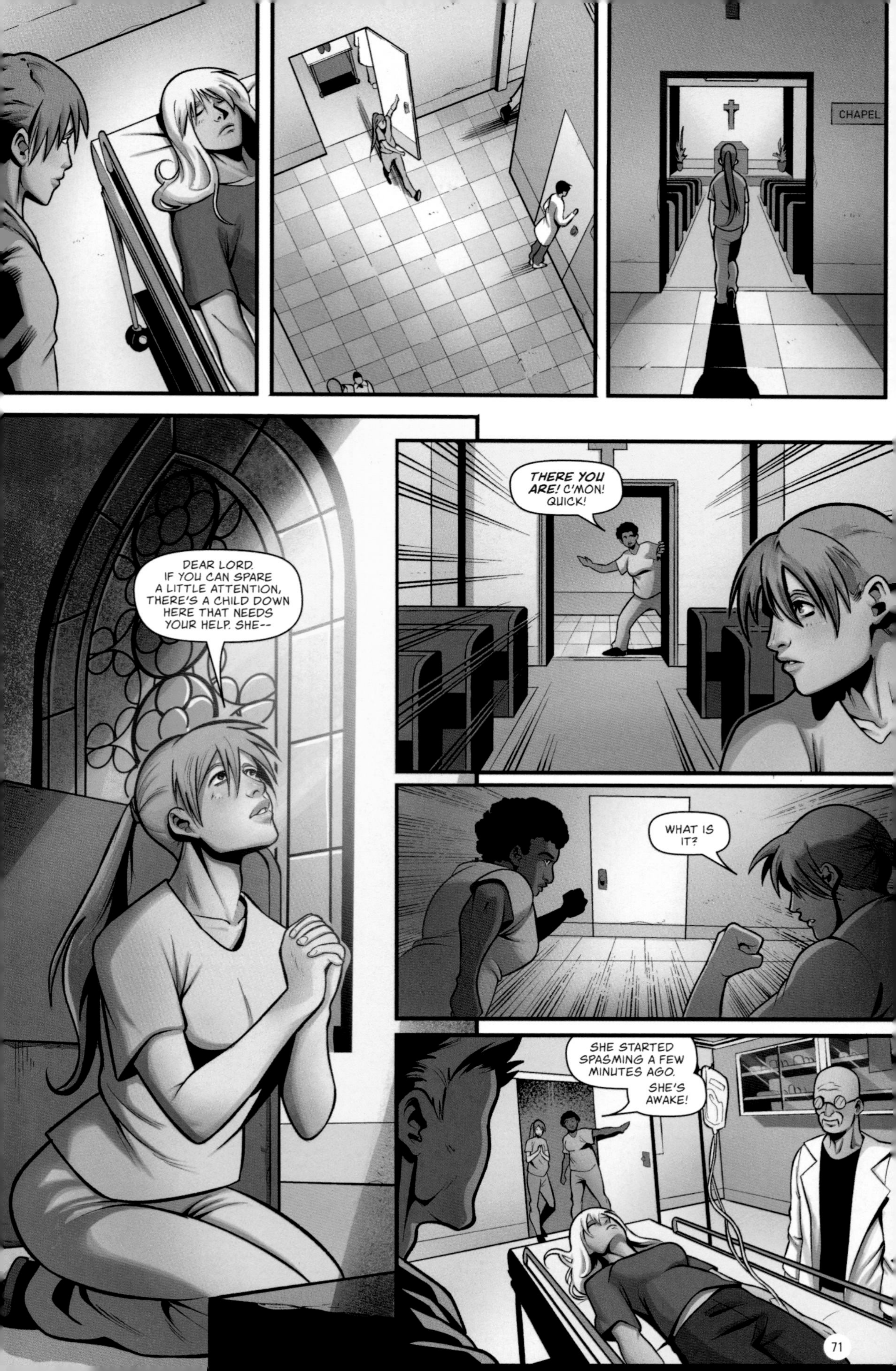
CHAPEL
DEAR LORD. IF YOU CAN SPARE A LITTLE ATTENTION, THERE'S A CHILD DOWN HERE THAT NEEDS YOUR HELP. SHE--
THERE YOU ARE! C'MON! QUICK!
WHAT IS IT?
SHE STARTED SPASMING A FEW MINUTES AGO.
SHE'S AWAKE!

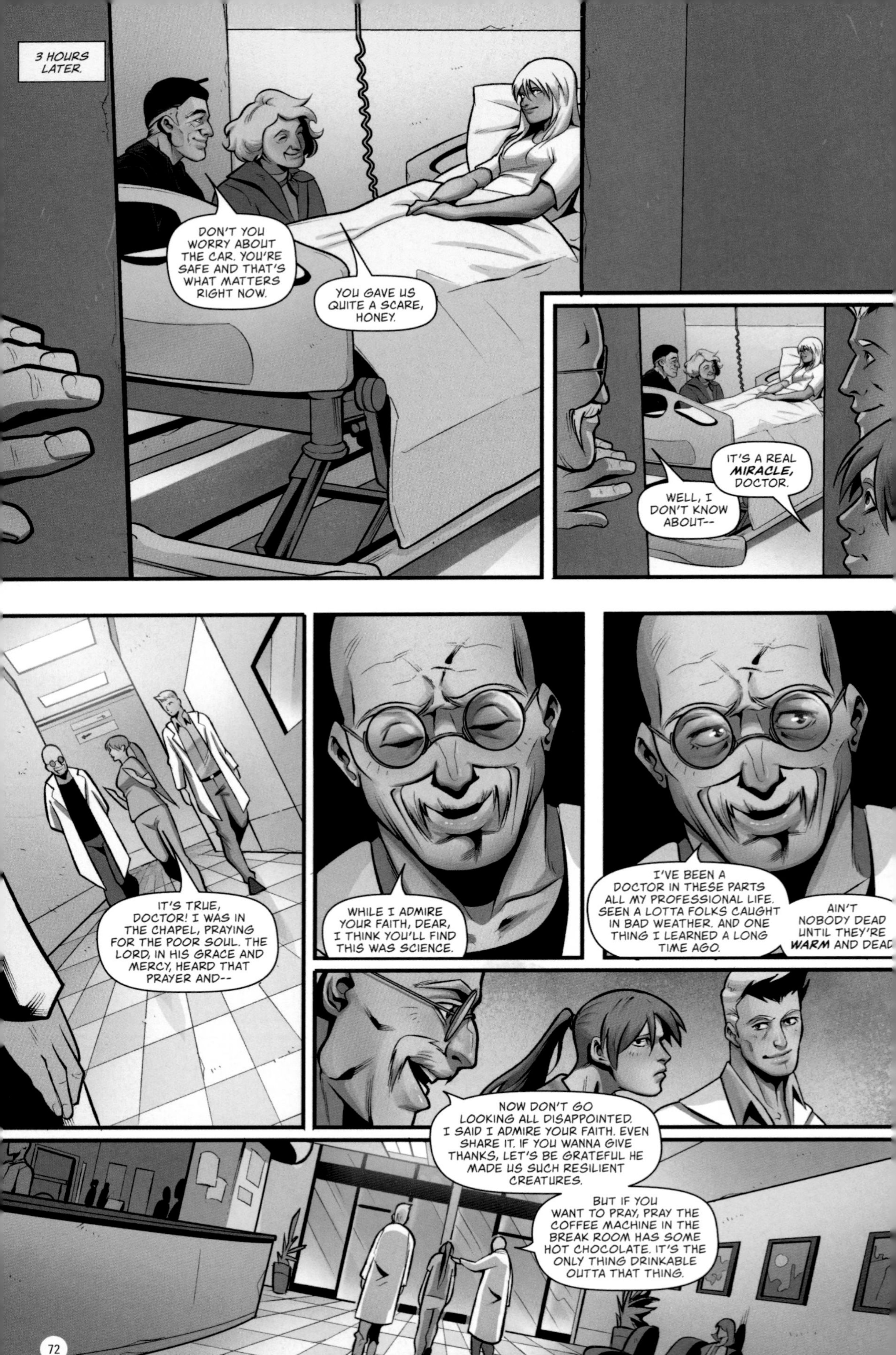
3 HOURS LATER.
DON'T YOU WORRY ABOUT THE CAR. YOU'RE SAFE AND THAT'S WHAT MATTERS RIGHT NOW.
YOU GAVE US QUITE A SCARE, HONEY.
IT'S A REAL MIRACLE, DOCTOR.
WELL, I DON'T KNOW ABOUT--
IT'S TRUE, DOCTOR! I WAS IN THE CHAPEL, PRAYING FOR THE POOR SOUL. THE LORD, IN HIS GRACE AND MERCY, HEARD THAT PRAYER AND--
WHILE I ADMIRE YOUR FAITH, DEAR, I THINK YOU'LL FIND THIS WAS SCIENCE.
I'VE BEEN A DOCTOR IN THESE PARTS ALL MY PROFESSIONAL LIFE. SEEN A LOTTA FOLKS CAUGHT IN BAD WEATHER. AND ONE THING I LEARNED A LONG TIME AGO.
AIN'T NOBODY DEAD UNTIL THEY'RE WARM AND DEAD
NOW DON'T GO LOOKING ALL DISAPPOINTED. I SAID I ADMIRE YOUR FAITH. EVEN SHARE IT. IF YOU WANNA GIVE THANKS, LET'S BE GRATEFUL HE MADE US SUCH RESILIENT CREATURES.
BUT IF YOU WANT TO PRAY, PRAY THE COFFEE MACHINE IN THE BREAK ROOM HAS SOME HOT CHOCOLATE. IT'S THE ONLY THING DRINKABLE OUTTA THAT THING.

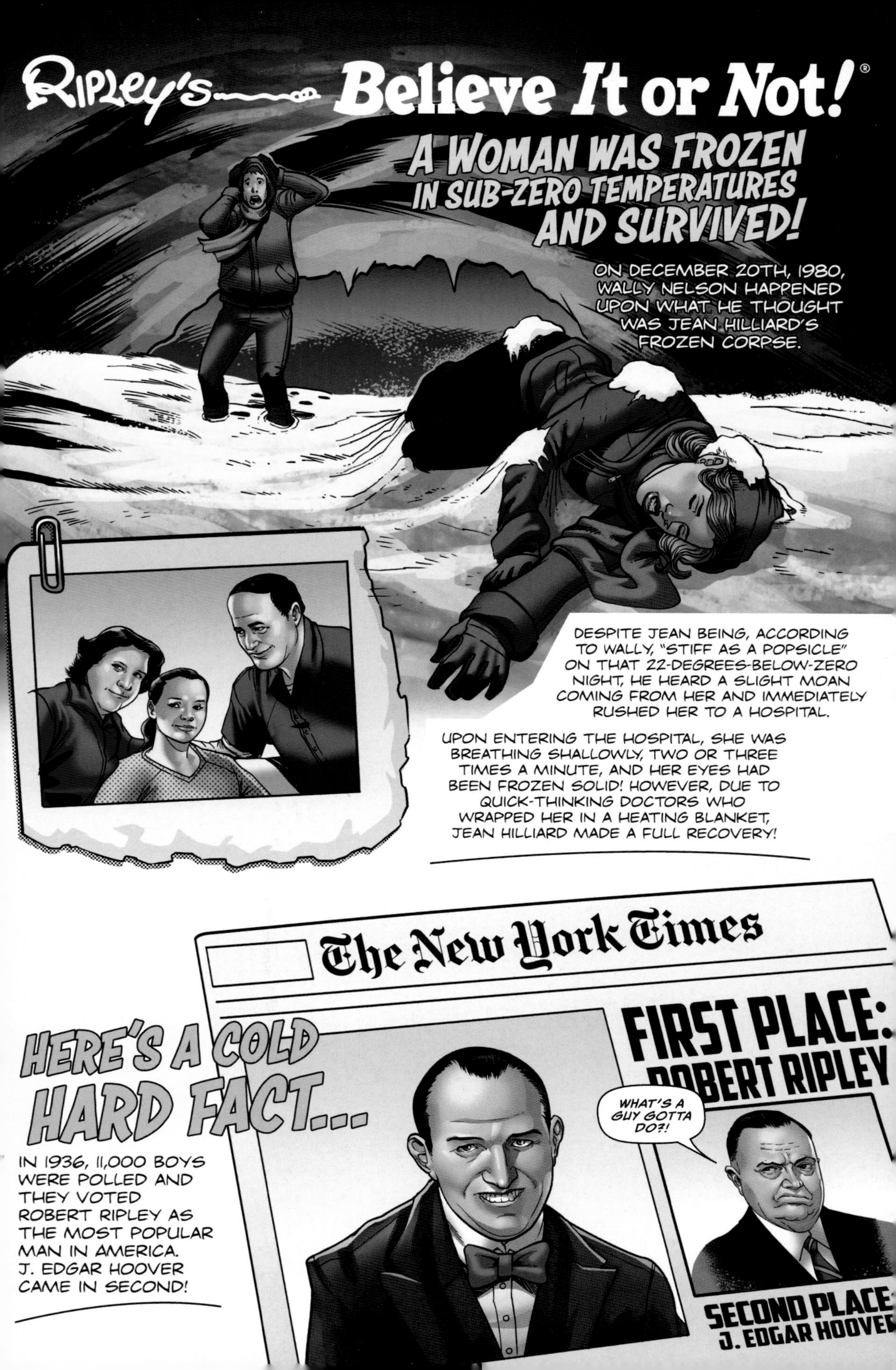
RIPLEY'S Believe It or Not!®
A WOMAN WAS FROZEN IN SUB-ZERO TEMPERATURES AND SURVIVED!
ON DECEMBER 20TH, 1980, WALLY NELSON HAPPENED UPON WHAT HE THOUGHT WAS JEAN HILLIARD'S FROZEN CORPSE.
DESPITE JEAN BEING, ACCORDING TO WALLY, "STIFF AS A POPSICLE" ON THAT 22-DEGREES-BELOW-ZERO NIGHT, HE HEARD A SLIGHT MOAN COMING FROM HER AND IMMEDIATELY RUSHED HER TO A HOSPITAL.
UPON ENTERING THE HOSPITAL, SHE WAS BREATHING SHALLOWLY, TWO OR THREE TIMES A MINUTE, AND HER EYES HAD BEEN FROZEN SOLID! HOWEVER, DUE TO QUICK-THINKING DOCTORS WHO WRAPPED HER IN A HEATING BLANKET, JEAN HILLIARD MADE A FULL RECOVERY!
HERE'S A COLD HARD FACT...
IN 1936, 11,000 BOYS WERE POLLED AND THEY VOTED ROBERT RIPLEY AS THE MOST POPULAR MAN IN AMERICA. J. EDGAR HOOVER CAME IN SECOND!
The New York Times
FIRST PLACE: ROBERT RIPLEY
WHAT'S A GUY GOTTA DO?!
SECOND PLACE: J. EDGAR HOOVER

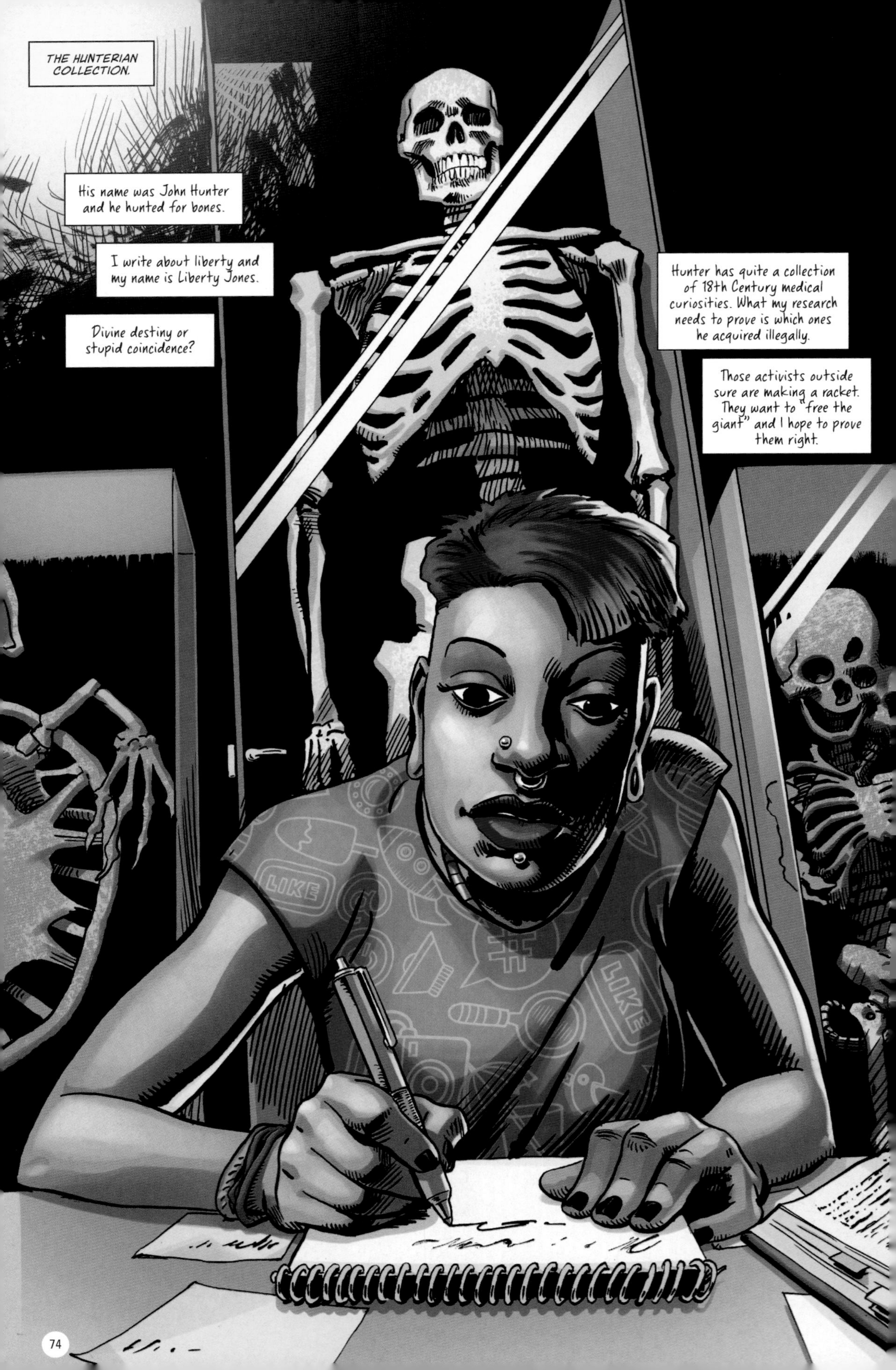
THE HUNTERIAN COLLECTION.
His name was John Hunter and he hunted for bones.
I write about liberty and my name is Liberty Jones.
Divine destiny or stupid coincidence?
Hunter has quite a collection of 18th Century medical curiosities. What my research needs to prove is which ones he acquired illegally.
Those activists outside sure are making a racket. They want to "free the giant" and I hope to prove them right.
LIKE
LIKE

SKITCH
SKITCH

Charles Byrne. The Irish Giant, celebrated and tragic.

Dr. Hunter was in such a rush to put you on display, he boiled the genetic secrets right out of your bones.

He missed the evidence in your skull. He could have discovered it was the pituitary gland that caused gigantism.

Mr. Smartypants Hunter blew it.

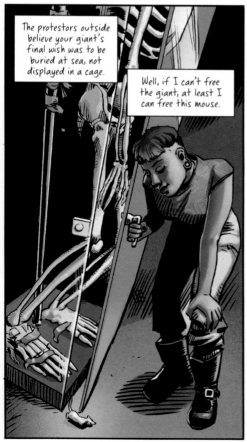

The protestors outside believe your giant's final wish was to be buried at sea, not displayed in a cage.

Well, if I can't free the giant, at least I can free this mouse.

WHOOPS!

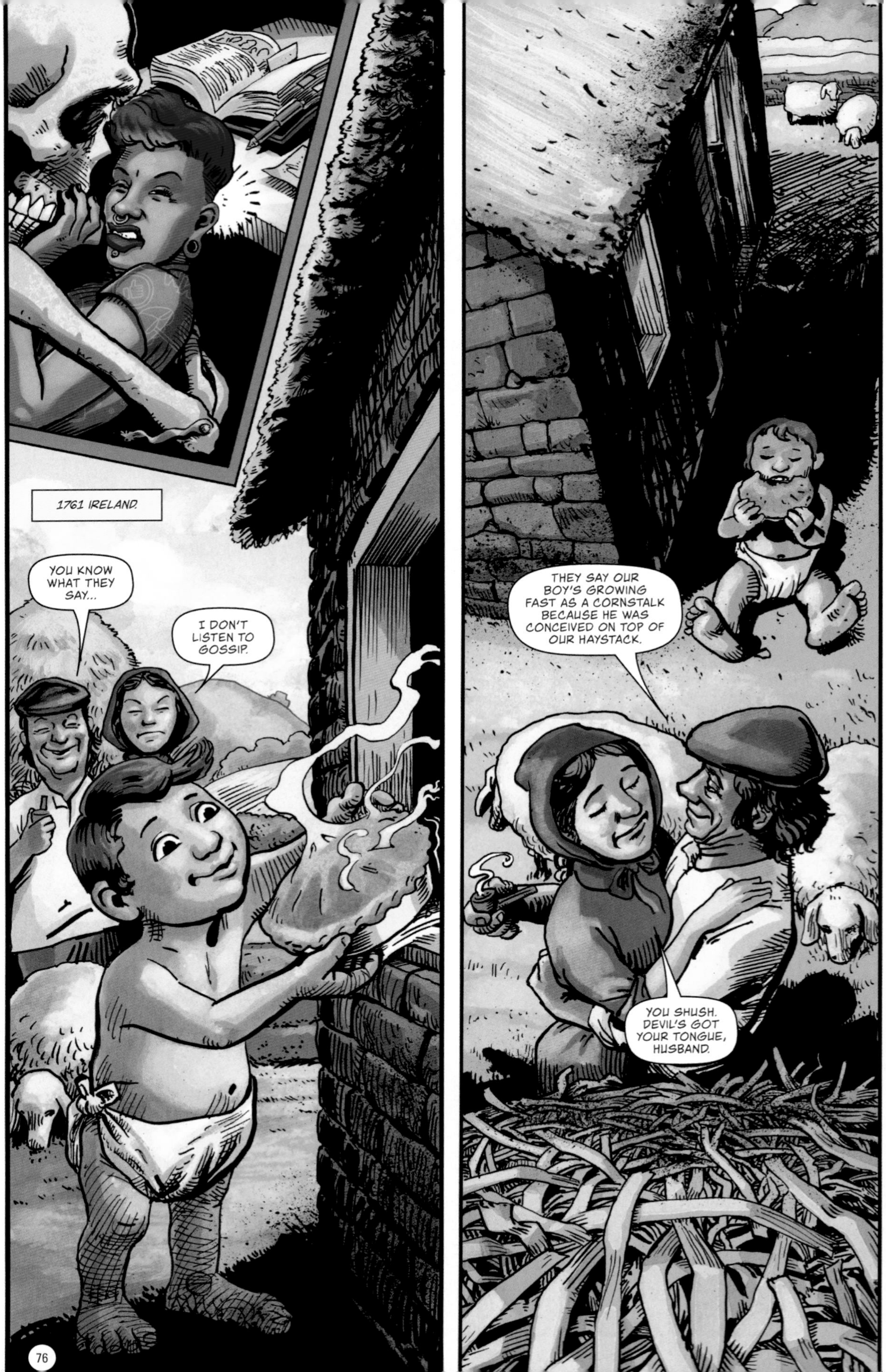
1761 IRELAND.
YOU KNOW WHAT THEY SAY...
I DON'T LISTEN TO GOSSIP.
THEY SAY OUR BOY'S GROWING FAST AS A CORNSTALK BECAUSE HE WAS CONCEIVED ON TOP OF OUR HAYSTACK.
YOU SHUSH. DEVIL'S GOT YOUR TONGUE, HUSBAND.

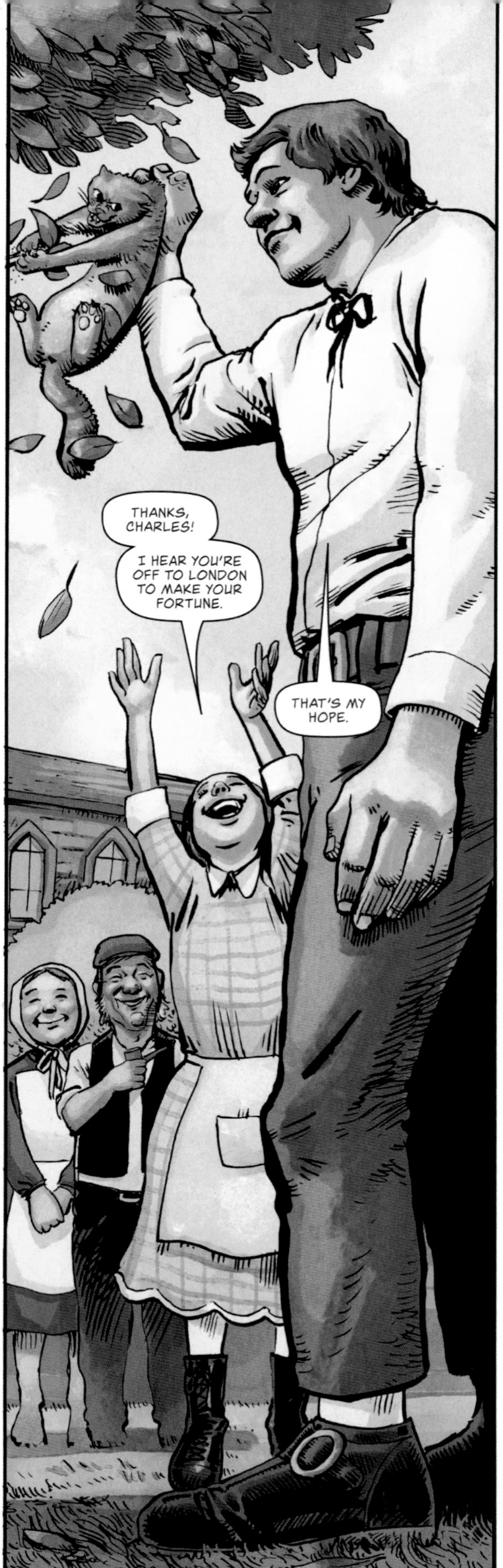
THANKS, CHARLES!
I HEAR YOU'RE OFF TO LONDON TO MAKE YOUR FORTUNE.
THAT'S MY HOPE.

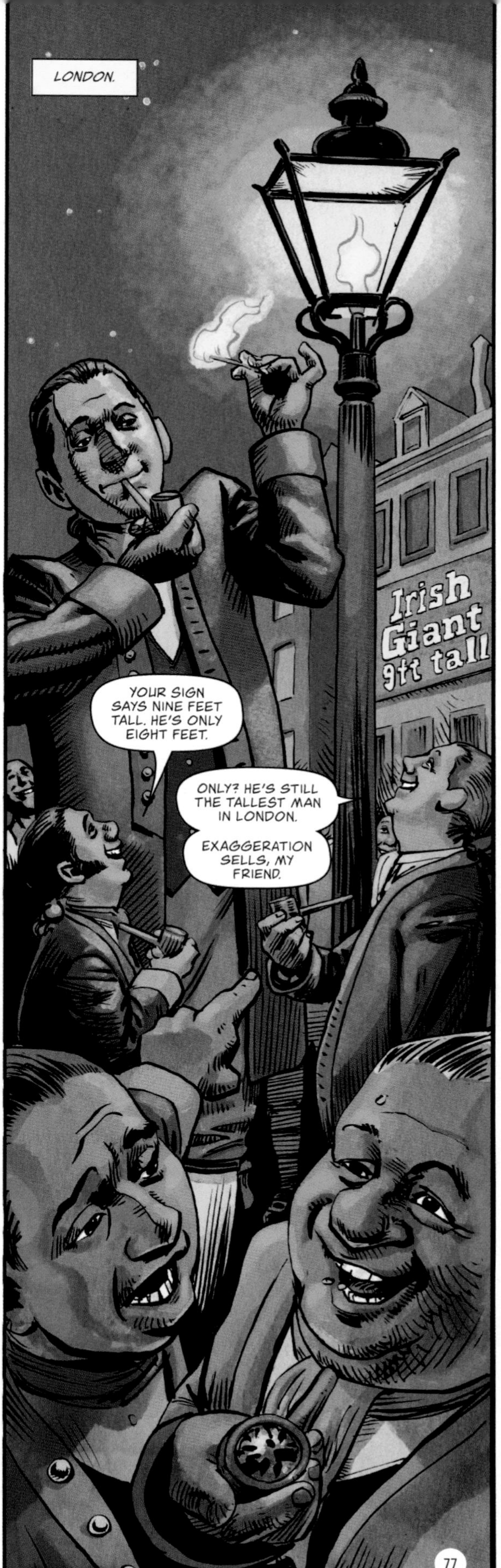
LONDON.
Irish Giant 9ft tall
YOUR SIGN SAYS NINE FEET TALL. HE'S ONLY EIGHT FEET.
ONLY? HE'S STILL THE TALLEST MAN IN LONDON.
EXAGGERATION SELLS, MY FRIEND.

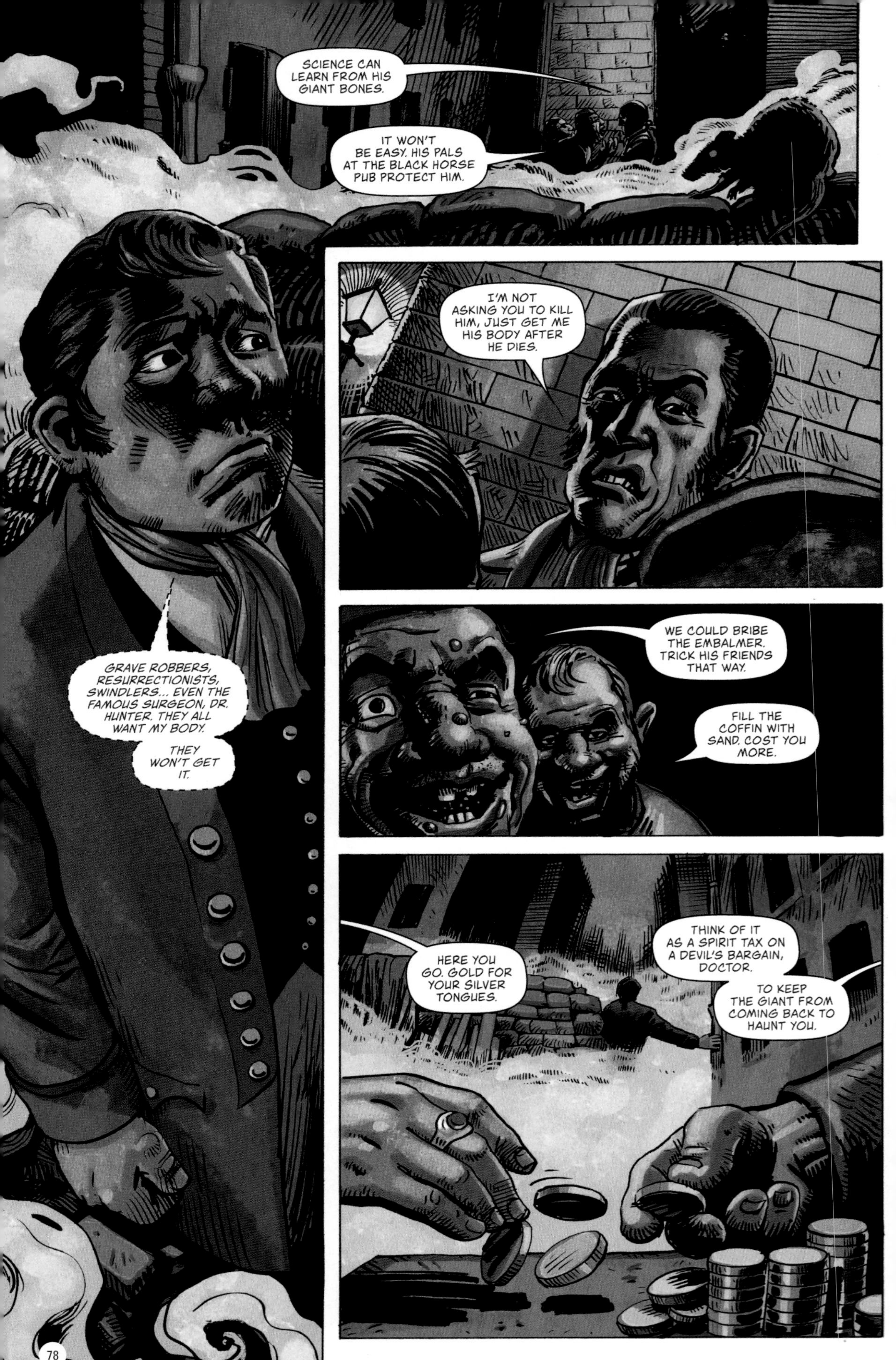
SCIENCE CAN LEARN FROM HIS GIANT BONES.
IT WON'T BE EASY. HIS PALS AT THE BLACK HORSE PUB PROTECT HIM.
I'M NOT ASKING YOU TO KILL HIM, JUST GET ME HIS BODY AFTER HE DIES.
GRAVE ROBBERS, RESURRECTIONISTS, SWINDLERS... EVEN THE FAMOUS SURGEON, DR. HUNTER. THEY ALL WANT MY BODY.
THEY WON'T GET IT.
WE COULD BRIBE THE EMBALMER. TRICK HIS FRIENDS THAT WAY.
FILL THE COFFIN WITH SAND. COST YOU MORE.
HERE YOU GO. GOLD FOR YOUR SILVER TONGUES.
THINK OF IT AS A SPIRIT TAX ON A DEVIL'S BARGAIN, DOCTOR.
TO KEEP THE GIANT FROM COMING BACK TO HAUNT YOU.

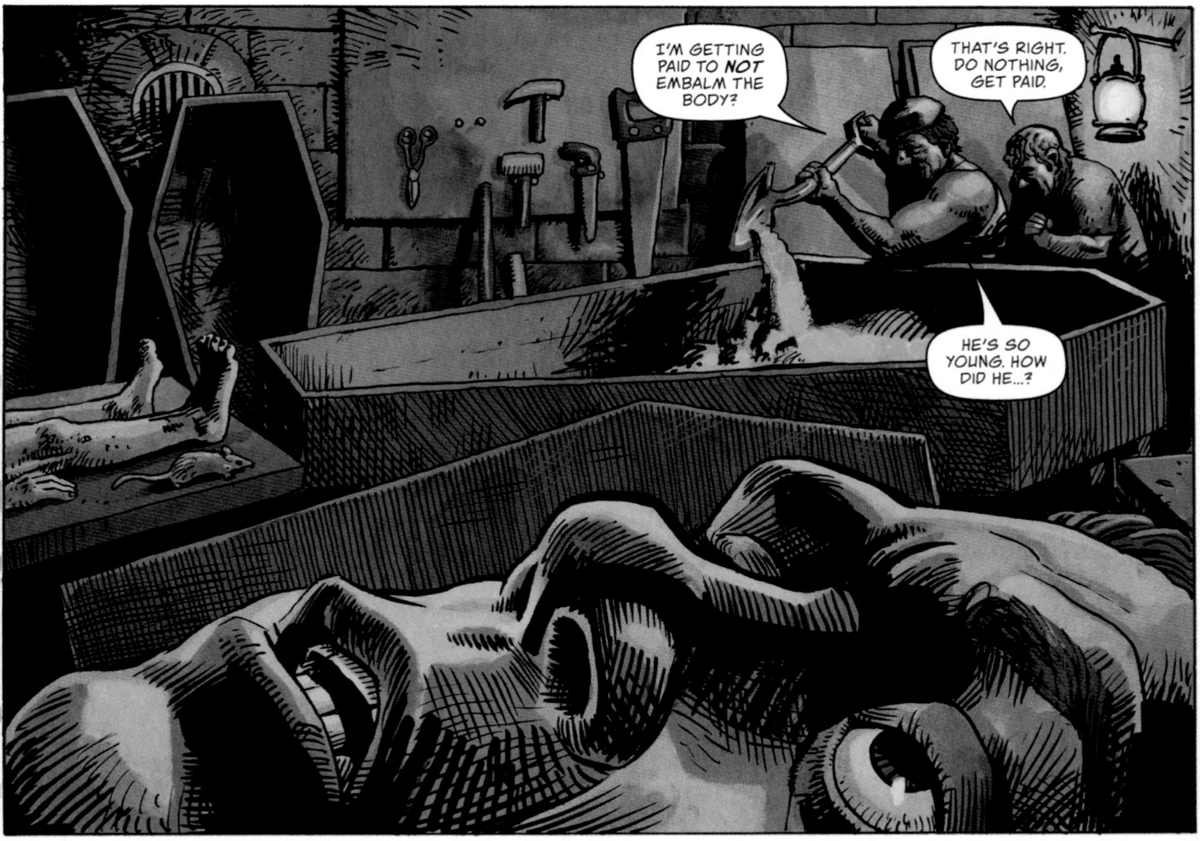
I'M GETTING PAID TO NOT EMBALM THE BODY?
THAT'S RIGHT. DO NOTHING, GET PAID.
HE'S SO YOUNG. HOW DID HE...?

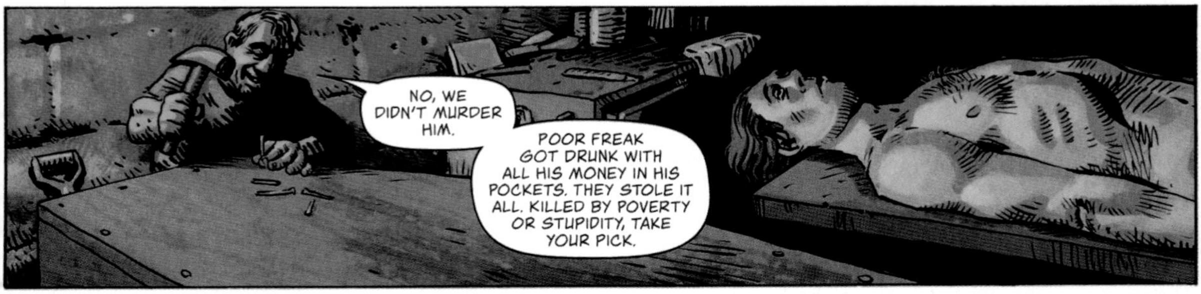
NO, WE DIDN'T MURDER HIM.
POOR FREAK GOT DRUNK WITH ALL HIS MONEY IN HIS POCKETS. THEY STOLE IT ALL. KILLED BY POVERTY OR STUPIDITY, TAKE YOUR PICK.

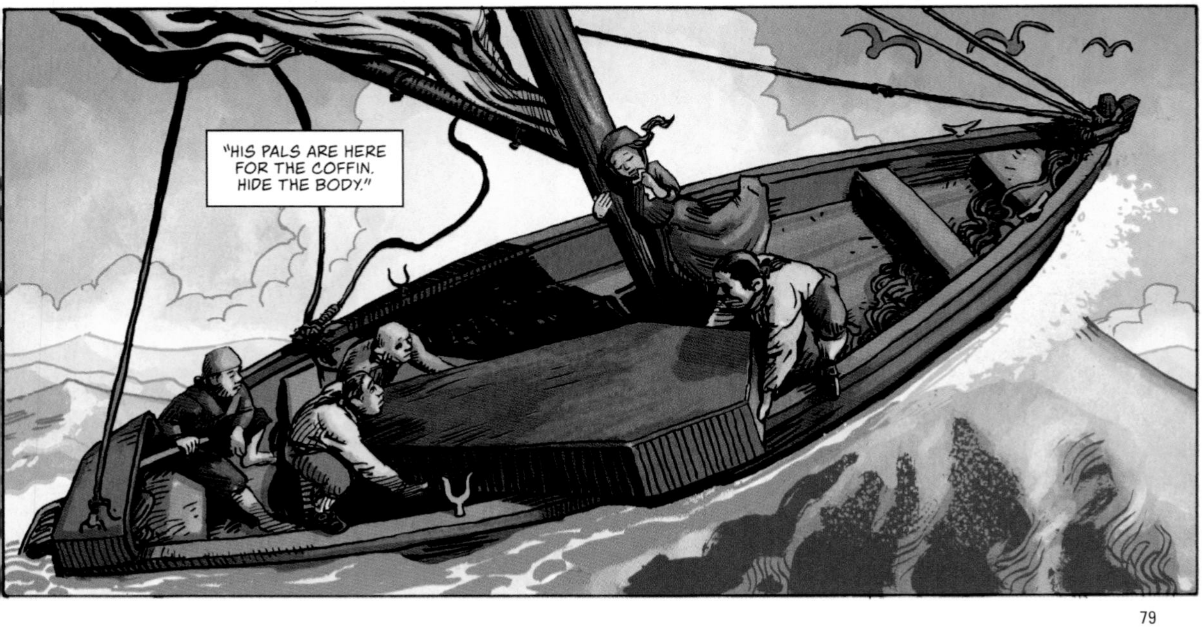
"HIS PALS ARE HERE FOR THE COFFIN. HIDE THE BODY."

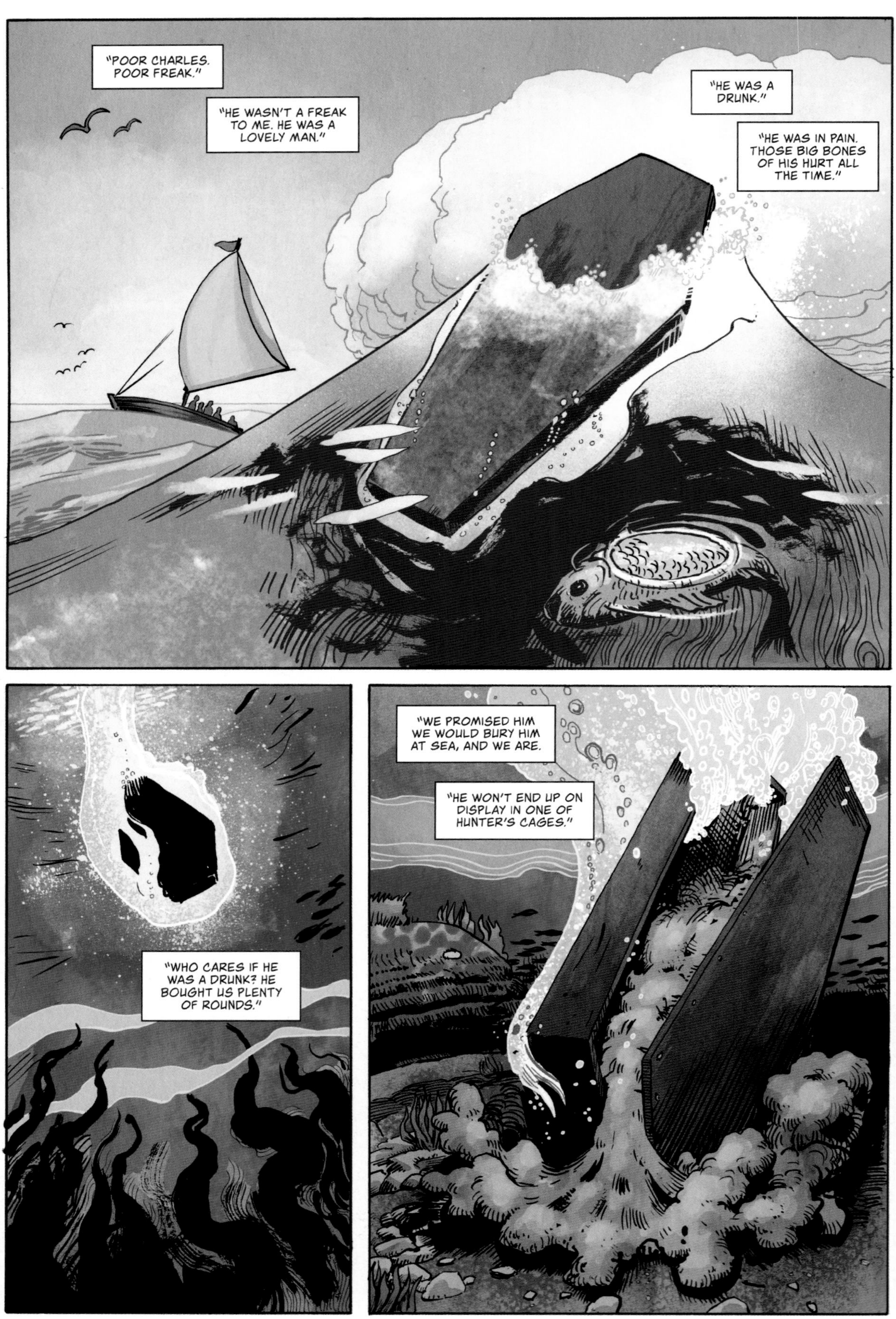
"POOR CHARLES. POOR FREAK."
"HE WASN'T A FREAK TO ME. HE WAS A LOVELY MAN."
"HE WAS A DRUNK."
"HE WAS IN PAIN. THOSE BIG BONES OF HIS HURT ALL THE TIME."
"WHO CARES IF HE WAS A DRUNK? HE BOUGHT US PLENTY OF ROUNDS."
"WE PROMISED HIM WE WOULD BURY HIM AT SEA, AND WE ARE.
"HE WON'T END UP ON DISPLAY IN ONE OF HUNTER'S CAGES."

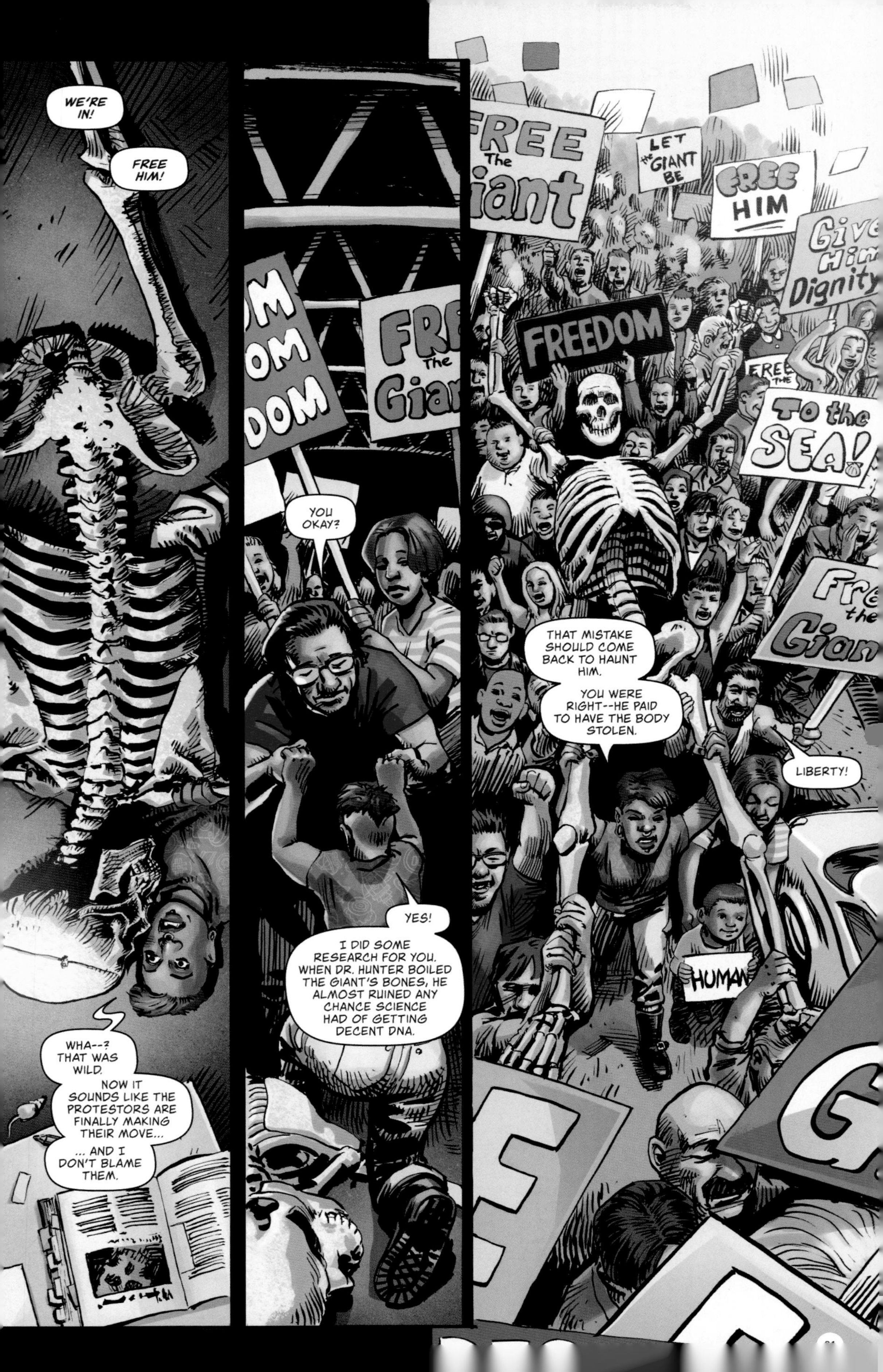

WE'RE IN!
FREE HIM!
WHA--? THAT WAS WILD.
NOW IT SOUNDS LIKE THE PROTESTORS ARE FINALLY MAKING THEIR MOVE...
... AND I DON'T BLAME THEM.
YOU OKAY?
YES!
I DID SOME RESEARCH FOR YOU. WHEN DR. HUNTER BOILED THE GIANT'S BONES, HE ALMOST RUINED ANY CHANCE SCIENCE HAD OF GETTING DECENT DNA.
LET THE GIANT BE
FREE HIM
Give Him Dignity
FREEDOM
To the SEA!
THAT MISTAKE SHOULD COME BACK TO HAUNT HIM.
YOU WERE RIGHT--HE PAID TO HAVE THE BODY STOLEN.
LIBERTY!

Ripley's Believe It or Not!®

THE IRISH GIANT!

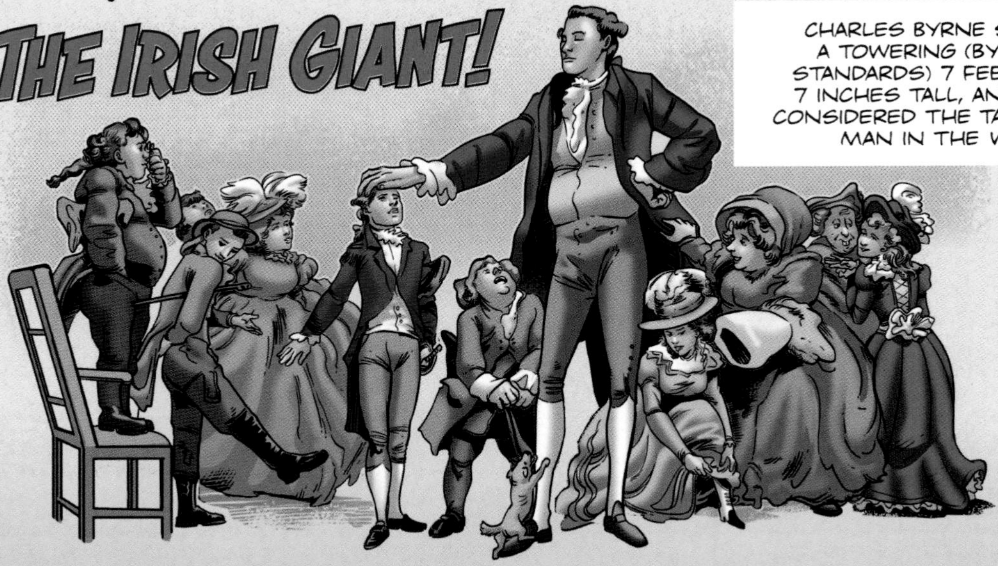

CHARLES BYRNE STOOD A TOWERING (BY 1780S STANDARDS) 7 FEET AND 7 INCHES TALL, AND WAS CONSIDERED THE TALLEST MAN IN THE WORLD!

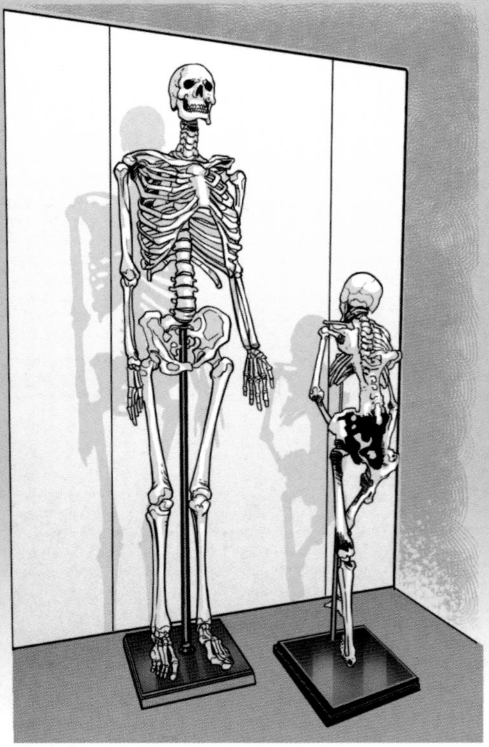

WHILE HIS PARENTS DID INDEED ATTRIBUTE HIS STATURE TO HIS CONCEPTION ATOP A HAYSTACK, IN ACTUALITY HIS SIZE WAS DUE TO A TUMOR IN HIS PITUITARY GLAND.

WHILE DEBATES CONTINUE TO THIS DAY AS TO WHETHER OR NOT CHARLES BYRNE'S REMAINS SHOULD BE BURIED AT SEA, HIS SKELETON STAYS ON DISPLAY AT THE HUNTERIAN MUSEUM IN ENGLAND. HOWEVER, HIS FINAL WISHES MAY BE CLOSE TO BECOMING A REALITY, SINCE SCIENTISTS HAVE FULLY SEQUENCED HIS D.N.A. AND POSSESS THE MEANS TO BUILD AN EXACT REPLICA OF HIS SKELETON!

FROM BIG TO SMALL!

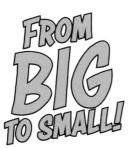

ROBERT RIPLEY WAS AT ONE POINT IN POSSESSION OF A 6.5-INCH MUMMIFIED BABY, DUBBED "ATTA-BOY." WHILE PHOTOGRAPHIC EVIDENCE PROVES ATTA-BOY'S EXISTENCE, THE SPECIMEN ITSELF HAS BEEN LOST FOR DECADES. ATTA-BOY IS CONSIDERED BY SOME TO BE "THE LOST HOLY GRAIL OF RIPLEY'S COLLECTION."

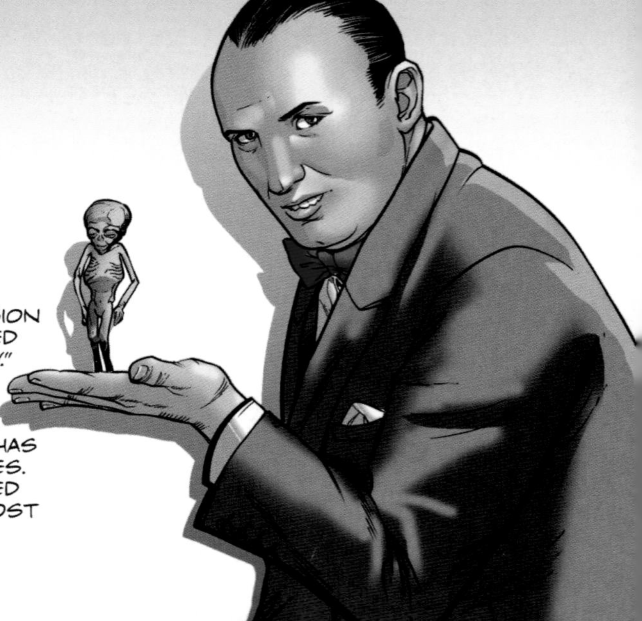

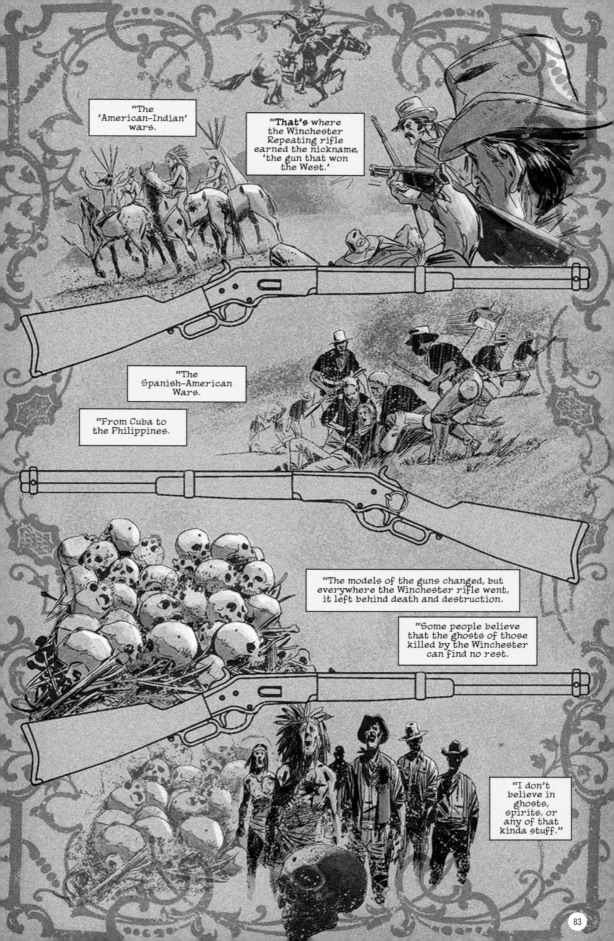

"The 'American-Indian' wars.

"**That's** where the Winchester Repeating rifle earned the nickname, 'the gun that won the West.'

"The Spanish-American Wars.

"From Cuba to the Philippines.

"The models of the guns changed, but everywhere the Winchester rifle went, it left behind death and destruction.

"Some people believe that the ghosts of those killed by the Winchester can find no rest.

"I don't believe in ghosts, spirits, or any of that kinda stuff."

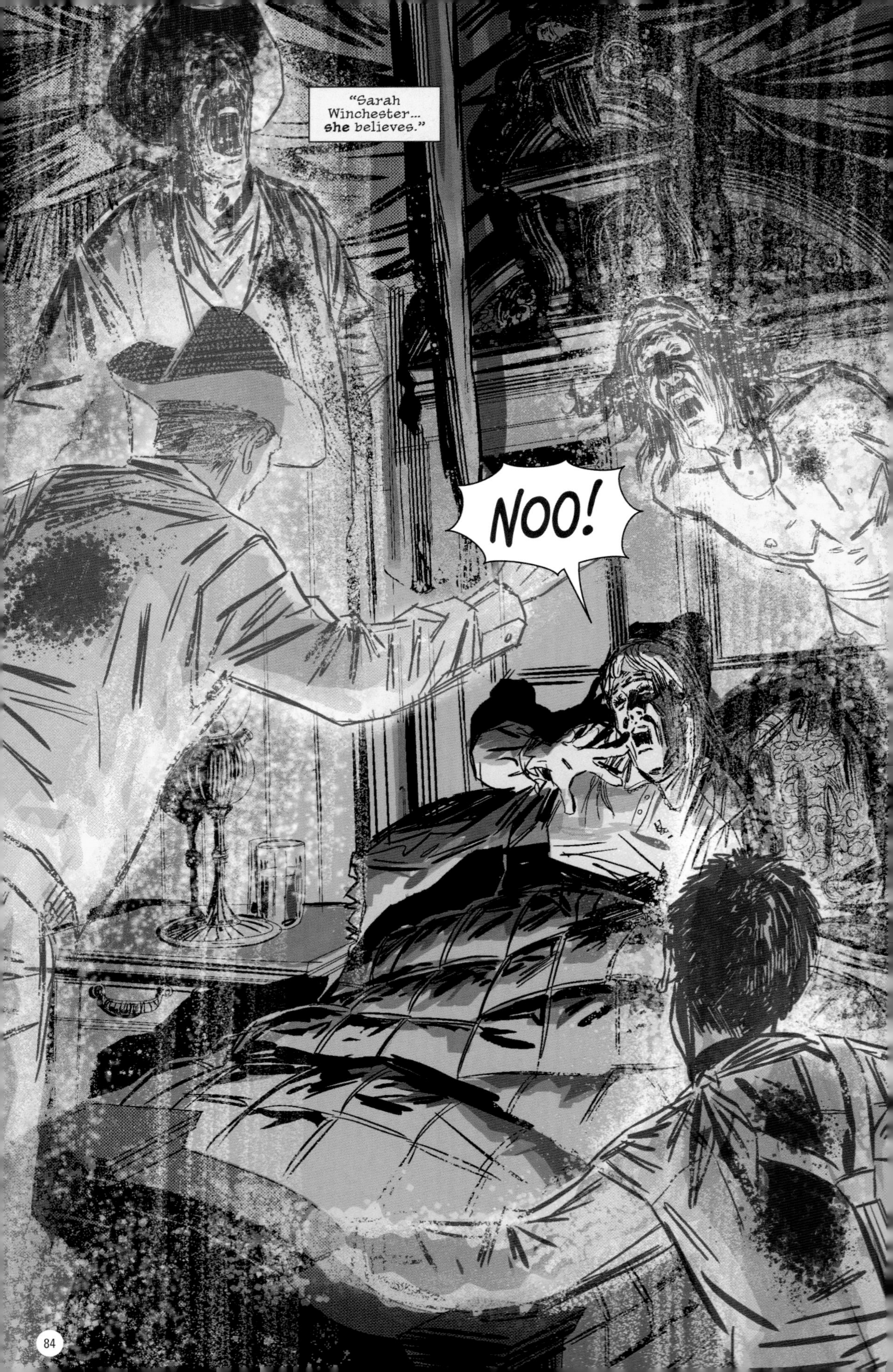
"Sarah Winchester... **she** believes."
NOO!

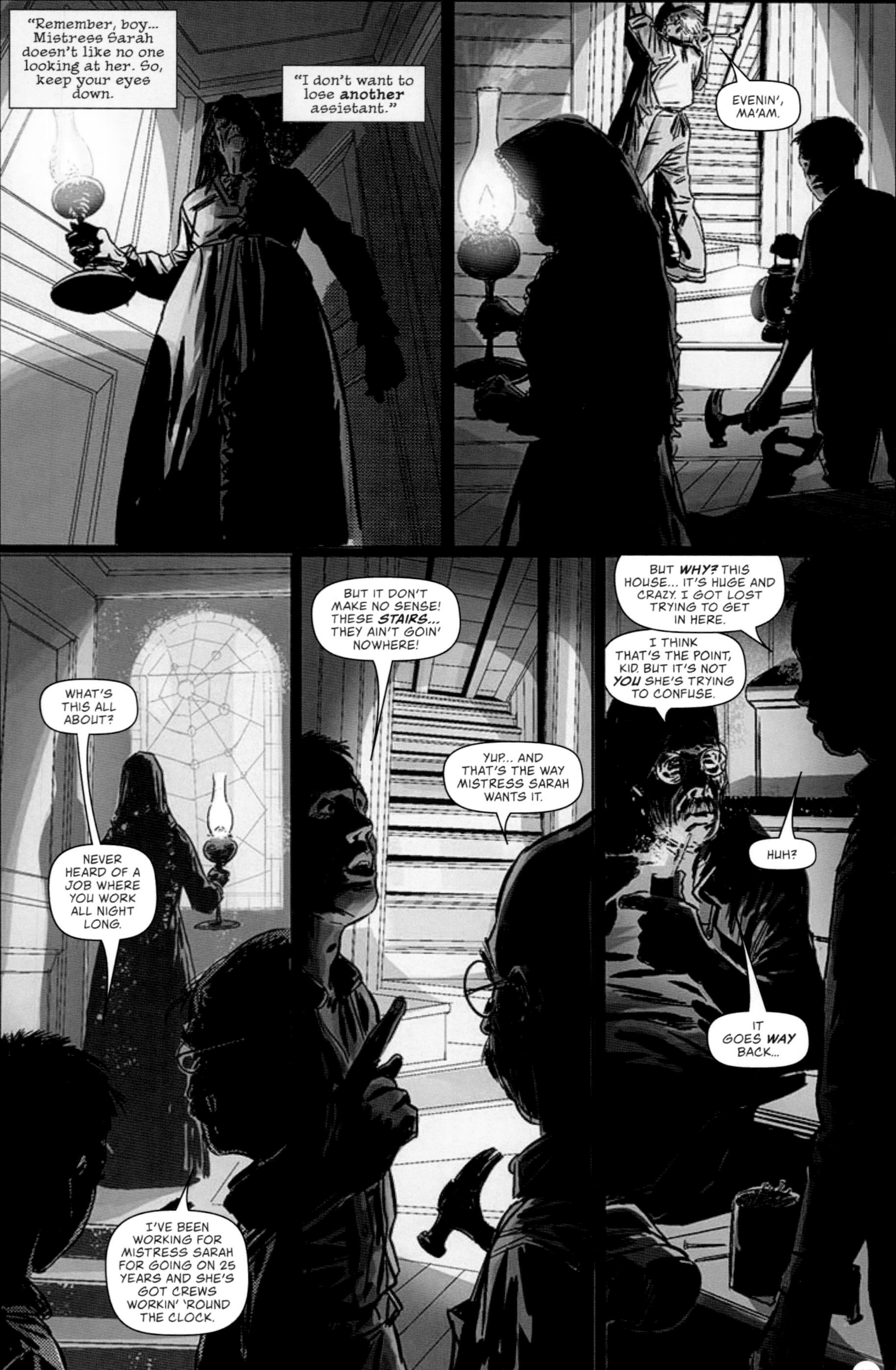
"Remember, boy... Mistress Sarah doesn't like no one looking at her. So, keep your eyes down.
"I don't want to lose **another** assistant."
EVENIN', MA'AM.
WHAT'S THIS ALL ABOUT?
NEVER HEARD OF A JOB WHERE YOU WORK ALL NIGHT LONG.
I'VE BEEN WORKING FOR MISTRESS SARAH FOR GOING ON 25 YEARS AND SHE'S GOT CREWS WORKIN' 'ROUND THE CLOCK.
BUT IT DON'T MAKE NO SENSE! THESE ***STAIRS...*** THEY AIN'T GOIN' NOWHERE!
YUP... AND THAT'S THE WAY MISTRESS SARAH WANTS IT.
BUT ***WHY?*** THIS HOUSE... IT'S HUGE AND CRAZY. I GOT LOST TRYING TO GET IN HERE.
I THINK THAT'S THE POINT, KID. BUT IT'S NOT ***YOU*** SHE'S TRYING TO CONFUSE.
HUH?
IT GOES ***WAY*** BACK...

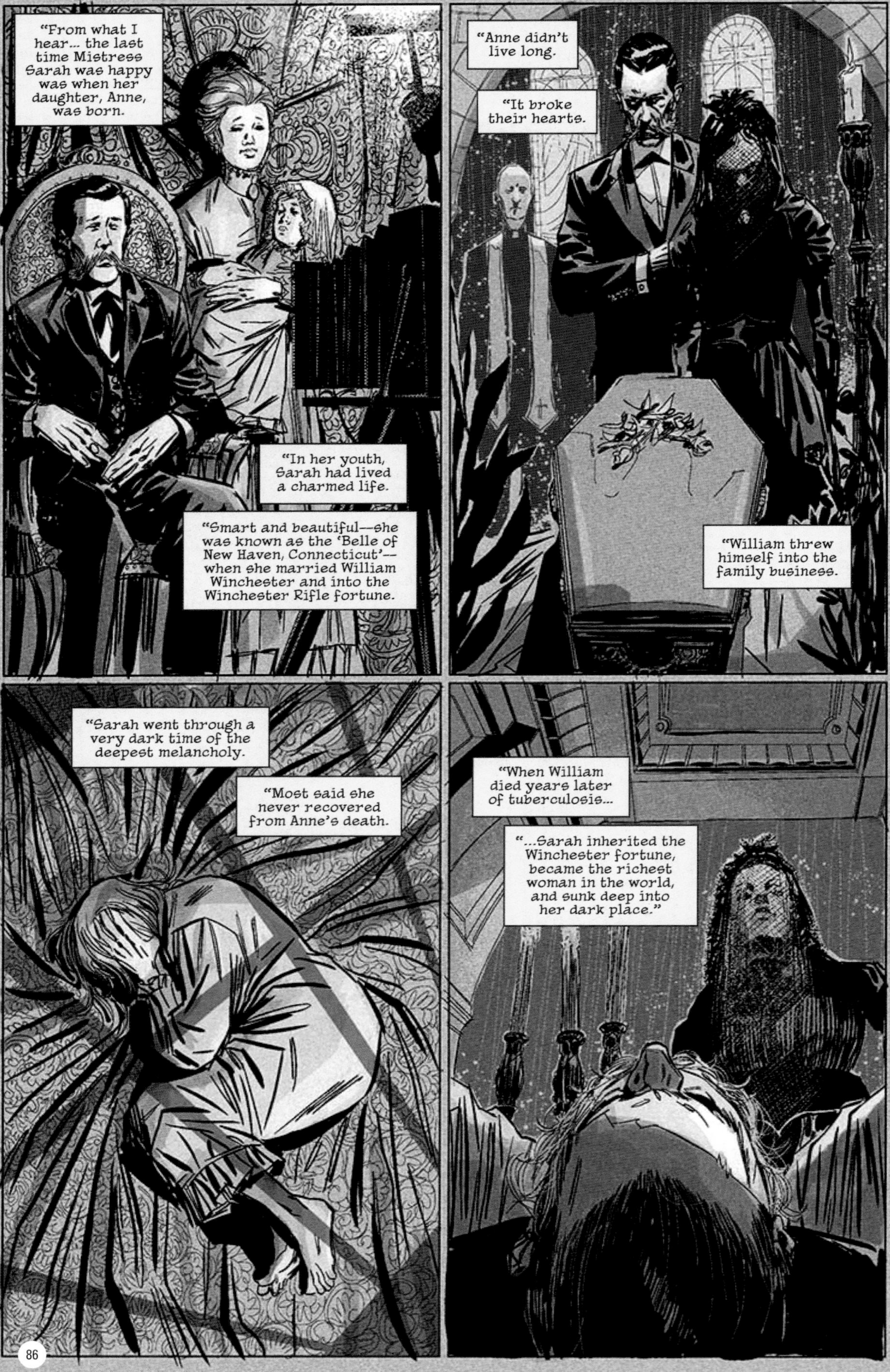
"From what I hear... the last time Mistress Sarah was happy was when her daughter, Anne, was born.
"In her youth, Sarah had lived a charmed life.
"Smart and beautiful—she was known as the 'Belle of New Haven, Connecticut'—when she married William Winchester and into the Winchester Rifle fortune.
"Anne didn't live long.
"It broke their hearts.
"William threw himself into the family business.
"Sarah went through a very dark time of the deepest melancholy.
"Most said she never recovered from Anne's death.
"When William died years later of tuberculosis...
"...Sarah inherited the Winchester fortune, became the richest woman in the world, and sunk deep into her dark place."

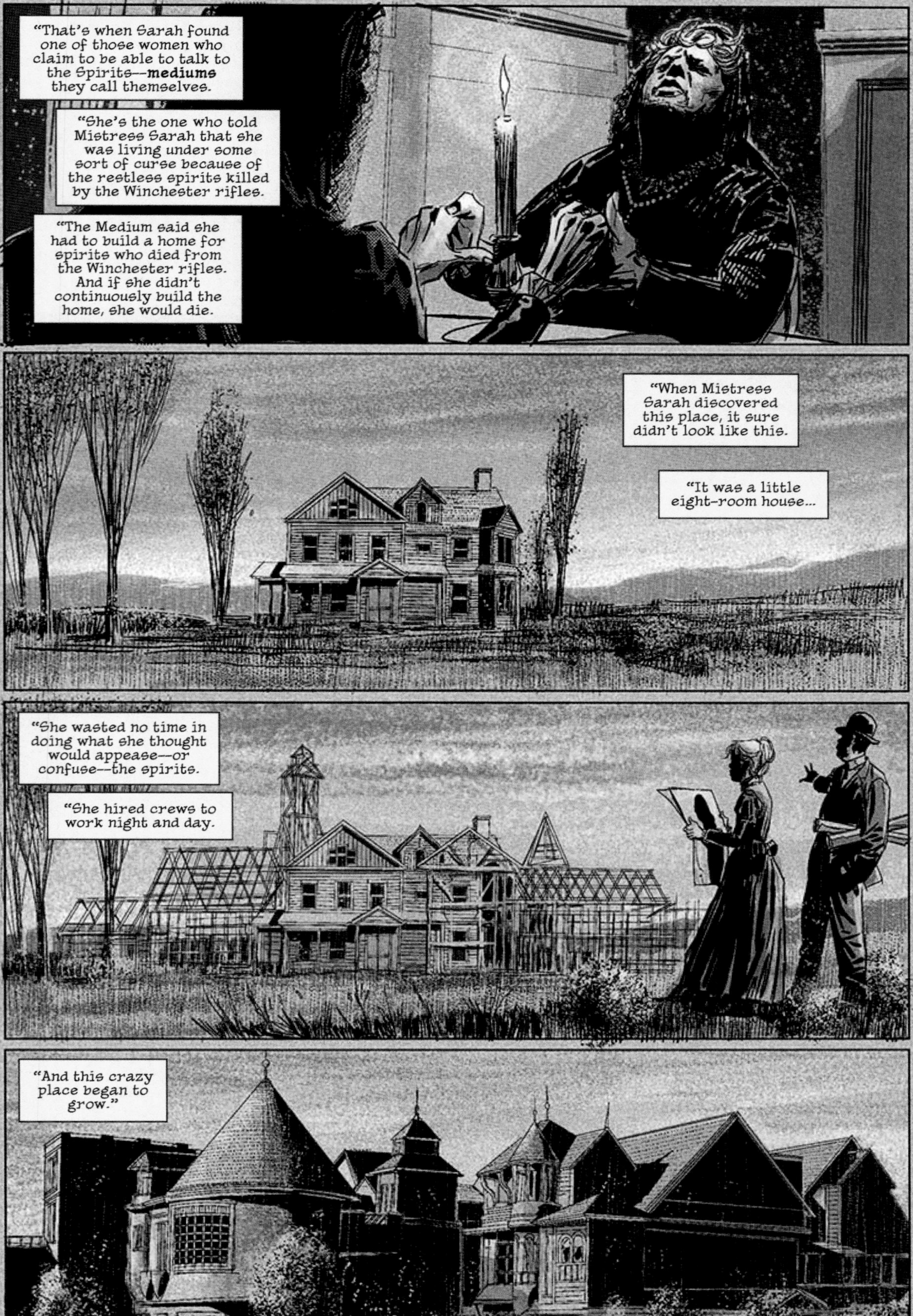
"That's when Sarah found one of those women who claim to be able to talk to the Spirits--**mediums** they call themselves.
"She's the one who told Mistress Sarah that she was living under some sort of curse because of the restless spirits killed by the Winchester rifles.
"The Medium said she had to build a home for spirits who died from the Winchester rifles. And if she didn't continuously build the home, she would die.
"When Mistress Sarah discovered this place, it sure didn't look like this.
"It was a little eight-room house...
"She wasted no time in doing what she thought would appease--or confuse--the spirits.
"She hired crews to work night and day.
"And this crazy place began to grow."

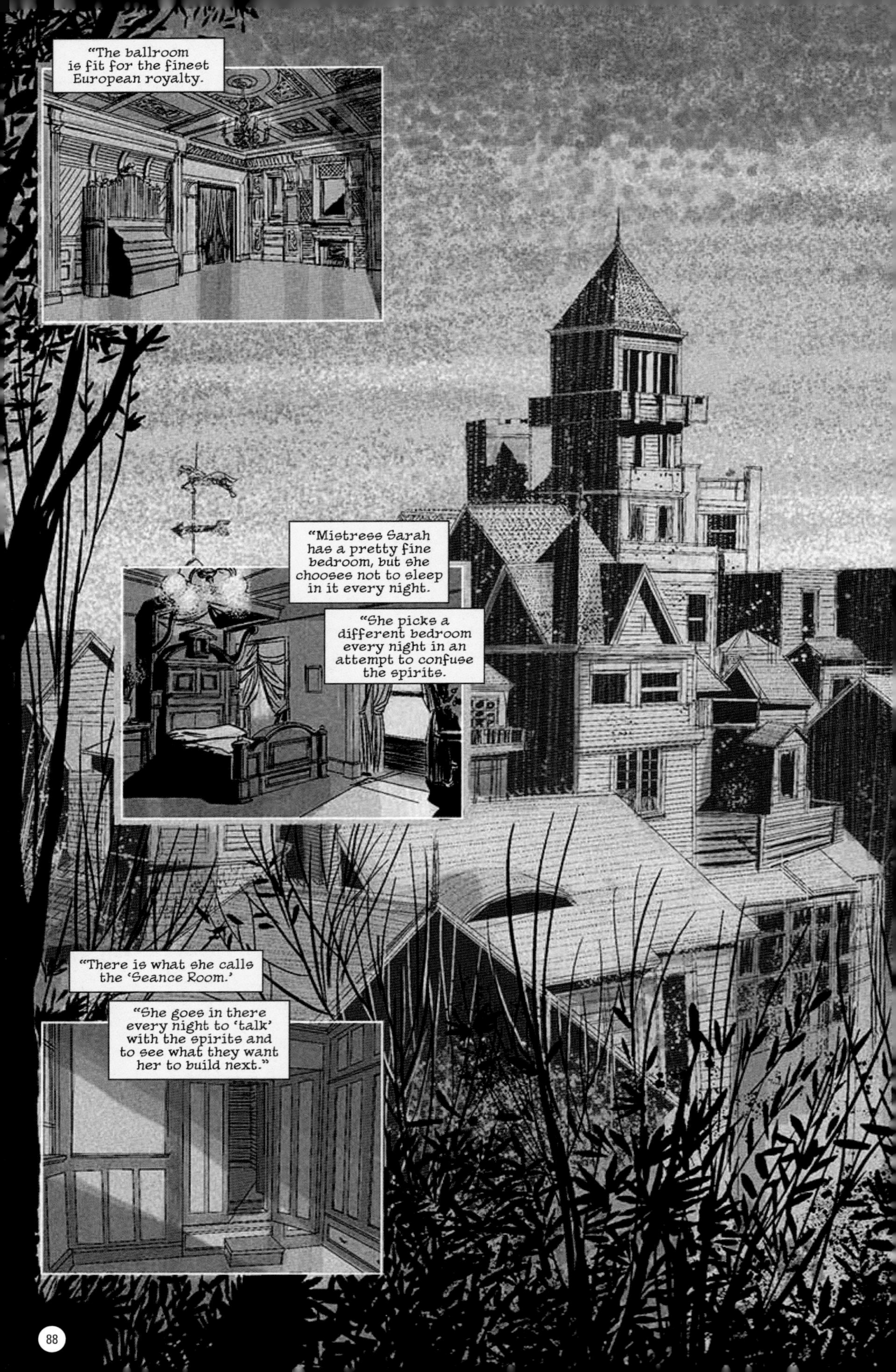
"The ballroom is fit for the finest European royalty.
"Mistress Sarah has a pretty fine bedroom, but she chooses not to sleep in it every night.
"She picks a different bedroom every night in an attempt to confuse the spirits.
"There is what she calls the 'Seance Room.'
"She goes in there every night to 'talk' with the spirits and to see what they want her to build next."

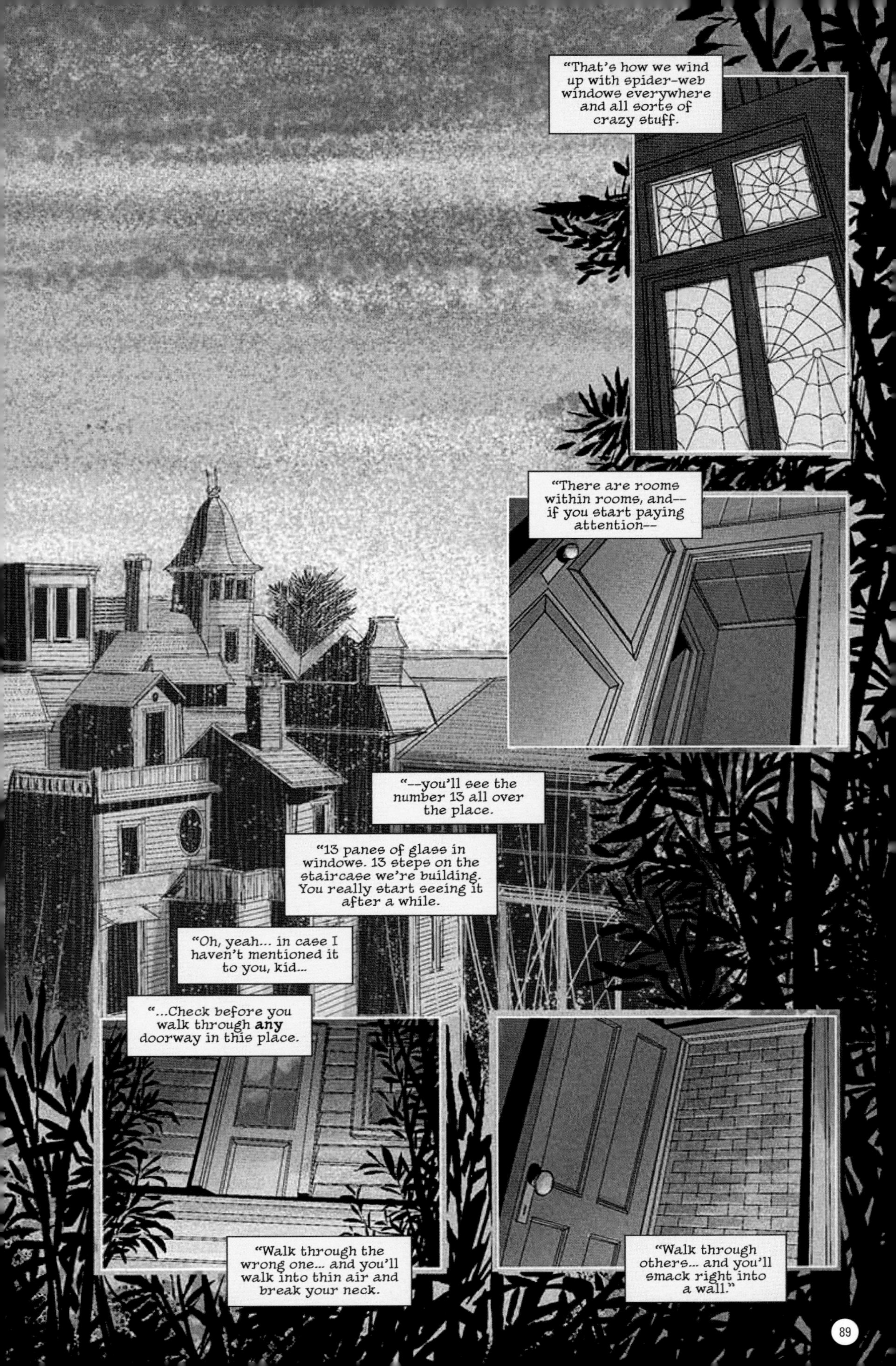
"That's how we wind up with spider-web windows everywhere and all sorts of crazy stuff.
"There are rooms within rooms, and-- if you start paying attention--
"--you'll see the number 13 all over the place.
"13 panes of glass in windows. 13 steps on the staircase we're building. You really start seeing it after a while.
"Oh, yeah... in case I haven't mentioned it to you, kid...
"...Check before you walk through **any** doorway in this place.
"Walk through the wrong one... and you'll walk into thin air and break your neck.
"Walk through others... and you'll smack right into a wall."

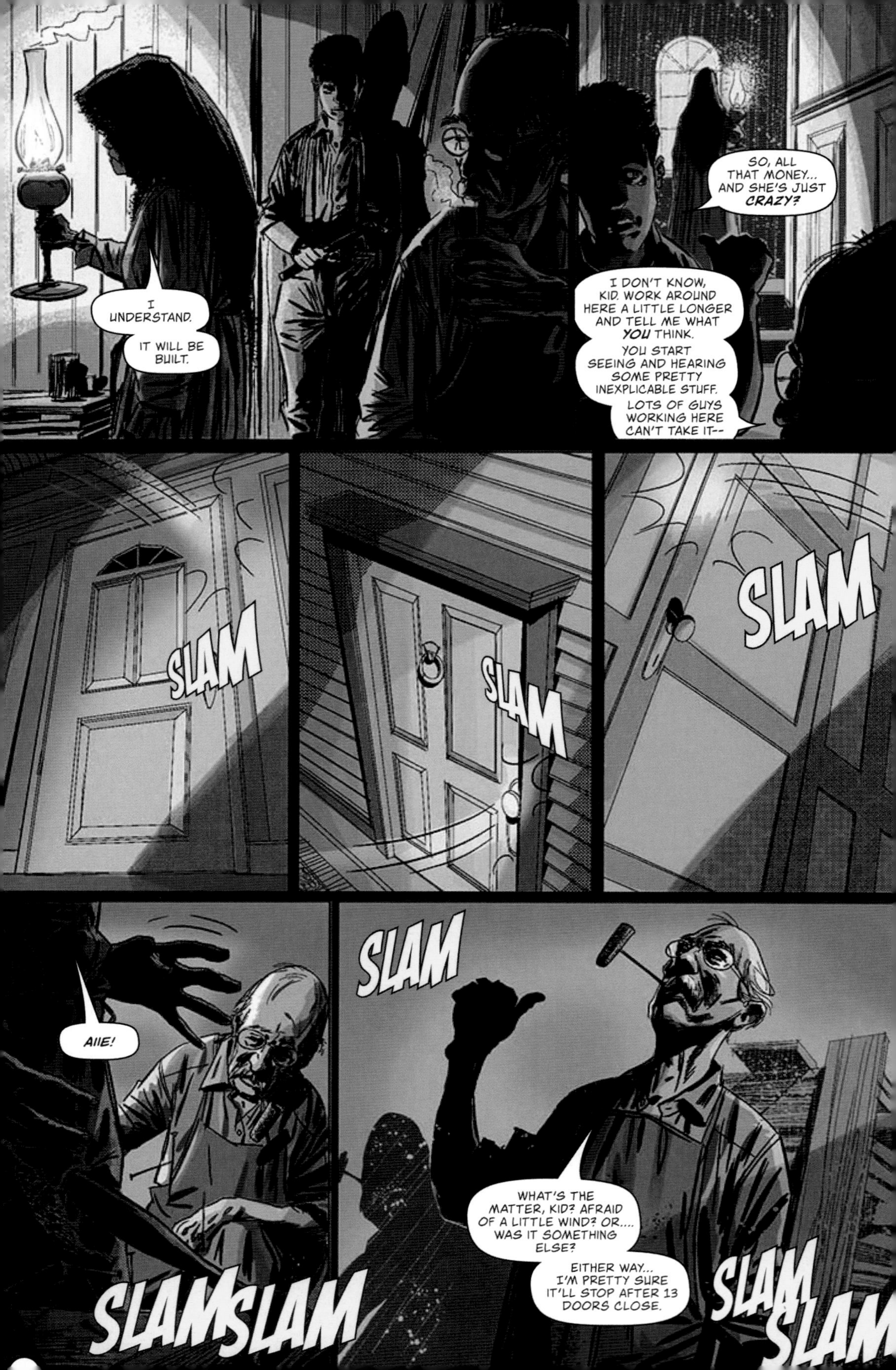
I UNDERSTAND.
IT WILL BE BUILT.
SO, ALL THAT MONEY... AND SHE'S JUST CRAZY?
I DON'T KNOW, KID. WORK AROUND HERE A LITTLE LONGER AND TELL ME WHAT YOU THINK.
YOU START SEEING AND HEARING SOME PRETTY INEXPLICABLE STUFF.
LOTS OF GUYS WORKING HERE CAN'T TAKE IT--
SLAM
SLAM
SLAM
AIIE!
SLAMSLAM
SLAM
WHAT'S THE MATTER, KID? AFRAID OF A LITTLE WIND? OR.... WAS IT SOMETHING ELSE?
EITHER WAY... I'M PRETTY SURE IT'LL STOP AFTER 13 DOORS CLOSE.
SLAM
SLAM

Ripley's Believe It or Not!®

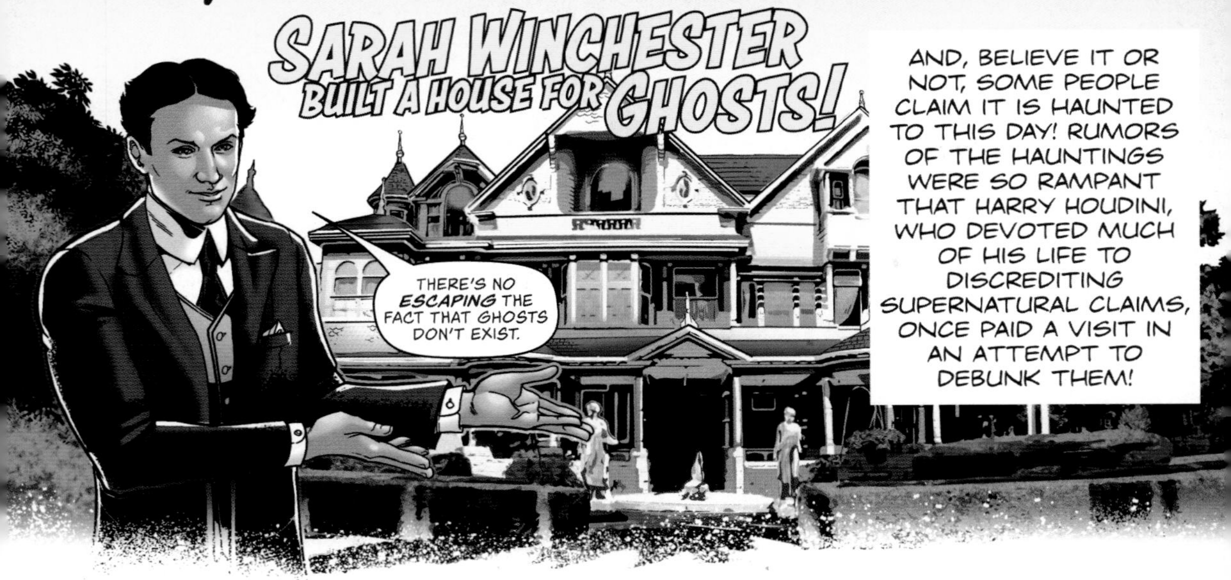
SARAH WINCHESTER BUILT A HOUSE FOR GHOSTS!
AND, BELIEVE IT OR NOT, SOME PEOPLE CLAIM IT IS HAUNTED TO THIS DAY! RUMORS OF THE HAUNTINGS WERE SO RAMPANT THAT HARRY HOUDINI, WHO DEVOTED MUCH OF HIS LIFE TO DISCREDITING SUPERNATURAL CLAIMS, ONCE PAID A VISIT IN AN ATTEMPT TO DEBUNK THEM!
THERE'S NO *ESCAPING* THE FACT THAT GHOSTS DON'T EXIST.

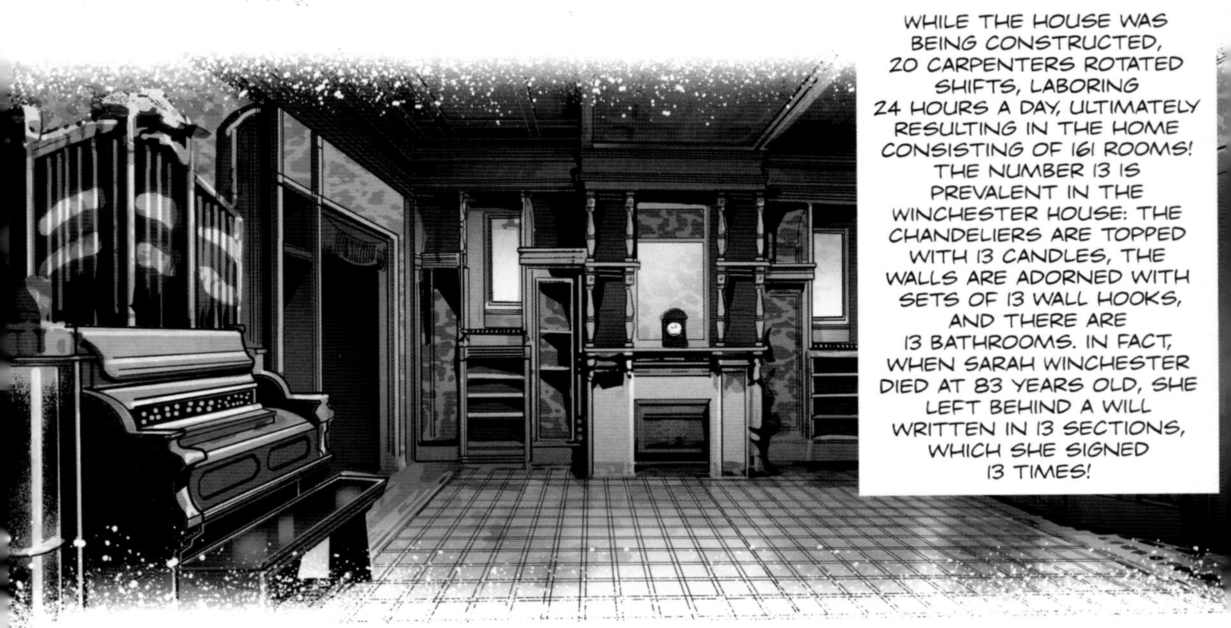
WHILE THE HOUSE WAS BEING CONSTRUCTED, 20 CARPENTERS ROTATED SHIFTS, LABORING 24 HOURS A DAY, ULTIMATELY RESULTING IN THE HOME CONSISTING OF 161 ROOMS! THE NUMBER 13 IS PREVALENT IN THE WINCHESTER HOUSE: THE CHANDELIERS ARE TOPPED WITH 13 CANDLES, THE WALLS ARE ADORNED WITH SETS OF 13 WALL HOOKS, AND THERE ARE 13 BATHROOMS. IN FACT, WHEN SARAH WINCHESTER DIED AT 83 YEARS OLD, SHE LEFT BEHIND A WILL WRITTEN IN 13 SECTIONS, WHICH SHE SIGNED 13 TIMES!

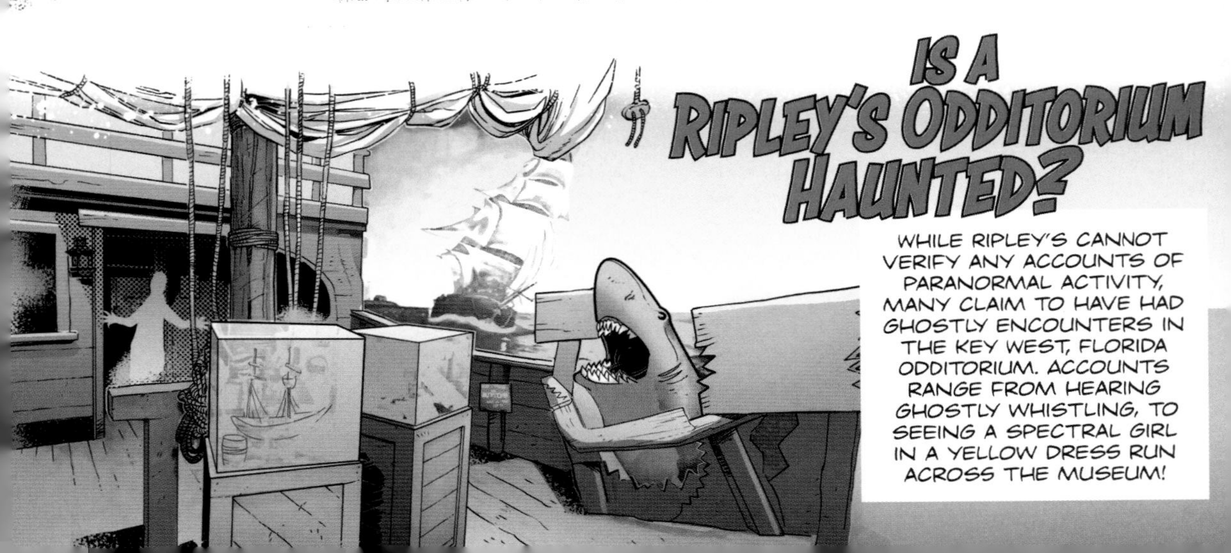
IS A RIPLEY'S ODDITORIUM HAUNTED?
WHILE RIPLEY'S CANNOT VERIFY ANY ACCOUNTS OF PARANORMAL ACTIVITY, MANY CLAIM TO HAVE HAD GHOSTLY ENCOUNTERS IN THE KEY WEST, FLORIDA ODDITORIUM. ACCOUNTS RANGE FROM HEARING GHOSTLY WHISTLING, TO SEEING A SPECTRAL GIRL IN A YELLOW DRESS RUN ACROSS THE MUSEUM!

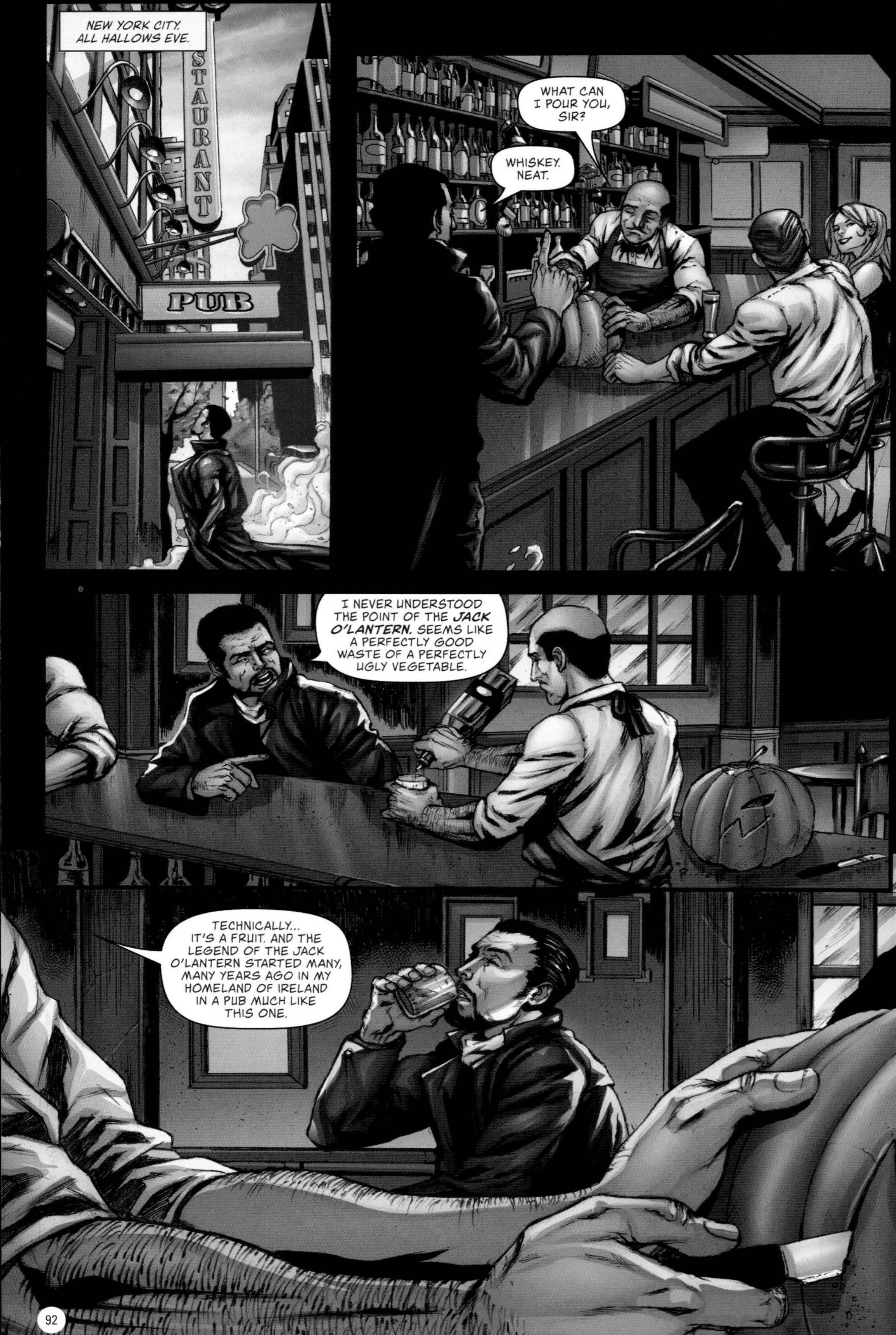
NEW YORK CITY. ALL HALLOWS EVE.
STAURANT
PUB
WHAT CAN I POUR YOU, SIR?
WHISKEY. NEAT.
I NEVER UNDERSTOOD THE POINT OF THE *JACK O'LANTERN.* SEEMS LIKE A PERFECTLY GOOD WASTE OF A PERFECTLY UGLY VEGETABLE.
TECHNICALLY... IT'S A FRUIT. AND THE LEGEND OF THE JACK O'LANTERN STARTED MANY, MANY YEARS AGO IN MY HOMELAND OF IRELAND IN A PUB MUCH LIKE THIS ONE.

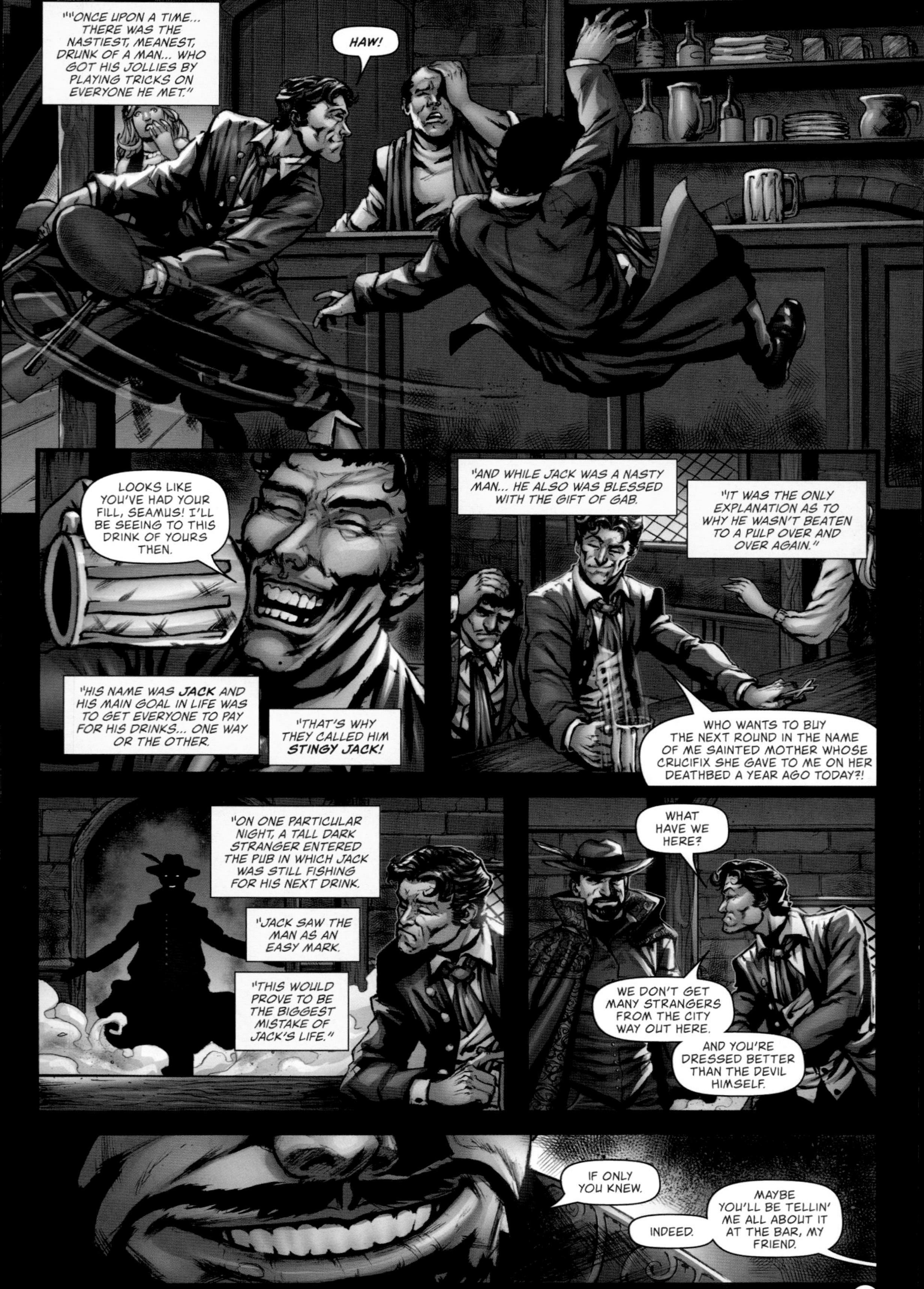
"'ONCE UPON A TIME... THERE WAS THE NASTIEST, MEANEST, DRUNK OF A MAN... WHO GOT HIS JOLLIES BY PLAYING TRICKS ON EVERYONE HE MET."
HAW!
LOOKS LIKE YOU'VE HAD YOUR FILL, SEAMUS! I'LL BE SEEING TO THIS DRINK OF YOURS THEN.
"HIS NAME WAS JACK AND HIS MAIN GOAL IN LIFE WAS TO GET EVERYONE TO PAY FOR HIS DRINKS... ONE WAY OR THE OTHER.
"THAT'S WHY THEY CALLED HIM STINGY JACK!
"AND WHILE JACK WAS A NASTY MAN... HE ALSO WAS BLESSED WITH THE GIFT OF GAB.
"IT WAS THE ONLY EXPLANATION AS TO WHY HE WASN'T BEATEN TO A PULP OVER AND OVER AGAIN."
WHO WANTS TO BUY THE NEXT ROUND IN THE NAME OF ME SAINTED MOTHER WHOSE CRUCIFIX SHE GAVE TO ME ON HER DEATHBED A YEAR AGO TODAY?!
"ON ONE PARTICULAR NIGHT, A TALL DARK STRANGER ENTERED THE PUB IN WHICH JACK WAS STILL FISHING FOR HIS NEXT DRINK.
"JACK SAW THE MAN AS AN EASY MARK.
"THIS WOULD PROVE TO BE THE BIGGEST MISTAKE OF JACK'S LIFE."
WHAT HAVE WE HERE?
WE DON'T GET MANY STRANGERS FROM THE CITY WAY OUT HERE.
AND YOU'RE DRESSED BETTER THAN THE DEVIL HIMSELF.
IF ONLY YOU KNEW.
MAYBE YOU'LL BE TELLIN' ME ALL ABOUT IT AT THE BAR, MY FRIEND.
INDEED.

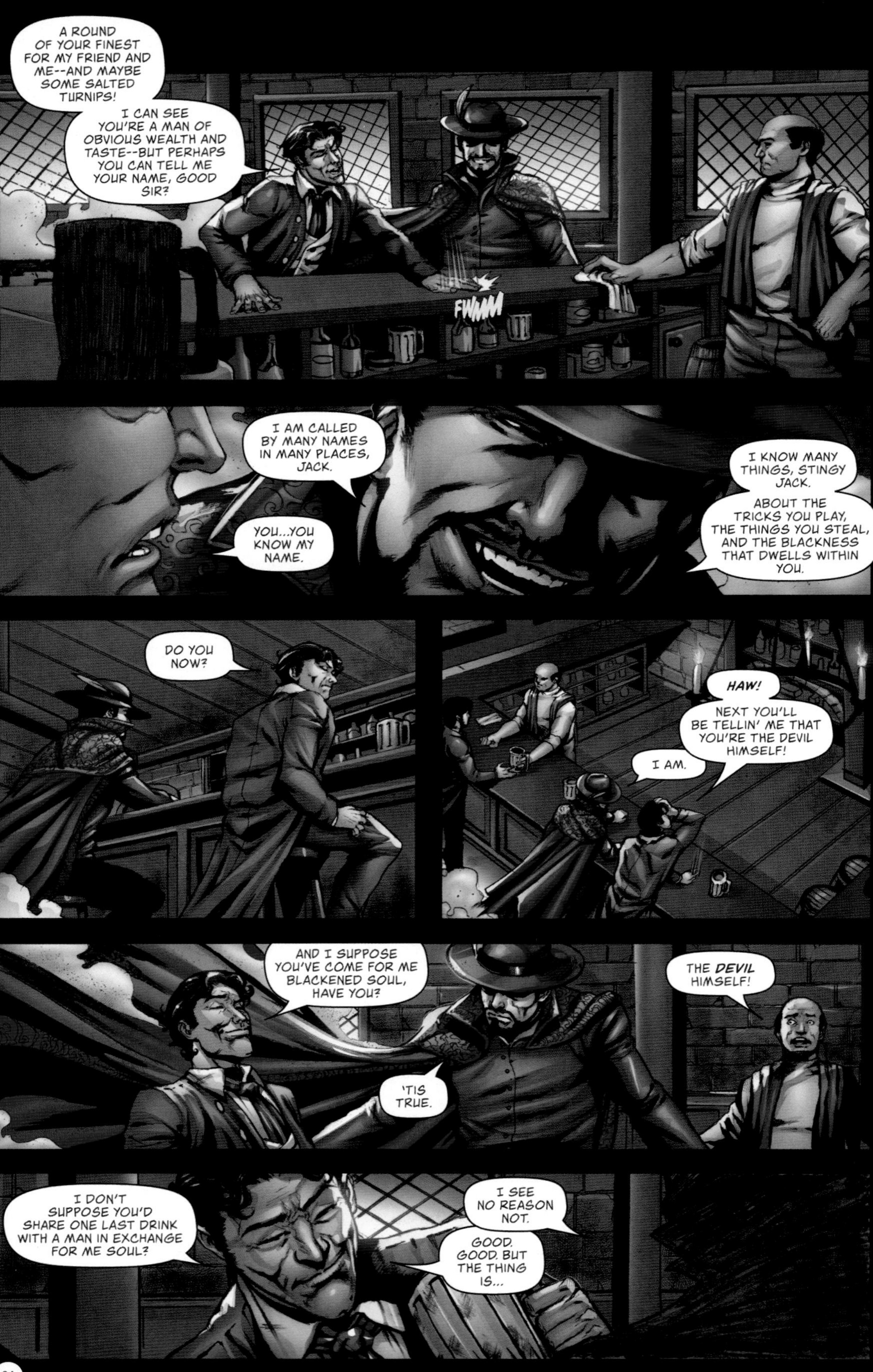
A ROUND OF YOUR FINEST FOR MY FRIEND AND ME--AND MAYBE SOME SALTED TURNIPS!
I CAN SEE YOU'RE A MAN OF OBVIOUS WEALTH AND TASTE--BUT PERHAPS YOU CAN TELL ME YOUR NAME, GOOD SIR?
FWMM
I AM CALLED BY MANY NAMES IN MANY PLACES, JACK.
YOU...YOU KNOW MY NAME.
I KNOW MANY THINGS, STINGY JACK.
ABOUT THE TRICKS YOU PLAY, THE THINGS YOU STEAL, AND THE BLACKNESS THAT DWELLS WITHIN YOU.
DO YOU NOW?
HAW!
NEXT YOU'LL BE TELLIN' ME THAT YOU'RE THE DEVIL HIMSELF!
I AM.
AND I SUPPOSE YOU'VE COME FOR ME BLACKENED SOUL, HAVE YOU?
'TIS TRUE.
THE *DEVIL* HIMSELF!
I DON'T SUPPOSE YOU'D SHARE ONE LAST DRINK WITH A MAN IN EXCHANGE FOR ME SOUL?
I SEE NO REASON NOT.
GOOD. GOOD. BUT THE THING IS...

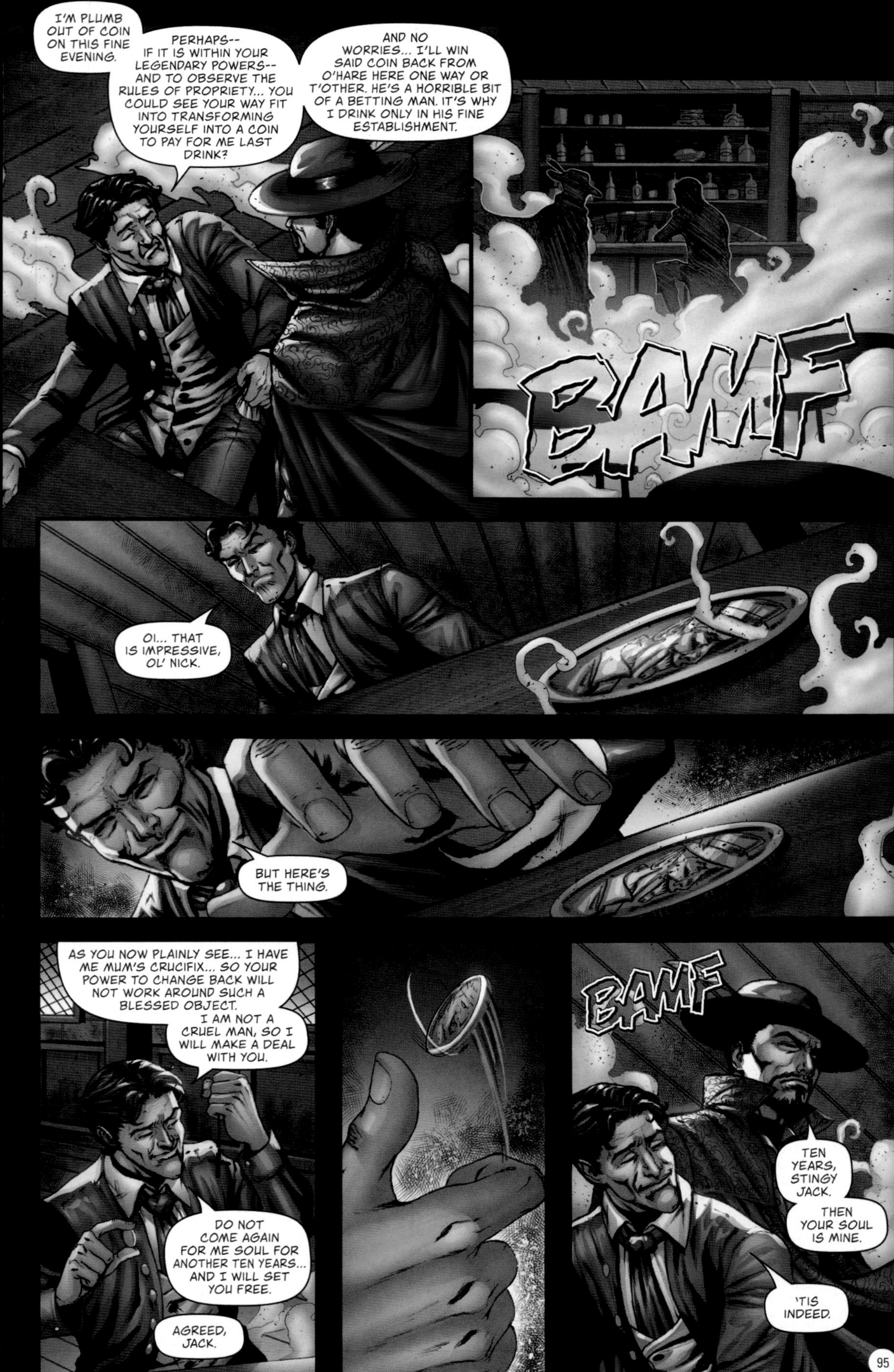
I'M PLUMB OUT OF COIN ON THIS FINE EVENING.
PERHAPS-- IF IT IS WITHIN YOUR LEGENDARY POWERS-- AND TO OBSERVE THE RULES OF PROPRIETY... YOU COULD SEE YOUR WAY FIT INTO TRANSFORMING YOURSELF INTO A COIN TO PAY FOR ME LAST DRINK?
AND NO WORRIES... I'LL WIN SAID COIN BACK FROM O'HARE HERE ONE WAY OR T'OTHER. HE'S A HORRIBLE BIT OF A BETTING MAN. IT'S WHY I DRINK ONLY IN HIS FINE ESTABLISHMENT.
BAMF
OI... THAT IS IMPRESSIVE, OL' NICK.
BUT HERE'S THE THING.
AS YOU NOW PLAINLY SEE... I HAVE ME MUM'S CRUCIFIX... SO YOUR POWER TO CHANGE BACK WILL NOT WORK AROUND SUCH A BLESSED OBJECT.
I AM NOT A CRUEL MAN, SO I WILL MAKE A DEAL WITH YOU.
DO NOT COME AGAIN FOR ME SOUL FOR ANOTHER TEN YEARS... AND I WILL SET YOU FREE.
AGREED, JACK.
BAMF
TEN YEARS, STINGY JACK.
THEN YOUR SOUL IS MINE.
'TIS INDEED.

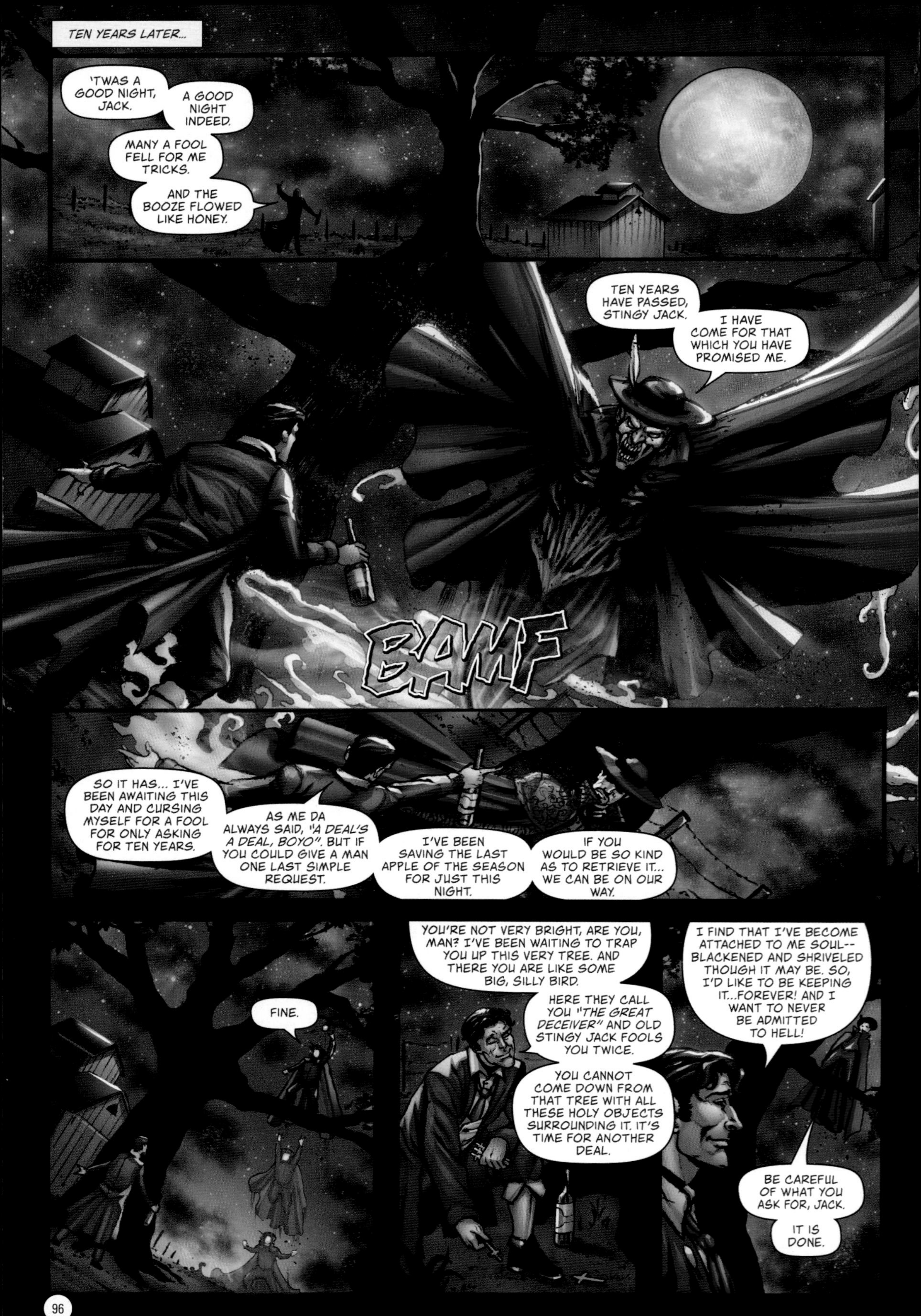
TEN YEARS LATER...
'TWAS A GOOD NIGHT, JACK.
A GOOD NIGHT INDEED.
MANY A FOOL FELL FOR ME TRICKS.
AND THE BOOZE FLOWED LIKE HONEY.
TEN YEARS HAVE PASSED, STINGY JACK.
I HAVE COME FOR THAT WHICH YOU HAVE PROMISED ME.
BAMF
SO IT HAS... I'VE BEEN AWAITING THIS DAY AND CURSING MYSELF FOR A FOOL FOR ONLY ASKING FOR TEN YEARS.
AS ME DA ALWAYS SAID, "A DEAL'S A DEAL, BOYO". BUT IF YOU COULD GIVE A MAN ONE LAST SIMPLE REQUEST.
I'VE BEEN SAVING THE LAST APPLE OF THE SEASON FOR JUST THIS NIGHT.
IF YOU WOULD BE SO KIND AS TO RETRIEVE IT... WE CAN BE ON OUR WAY.
FINE.
YOU'RE NOT VERY BRIGHT, ARE YOU, MAN? I'VE BEEN WAITING TO TRAP YOU UP THIS VERY TREE. AND THERE YOU ARE LIKE SOME BIG, SILLY BIRD.
HERE THEY CALL YOU "THE GREAT DECEIVER" AND OLD STINGY JACK FOOLS YOU TWICE.
YOU CANNOT COME DOWN FROM THAT TREE WITH ALL THESE HOLY OBJECTS SURROUNDING IT. IT'S TIME FOR ANOTHER DEAL.
I FIND THAT I'VE BECOME ATTACHED TO ME SOUL-- BLACKENED AND SHRIVELED THOUGH IT MAY BE. SO, I'D LIKE TO BE KEEPING IT...FOREVER! AND I WANT TO NEVER BE ADMITTED TO HELL!
BE CAREFUL OF WHAT YOU ASK FOR, JACK.
IT IS DONE.

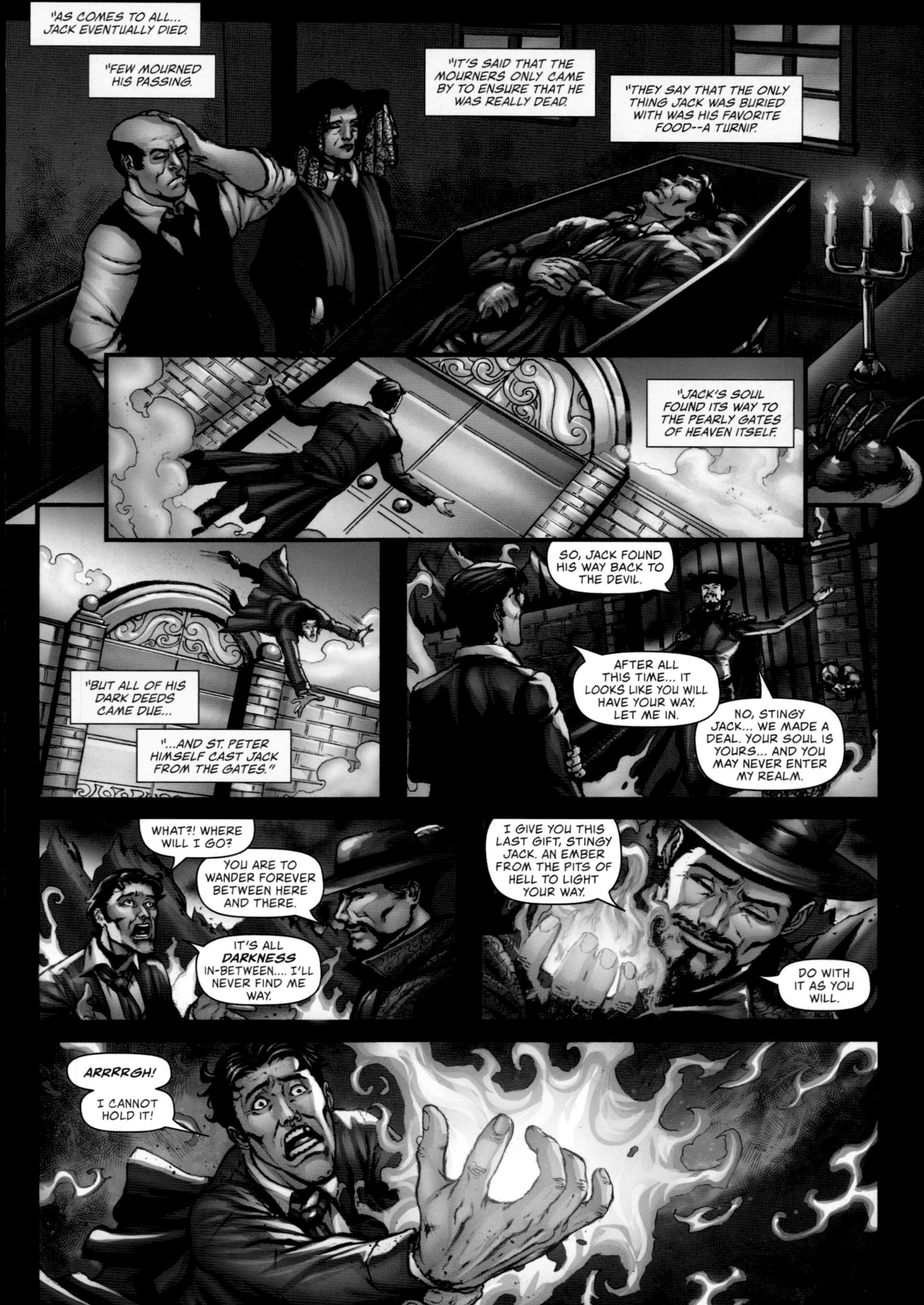
"AS COMES TO ALL... JACK EVENTUALLY DIED.
"FEW MOURNED HIS PASSING.
"IT'S SAID THAT THE MOURNERS ONLY CAME BY TO ENSURE THAT HE WAS REALLY DEAD.
"THEY SAY THAT THE ONLY THING JACK WAS BURIED WITH WAS HIS FAVORITE FOOD--A TURNIP.
"JACK'S SOUL FOUND ITS WAY TO THE PEARLY GATES OF HEAVEN ITSELF.
"BUT ALL OF HIS DARK DEEDS CAME DUE...
"...AND ST. PETER HIMSELF CAST JACK FROM THE GATES."
SO, JACK FOUND HIS WAY BACK TO THE DEVIL.
AFTER ALL THIS TIME... IT LOOKS LIKE YOU WILL HAVE YOUR WAY. LET ME IN.
NO, STINGY JACK... WE MADE A DEAL. YOUR SOUL IS YOURS... AND YOU MAY NEVER ENTER MY REALM.
WHAT?! WHERE WILL I GO?
YOU ARE TO WANDER FOREVER BETWEEN HERE AND THERE.
IT'S ALL DARKNESS IN-BETWEEN.... I'LL NEVER FIND ME WAY.
I GIVE YOU THIS LAST GIFT, STINGY JACK. AN EMBER FROM THE PITS OF HELL TO LIGHT YOUR WAY.
DO WITH IT AS YOU WILL.
ARRRRGH!
I CANNOT HOLD IT!

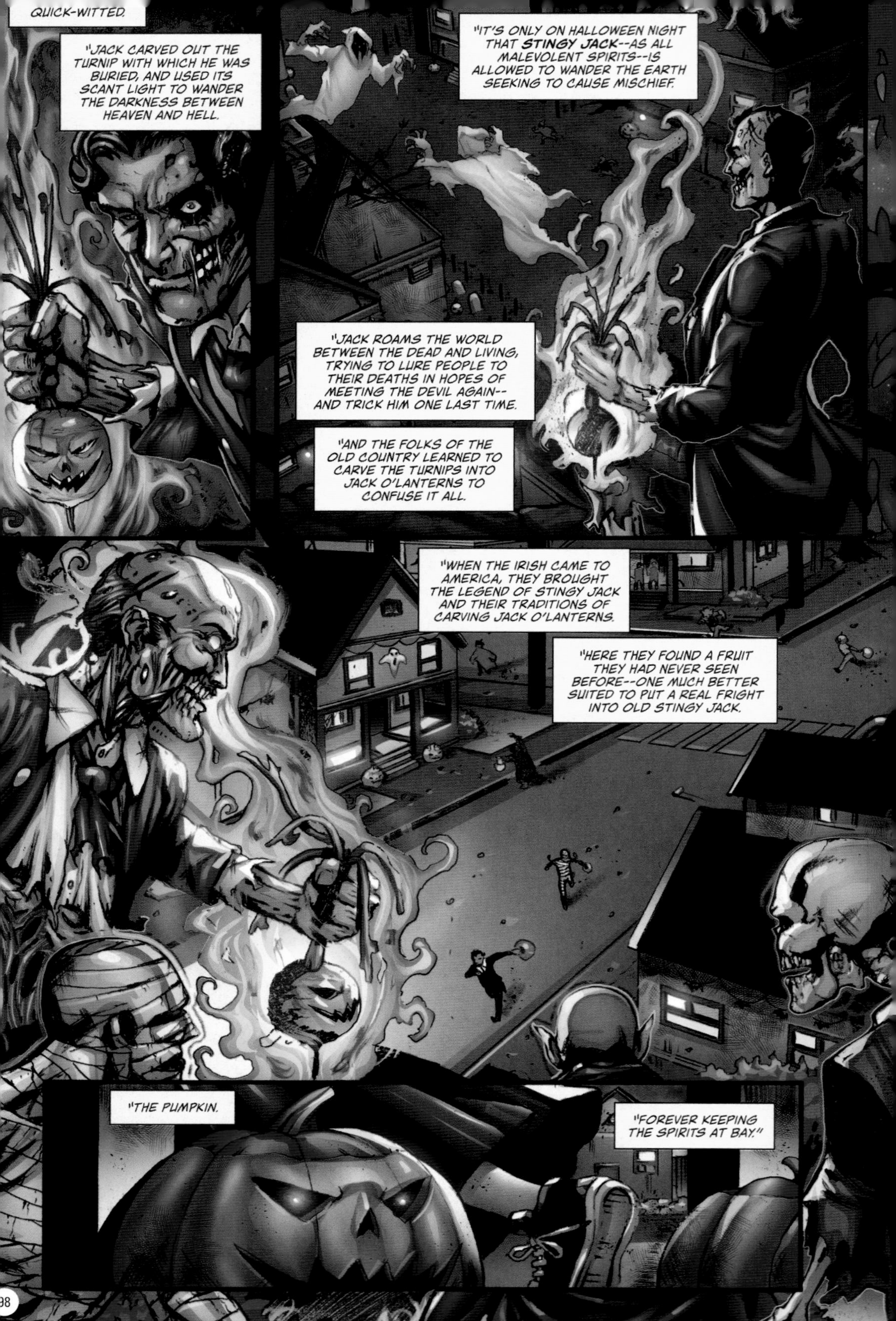
QUICK-WITTED.
"JACK CARVED OUT THE TURNIP WITH WHICH HE WAS BURIED, AND USED ITS SCANT LIGHT TO WANDER THE DARKNESS BETWEEN HEAVEN AND HELL.
"IT'S ONLY ON HALLOWEEN NIGHT THAT STINGY JACK--AS ALL MALEVOLENT SPIRITS--IS ALLOWED TO WANDER THE EARTH SEEKING TO CAUSE MISCHIEF.
"JACK ROAMS THE WORLD BETWEEN THE DEAD AND LIVING, TRYING TO LURE PEOPLE TO THEIR DEATHS IN HOPES OF MEETING THE DEVIL AGAIN-- AND TRICK HIM ONE LAST TIME.
"AND THE FOLKS OF THE OLD COUNTRY LEARNED TO CARVE THE TURNIPS INTO JACK O'LANTERNS TO CONFUSE IT ALL.
"WHEN THE IRISH CAME TO AMERICA, THEY BROUGHT THE LEGEND OF STINGY JACK AND THEIR TRADITIONS OF CARVING JACK O'LANTERNS.
"HERE THEY FOUND A FRUIT THEY HAD NEVER SEEN BEFORE--ONE MUCH BETTER SUITED TO PUT A REAL FRIGHT INTO OLD STINGY JACK.
"THE PUMPKIN.
"FOREVER KEEPING THE SPIRITS AT BAY."

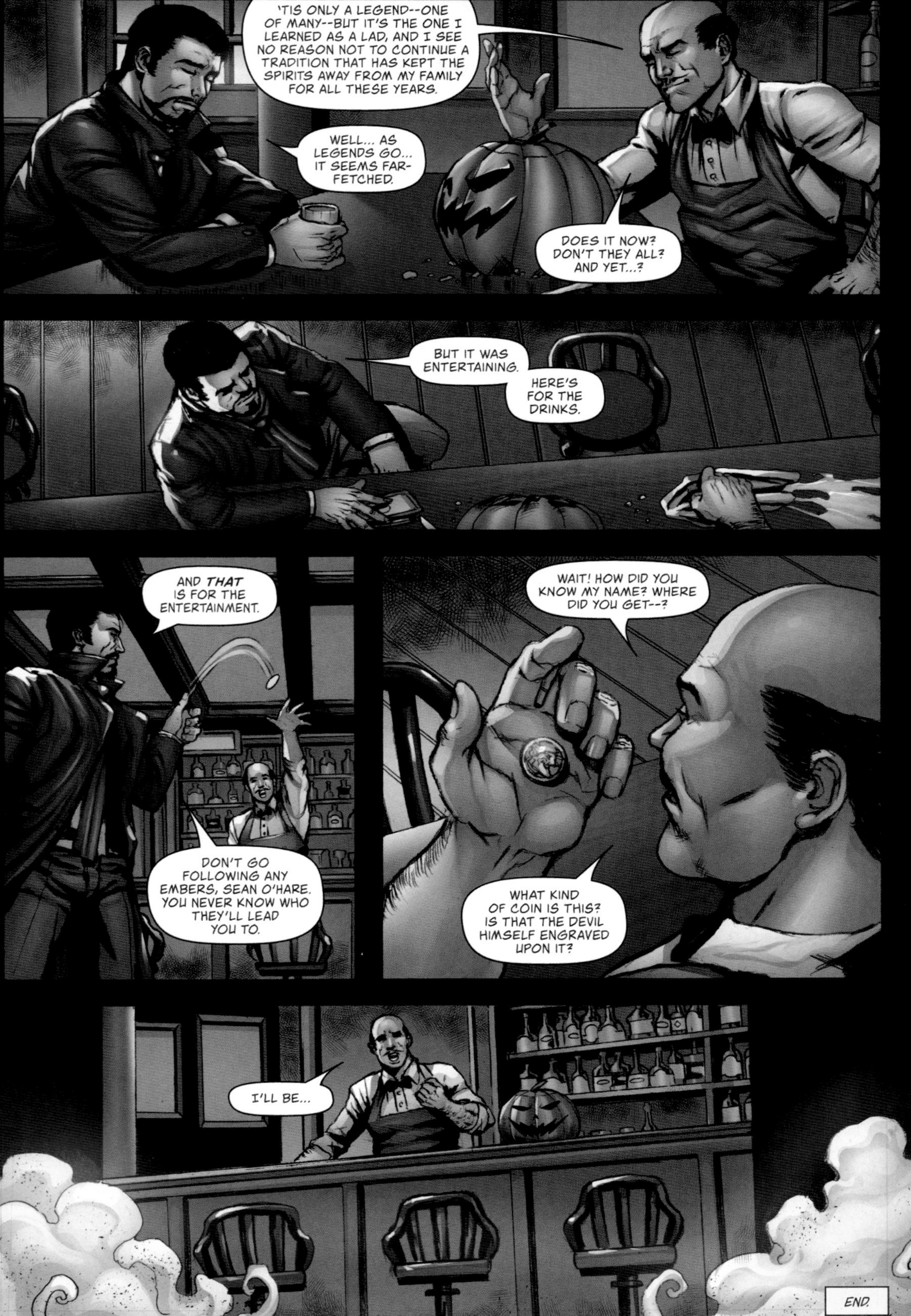
'TIS ONLY A LEGEND--ONE OF MANY--BUT IT'S THE ONE I LEARNED AS A LAD, AND I SEE NO REASON NOT TO CONTINUE A TRADITION THAT HAS KEPT THE SPIRITS AWAY FROM MY FAMILY FOR ALL THESE YEARS.
WELL... AS LEGENDS GO... IT SEEMS FAR-FETCHED.
DOES IT NOW? DON'T THEY ALL? AND YET...?
BUT IT WAS ENTERTAINING.
HERE'S FOR THE DRINKS.
AND *THAT* IS FOR THE ENTERTAINMENT.
DON'T GO FOLLOWING ANY EMBERS, SEAN O'HARE. YOU NEVER KNOW WHO THEY'LL LEAD YOU TO.
WAIT! HOW DID YOU KNOW MY NAME? WHERE DID YOU GET--?
WHAT KIND OF COIN IS THIS? IS THAT THE DEVIL HIMSELF ENGRAVED UPON IT?
I'LL BE...
END.

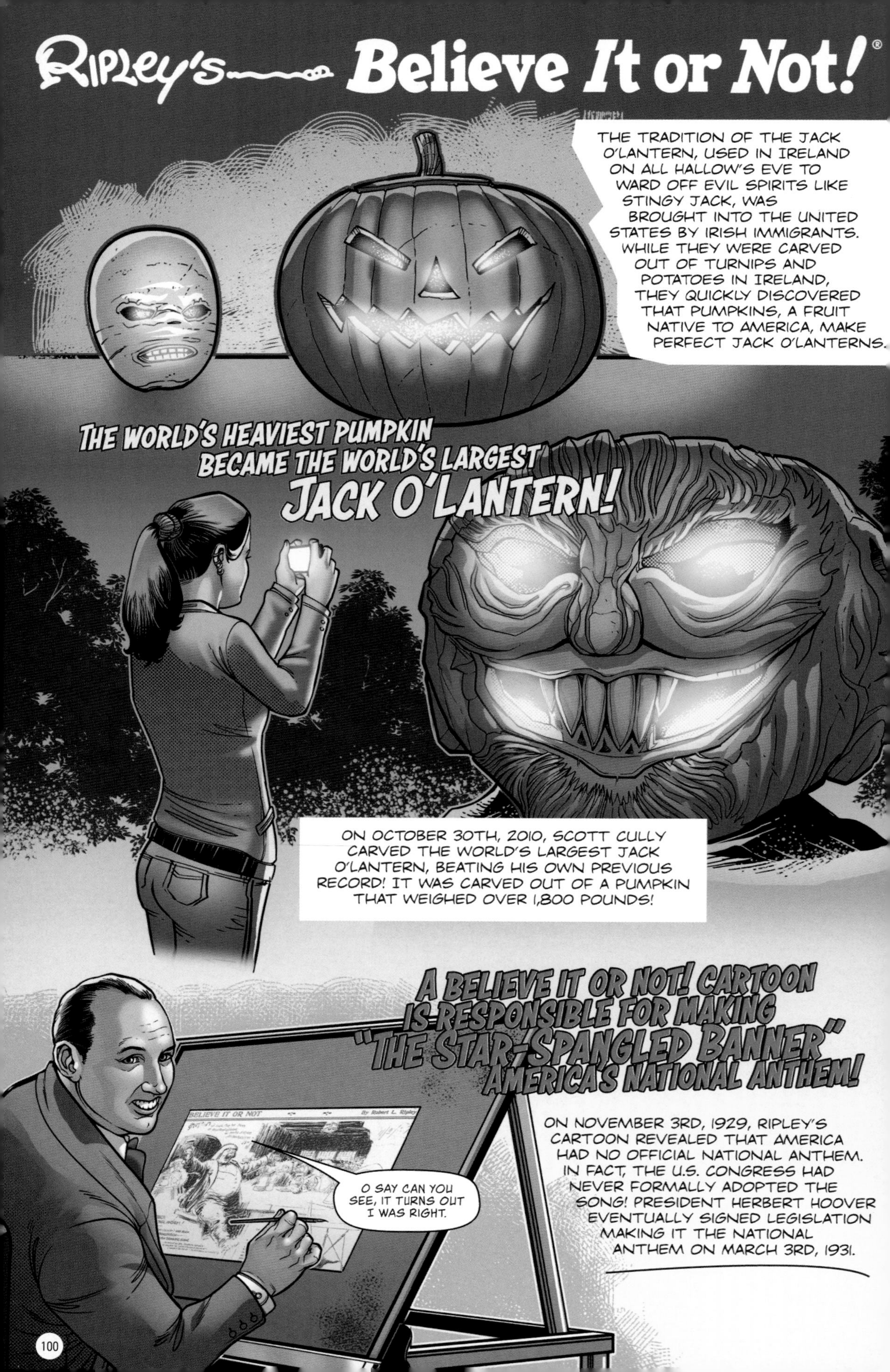

RIPLEY'S Believe It or Not!®
THE TRADITION OF THE JACK O'LANTERN, USED IN IRELAND ON ALL HALLOW'S EVE TO WARD OFF EVIL SPIRITS LIKE STINGY JACK, WAS BROUGHT INTO THE UNITED STATES BY IRISH IMMIGRANTS. WHILE THEY WERE CARVED OUT OF TURNIPS AND POTATOES IN IRELAND, THEY QUICKLY DISCOVERED THAT PUMPKINS, A FRUIT NATIVE TO AMERICA, MAKE PERFECT JACK O'LANTERNS.
THE WORLD'S HEAVIEST PUMPKIN BECAME THE WORLD'S LARGEST JACK O'LANTERN!
ON OCTOBER 30TH, 2010, SCOTT CULLY CARVED THE WORLD'S LARGEST JACK O'LANTERN, BEATING HIS OWN PREVIOUS RECORD! IT WAS CARVED OUT OF A PUMPKIN THAT WEIGHED OVER 1,800 POUNDS!
A BELIEVE IT OR NOT! CARTOON IS RESPONSIBLE FOR MAKING "THE STAR-SPANGLED BANNER" AMERICA'S NATIONAL ANTHEM!
BELIEVE IT OR NOT
By Robert L. Ripley
O SAY CAN YOU SEE, IT TURNS OUT I WAS RIGHT.
ON NOVEMBER 3RD, 1929, RIPLEY'S CARTOON REVEALED THAT AMERICA HAD NO OFFICIAL NATIONAL ANTHEM. IN FACT, THE U.S. CONGRESS HAD NEVER FORMALLY ADOPTED THE SONG! PRESIDENT HERBERT HOOVER EVENTUALLY SIGNED LEGISLATION MAKING IT THE NATIONAL ANTHEM ON MARCH 3RD, 1931.

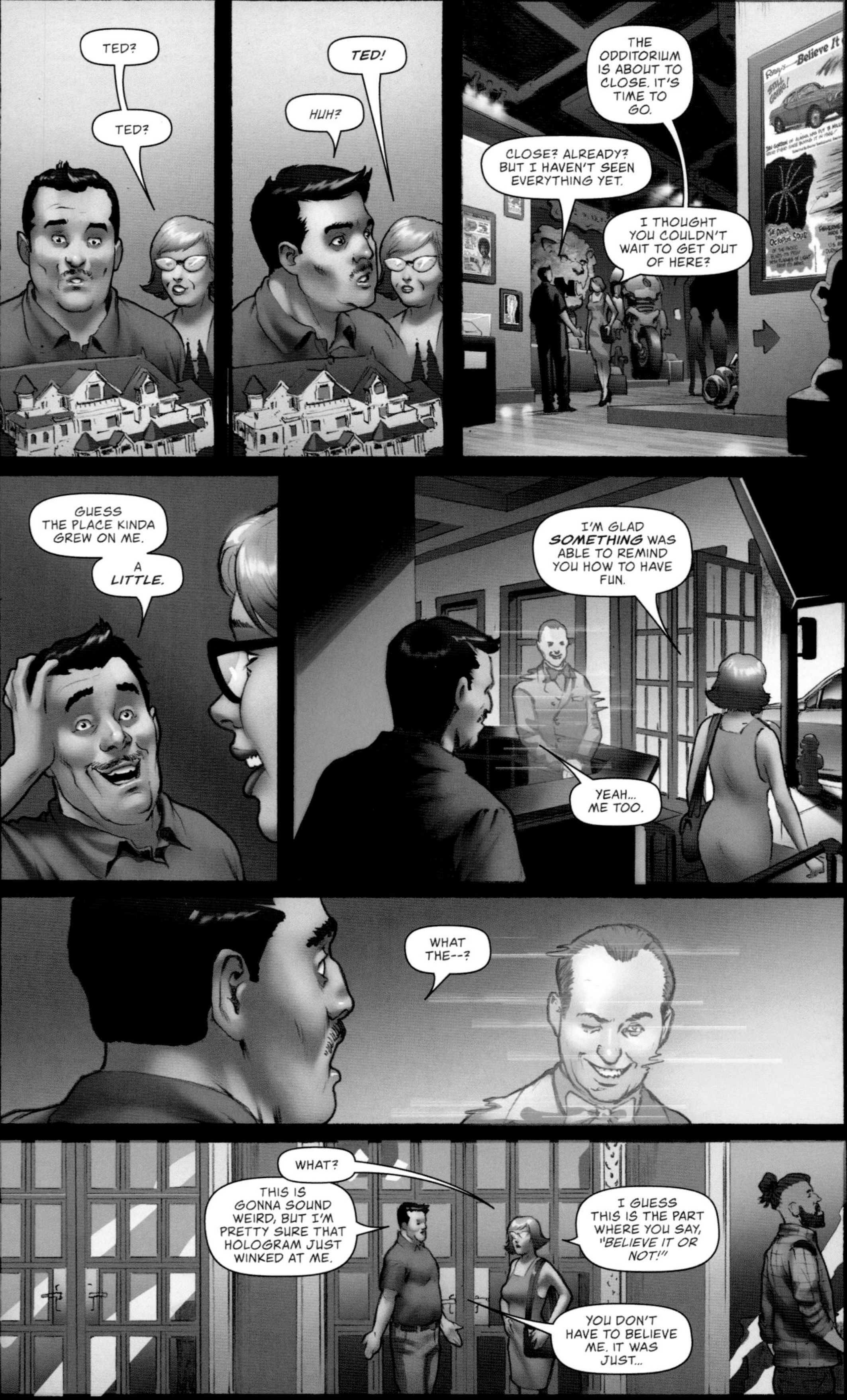
TED?
TED?
HUH?
TED!
THE ODDITORIUM IS ABOUT TO CLOSE. IT'S TIME TO GO.
CLOSE? ALREADY? BUT I HAVEN'T SEEN EVERYTHING YET.
I THOUGHT YOU COULDN'T WAIT TO GET OUT OF HERE?
GUESS THE PLACE KINDA GREW ON ME.
A *LITTLE.*
I'M GLAD ***SOMETHING*** WAS ABLE TO REMIND YOU HOW TO HAVE FUN.
YEAH... ME TOO.
WHAT THE--?
WHAT?
THIS IS GONNA SOUND WEIRD, BUT I'M PRETTY SURE THAT HOLOGRAM JUST WINKED AT ME.
I GUESS THIS IS THE PART WHERE YOU SAY, *"BELIEVE IT OR NOT!"*
YOU DON'T HAVE TO BELIEVE ME. IT WAS JUST...

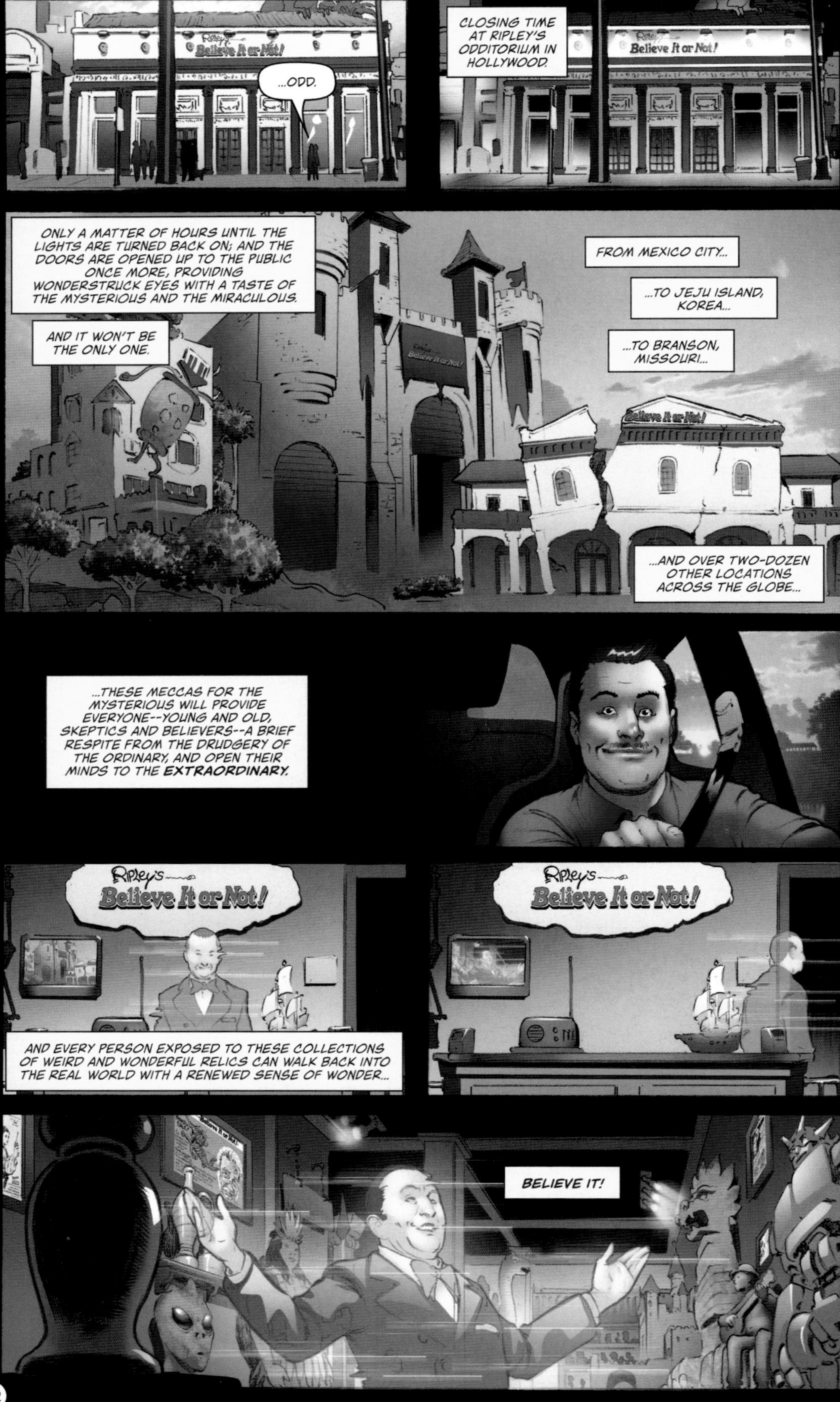

Ripley's Believe It or Not!
...ODD.
CLOSING TIME AT RIPLEY'S ODDITORIUM IN HOLLYWOOD.
Ripley's Believe It or Not!
ONLY A MATTER OF HOURS UNTIL THE LIGHTS ARE TURNED BACK ON; AND THE DOORS ARE OPENED UP TO THE PUBLIC ONCE MORE, PROVIDING WONDERSTRUCK EYES WITH A TASTE OF THE MYSTERIOUS AND THE MIRACULOUS.
AND IT WON'T BE THE ONLY ONE.
FROM MEXICO CITY...
...TO JEJU ISLAND, KOREA...
...TO BRANSON, MISSOURI...
Believe It or Not!
Believe It or Not!
...AND OVER TWO-DOZEN OTHER LOCATIONS ACROSS THE GLOBE...
...THESE MECCAS FOR THE MYSTERIOUS WILL PROVIDE EVERYONE--YOUNG AND OLD, SKEPTICS AND BELIEVERS--A BRIEF RESPITE FROM THE DRUDGERY OF THE ORDINARY, AND OPEN THEIR MINDS TO THE EXTRAORDINARY.
Ripley's Believe It or Not!
AND EVERY PERSON EXPOSED TO THESE COLLECTIONS OF WEIRD AND WONDERFUL RELICS CAN WALK BACK INTO THE REAL WORLD WITH A RENEWED SENSE OF WONDER...
Ripley's Believe It or Not!
Believe It or Not!
BELIEVE IT!

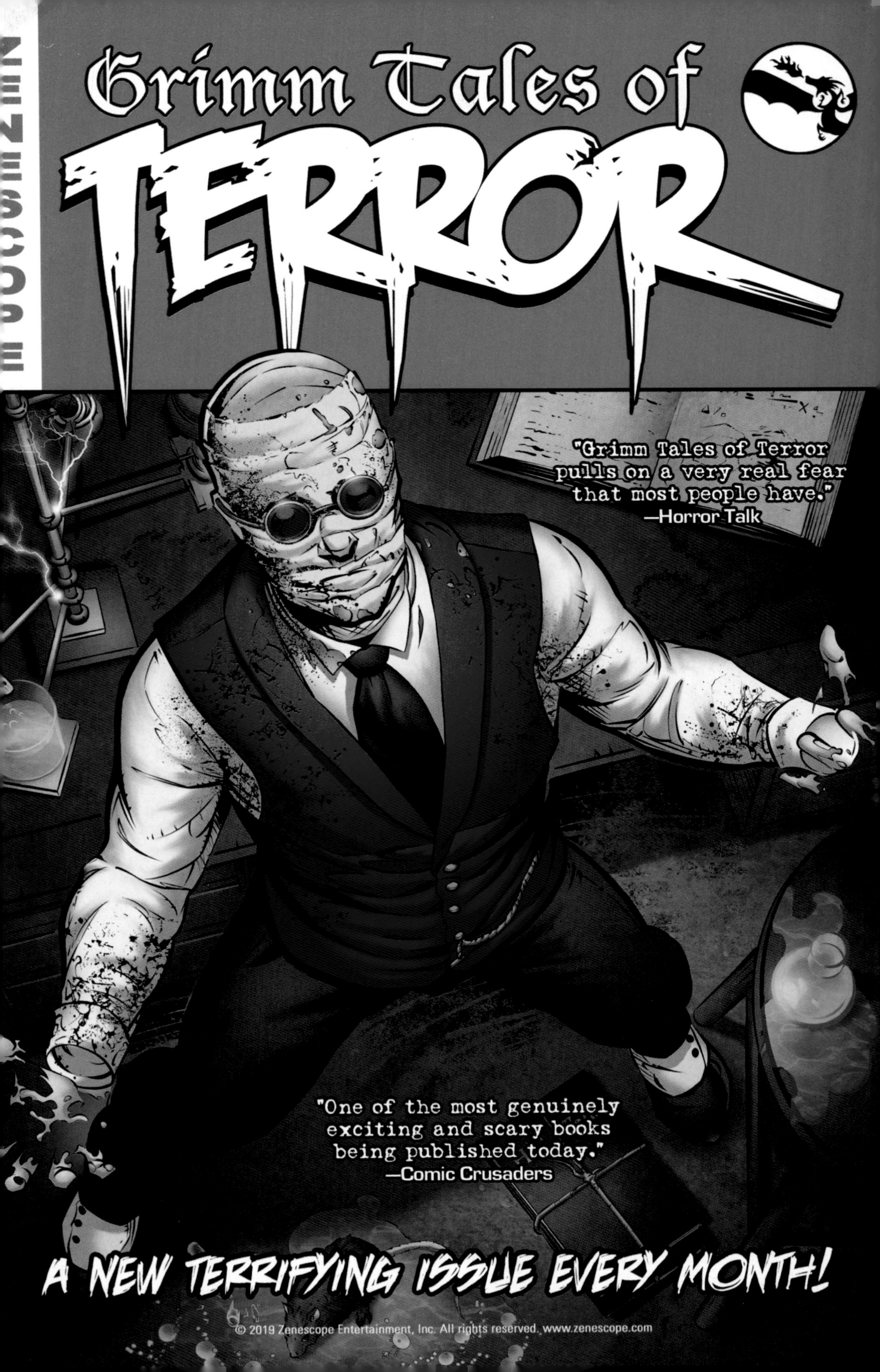

ZENESCOPE
Grimm Tales of
TERROR
"Grimm Tales of Terror pulls on a very real fear that most people have."
—Horror Talk
"One of the most genuinely exciting and scary books being published today."
—Comic Crusaders
A NEW TERRIFYING ISSUE EVERY MONTH!
© 2019 Zenescope Entertainment, Inc. All rights reserved. www.zenescope.com

Ripley's
Believe It
or Not!®